Primary MATLAB® for Life Sciences: Guide for Beginners

Authored By

Leonid Burstein

Kinneret Academic College on the Sea of Galilee
School of Engineering
Quality Assurance Engineering Department
Israel

CONTENTS

PREFACE

The last two-three decades are a remarkable, revolutionary time, in which computer- and life sciences have been contributing much to one another. Computer engineers are actively working in bio-areas while life science specialists are working on bio-computers, cell lasers, and other amazing devices recently introduced into the non-biological domain. Therefore, today is a real need to familiarize biotechnologists with the computing software used by 'classical' engineers. The present book is a short introductory MATLAB® guide addressed to a wide life science audience - undergraduate and graduate students and practicing engineers. It provides the MATLAB® fundamentals with a variety of application examples and problems from current biotechnology, computational biology, molecular biology, bio-kinetics, biomedicine, ecology, population dynamics, and bioengineering. I hope that many non-programmer students, engineers and scientists from this area will find the software user-friendly and extremely convenient in solving their specific problems.

The book was planned at a time when its predecessor "MATLAB® in bioscience and biotechnology" (L. Burstein, Biohealthcare Publishing (Oxford) Limited, Oxford-New York, 2011, pp. 230) was still in production and thus unavailable. Accordingly, their sections 2, dealing with MATLAB® basics, are similar. Otherwise, the book is tailored to the level of a newcomer in computer calculations, and contains topics and examples not given in the predecessor. Most of the problems required in the latter to be solved by the reader, are reproduced with their solutions – and *vice versa*. The used sample data and at least 80% of the problems were revised or completely reformulated in this book, which contains a new chapter on useful tools such as the Basic Fitting and Time Series interfaces.

The book accumulates the experience of many years of MATLAB teaching in introductory and advanced courses for students, engineers and scientists specializing in the area in question.

I hope this book will prove useful to students and engineers in both the natural and life sciences and enable them to work with one of the finest software tools.

Leonid Burstein
Kinneret College on the Sea of Galilee
School of Engineering
Quality Assurance Department
M.P. Jordan Valley, 15132
Israel
E-mail: leonidburstein@gmail.com

ACKNOWLEDGEMENTS

I thank MathWorks Inc[1], who kindly granted permission to use certain material. I am also grateful to the Biohealthcare Publishing (Oxford) Limited[2] for permission to use the text, tables, figures, and screenshots from the following pages of the previous book: Chapter 2, pp. 2-11, 13, 15-28, 32-35, 38, 41-46, 48; Chapter 3, Table **3.3**; Chapter 5, Table **5.1** (cited tables are referred to also in the text of this book). I would like to thank the research Fund of Kinneret Academic College for funding the editing the text of the 2 -6 Chapters of the book. I would like to thank the research Fund of Kinneret Academic College for funding the 2 - 6 Chapters editing.

[1]The MathWorks, Inc., 3Apple Hill Drive, Natick, MA, 01760-2098 USA, Tel: 508-647-7000, Fax: 508-647-7001, E-mail: info@mathworks.com, Web: www.mathworks.com

[2]The Biohealthcare Publishing (Oxford) Limited was acquired in March 2102 by the Woodhead Publishing Limited, 80 High Street, Sawston, Cambridge CB22 3HJ, UK, Tel: 1233 499140 ext. 130., Fax: 1223 832819, E-mail: wp@woodheadpublishing.com, Web: www.woodheadpublishing.com

DEDICATION

In memory of my father Matvey

To my mother Leda, my wife Inna, and my son Dmitri

Send Orders for Reprints to reprints@benthamscience.net
Primary MATLAB® for Life Sciences: Guide for Beginners, 2013, 3-7

CHAPTER 1

Introduction

Abstract: The purposes, principal audience, the main topics, and chapter design are described here. MATLAB® advances in comparison to such popular software as Mathematica, Mathcad, Maple, and R, are briefly lightened. The differences between the present and author's previous book are discussed briefly.

Keywords: Introduction; purposes; principal audience; MATLAB® releases, Mathematica; Mathcad; Maple; R- software; chapter design; presentation order.

Live science, or biology[1], is the large branch of the natural sciences concerned with the living organisms – microspecies, plants, animals, and humans. While general in natural sciences mathematical, physical, and computerized methods have long been in widespread use, the live sciences, their accession is relatively recent. It was commonly held that the biologist is not oriented towards math and computers, whereas the mathematician, computer scientist and engineer do not know biology. During past few decades this situation changed dramatically, with mutual interpenetration on both "sides". Today computer engineers serve in biotechnological companies, and biotechnologists widely and actively use mathematics and computers in their daily work. At present, knowledge of computers and ability to implement relevant computer programs are of vital importance for representatives of life science.

In recent years MATLAB®, as one of the most popular programs for technical computing [3], has spread into new areas such as biosciences, biotechnology and medicine. As a result, a large new community of specialists is in need of a short and comprehensive text, easy to understand and providing access to the tool.

MATLAB® AND OTHER SOFTWARE

MATLAB® competes with other widespread software such as Mathematica, Mathcad, and Maple, and has gained acceptance in engineering, which is today the area for which it is intended. In some respects MATLAB® is comparable with open programs such as R, SciPy, Octave, Scilab and other packages each of which

[1]From ancient Greek: bio – life, logos – word, speech, reasoning.

Leonid Burstein

is associated with a particular area (statistics, scientific libraries, *etc.*). Without going into details, we list here some of the factors which, combine, give the advantage to MATLAB®:

- Suitability for solution of both simple and complex program-oriented problems;
- Adaptability for various fields of science and engineering, with the specialized tools;
- Convenience and diversity of visualization;
- Quick access to well organized and comprehensive documentation.

PURPOSE AND PRINCIPAL AUDIENCE OF THE BOOK

The advantages listed above assured the popularity of the software in non-biological audiences, and the purpose of this book to guide biology students, teachers, engineers and scientists towards it. It is assumed that the reader has no prior programming experience and will be using the software for the first time. In order to make clear to the target audience the primary programming steps and use of commands, they are illustrated by problems from different areas of life science and bioengineering.

ABOUT THE TOPICS

The topics were chosen on the basis of several years of experience in teaching MATLAB® to biotechnologists and other specialists and are presented so that the beginner can progress gradually, with only the previously acquired material as prerequisite for each new chapter.

The basic MATLAB® features such as environment, language design, help options, variables, matrix and array manipulations, elementary and special functions, flow chart control, conditional statements, *etc.* - are introduced in the second chapter.

In the third chapter the visualization tool is introduced by the examples of graphical representation of calculations. The material of these two (second and third) chapters enables the reader to create simple MATLAB® programs.

The fourth chapter explains how to write programs in the script- or function form and save it as an m-file; here are added the commands for common numerical calculations such as inter- and extrapolation, differentiation, and integration.

In the fifth chapter the specific solver commands intended for solving ordinary differential equation (ODE) are briefly presented with examples for bio-systems that can be represented by such equations, one or a set. Reader's familiarity with mathematics on a somewhat higher level is assumed during the course of this chapter.

In the final chapter the special tools for curve fitting and time series are introduced with emphasis on use of the appropriate interface for problems, such population data approximation, time series forecasting, *etc.*

The Appendix 1 lists the complete collections of the studied MATLAB® commands and functions.

The Appendix II describes the changes in the Desktop, Help and Editor Windows that were appeared at the time when the book already reached completion.

CHAPTER DESIGN

Each chapter begins with a short description of the targets, and then of the new tool and main commands for its realization are presented. Each command is explained in one or two simplest forms and possible extensions are given; additional information is available in the MATLAB® help or original MATLAB® documentation. Each topic is considered in concentrated form as completely as possible. Tables list the additionally available commands and their description and examples.

At the end - and sometimes in the middle - of each chapter, life science application problems are introduced with their solutions by the commands accessible to the reader; the given solutions are the easiest to understand, but not necessarily the shortest or original. Readers are encouraged to try their own solutions and compare the results with those in the book. For better assimilation of the material, problems and questions for self-checking are given at the end of each chapter, and I recommend to solve them for better MATLAB understanding. The answers to some of these problems and questions are also given in the end of each chapter.

The numerical values and contexts used in the problems are not factual data and serve for learning purposes only.

THE MATLAB® RELEASES

Like every popular software, MATLAB® is constantly updated and extended; two new versions appear every year. The version used in the book is R2012a. Each new version is designed so as to allow work with previously written commands; thus the basic commands in this book will remain valid in future versions. It is assumed that the reader has installed MATLAB® in his/her computer and will be able to perform all basic operations presented in the book.

THE ORDER OF PRESENTATION

The book is intended for a newcomer in computer calculations and topics are arranged accordingly, but teachers using it may find it useful to choose their own order. For example, the polynomial fitting (Subsection 6.1) and Basic Fitting interface (Subsections 6.2 and 6.3) can be presented immediately after the script- and function-files of Chapter 4, and the Time Series Tools (Subsection 6.4) before the ordinal differential equation solvers (Chapter 5); script files (Subsection 4.1) can be moved to Chapter 2 directly before the first application examples (Subsection 2.2) to allow students to write programs already during the first steps; logical and relational operators (subsection 2.3.1) can be presented after Chapter 3.

THE DIFFERENCES BETWEEN THE PRESENT BOOK AND AUTHOR'S PREVIOUS BOOK ON THIS SUBJECT

The competitor[2] to the present book is the author's 'MATLAB® in bioscience and biotechnology' (L. Burstein, Biohealthcare Publishing (Oxford) Limited, Oxford-

[2]During the time this book was written, new books [4, 5, 6] on this subject were published; these books are focused on specific bioareas (bio-mathematics, biomedicine, *etc.*) and are not MATLAB® primer.

New York, 2011, pp. 230), which was still in production and thus unavailable when the present one was planned. The above book was intended for beginners but in turned out to be suitable for an advanced audience. The present book, by contrast, is intended address for any newcomer to computer calculations, and includes the topics and examples are unavailable in the previous book; most of problems and questions, given in the previous book to be solved by the readers, are presented here complete with their solution, and *vice versa*. The used sets of data and at least 80% of the problems were revised or completely reformulated in this book. Moreover, the chapter on Bioinformatics toolbox™ replaced by a description of such basic and useful tools as the Basic Fitting and Time Series interfaces.

CHAPTER 2

Basics

Abstract: The MATLAB® windows, starting procedures; basic language constructions and commands; vectors, matrix and array manipulations, flow control operations are presented in this chapter. Basic commands are demonstrated on various bio-applications such as RNA volume computing, Arrhenius' equation, RNA bases, and many others. The questions and life-science problems together with answers to some of them are given in conclusion.

Keywords: MATLAB® basics; commands, matrices and arrays; flow control; logical and relational operations; application examples; RNA bases; Arrhenius' equation.

INTRODUCTION

In the late seventies of the last century, the American mathematician and programmer Cleve Moler created a programming tool for mathematicians and educators. The tool was quickly adopted by engineers as an effective tool for technical computing and is now actively employed in the life sciences. This tool and its language were named MATLAB®, comprising the words 'Matrix' and 'Laboratory', which emphasize that the main element of this language is the matrix. Such an approach permitted the unification of the processes of various calculations, graphics, modeling, simulations, and algorithm development. This chapter introduces the starting procedure and the main windows; it describes the main commands for simple arithmetic, algebraic and matrix operations; and finally, presents the basic loops and relational and logical operators.

2.1. STARTING MATLAB®[1]

Computers are managed through a set of programs called 'operating system', OS. This can take different forms, and the program language the user chooses to solve his tasks should be suitable for the specified OS. MATLAB® can be installed on computers with different operation systems, it is assumed here that the reader uses a

[1]The text, screenshots and tables used in this subsection are partly taken from pp. 2-11, 13 of the author's book [2] with the permission of Biohealthcare Publishing (Oxford) Limited.

Leonid Burstein

personal computer with an installed Windows operating system. To start, simply click on the icon representing red L-shaped membrane (Fig. **2.1**), provided with the MATLAB® -version subscription; the icon is placed on the Quick Launch bar or on the Windows Desktop. It is possible to start by selecting MATLAB® R2012a in the MATLAB-directory in the 'All Programs' option of the Windows 'Start' menu.

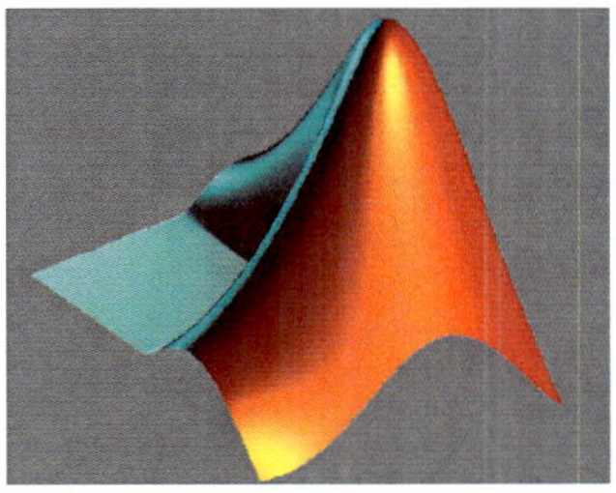

Figure 2.1: Surface plot of the L-shaped membrane, the MATLAB® logo[2].

2.1.1. MATLAB® Desktop

After start the opened window is the MATLAB® Desktop, shown in Fig. **2.2**. It comprises four windows: Command, Current Folder, Workspace and Command History.

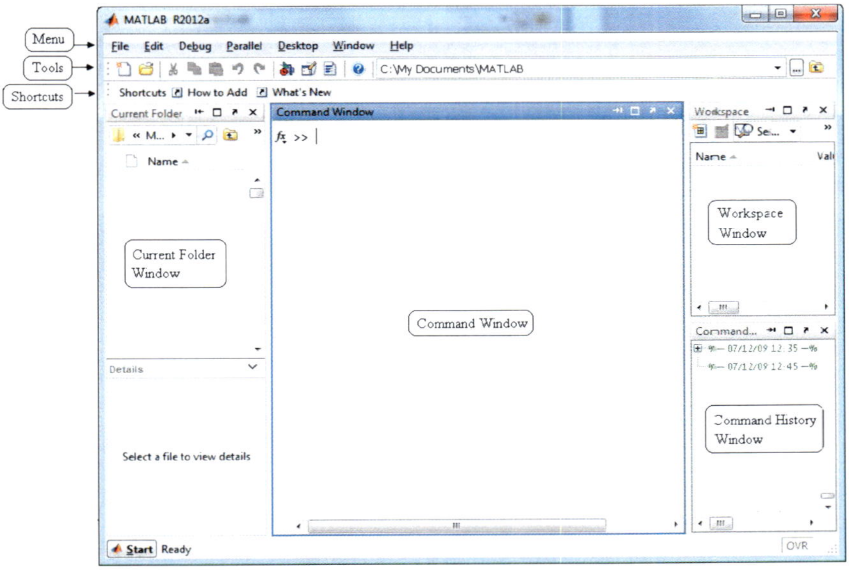

Figure 2.2: MATLAB® Desktop.

---

[2]The image produced by the logo command; the background color changed.

These windows are used intensively and will be briefly described below. There are also Help, Editor, and Figure windows which do not appear with MATLAB® Desktop; they are described within the chapters where they are used.

The Desktop also contains: the Menu, which can be changed depending on the tool in use; the MATLAB® Tools bar with the more common functions; the Shortcuts bar, where one can place icons for quick running of MATLAB® programs or group commands; and the Start button for accessing various tools, demos, shortcuts, and documentation.

Command Window, where commands are entered and results displayed, is the main desktop outlet. It can be separated from the desktop, for convenience, by clicking to the right of the title bar. Such separation is possible for all Desktop windows. To combine windows, click on or select the Default line in the Desktop Layout of the Desktop option at the Menu bar.

Workspace is the graphic interface that permits viewing and manages the variables and other objects of the MATLAB® workspace; it also displays and automatically updates the values of each variable.

Current Folder presents a browser that shows the full path to the current folder and displays the contents of the current folder. By staring MATLAB® here we can view the starting directory, hence called startup directory. After selecting a file, information about the file appears in the Details panel of this window.

Command History preserves most commands entered recently in the Command Window and shows the timestamps and a log of the statements you ran in current and earlier sessions.

2.1.2. Elementary Functions and Interactive Calculations

Two main working modes are available in MATLAB® – interactive mode and m-files mode. I will explain the latter in later chapters. The interactive mode is briefly presented here.

To enter and execute a command, type it in the Command Window immediately after the command prompt >>. Fig. **2.3** shows this window with some elementary commands.

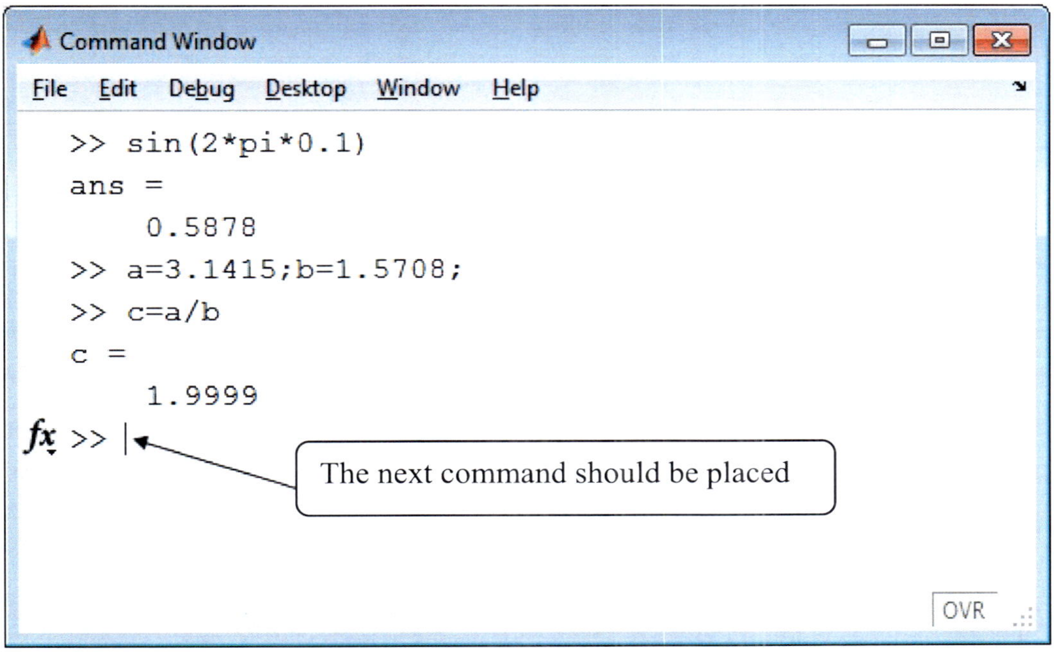

Figure 2.3: The Command Window, as it appears after separation from the desktop.

The symbol *fx*, which appears to the left of the command prompt, is called Function Browser. It helps find the needed function and information about its syntaxes and usage.

Entering a command and manipulating with it require us to master the following operations:

- The command must be typed next to the prompt >>;
- The Enter key must be clicked for execution;
- A command in a preceding line cannot be changed; to correct or repeat an executed command click up-arrow key ↑;
- A long command can be continued on the next line by typing … (three periods); the total length of the lines should not be greater than 4096 characters for one command.

- Commands in the same line should be divided by semicolons (;) or by commas (,);
- A semicolon at the end of the command withholds displaying the answer;
- The symbol % (percent symbol) designates comments be written in the line following it, the comments are not executed after entering;
- The command clc clears the Command Window.

The Command Window can be used as a calculator by using the following symbols for arithmetic operations: + (addition), - (subtraction), * (multiplication), / (right division), \ (left division, used mostly for matrices), and ^ (exponentiation).

These operations are applicable to a wide variety of elementary and trigonometric functions, which should be written with the name and the argument in parentheses. For example, sin x should be written as sin(x); in trigonometric functions the argument x should be given in radians; in trigonometric functions written with the ending letter d, *e.g.* sind(x), the argument x should be written in degrees; inverse trigonometric functions with the ending d produce results in degrees. A short list of such functions and variables appears in Table **2.1**. Hereinafter the operations executed in the Command Window are written after the command line prompt (>>); and it is also meant that the user presses the Enter key after entering one or more commands written in one command line.

Table 2.1: Elementary and trigonometric mathematical functions

Functions and Constants in Math	**MATLAB® Presentation**	**MATLAB® Example (Inputs and Outputs)**
$\|x\|$ - absolute value	abs(x)	>> abs(-15.1234) ans = 15.1234
e^x – exponential function	exp(x)	>> exp(2.7) ans = 14.8797
$ln\ x$ – natural (base e) logarithm	log(x)	>> log(10) ans =

		2.3026
$log_{10}x$ – Napierian (base 10) logarithm	log10(x)	>> log10(10) ans = 1
$\sqrt{x}$ – square root	sqrt(x)	>> sqrt(2/3) ans = 0.8165
π - the number π (circumference-to-diameter ratio of circle)	pi	>> 2*pi ans = 6.2832
Round towards minus infinity	floor(x)	>> floor(-12.1) ans = -13
Round to the nearest integer	round(x)	>>round(12.6) ans = 13
sin x – sine	sin(x)	>> sin(pi/3) ans = 0.8660
sind x – sine with x in degrees	sind(x)	>> sind(60) ans = 0.8660
cos x - cosine	cos(x)	>> cos(pi/3) ans = 0.5000
cosd x – cosine with x in degrees	cosd(x)	>> cosd(60) ans = 0.5000
tan x - tangent	tan(x)	>> tan(pi/3) ans = 1.7321
tand x – tangent with x in degrees	tand(x)	>> tand(60) ans = 1.7321
cot x - cotangent	cot(x)	>> cot(pi/3) ans = 0.5774
cotd x –cotangent with *x* in degrees	cotd(x)	>> cotd(60) ans = 0.5774
arcsin x – inverse sine	asin(x)	>> asin(1)

		ans = 1.5708
arsind x – inverse sine with *x* between -1 and 1; result in degrees between -90° and 90°	asind(x)	>> asind(pi/6) ans = 31.5740
arccos x - inverse cosine	acos(x)	>> acos(1) ans = 0
arccosd x - inverse cosine with *x* between -1 and 1; result in degrees between 0° and 180°	acosd(x)	>> acosd(pi/6) ans = 58.4260
arctan x - inverse tangent	atan(x)	>> atan(1) ans = 0.7854
arctand x - inverse tangent; result in degrees between -90° and 90° (asymptotically)	atand(x)	>> atand(pi/6) ans = 27.6365
arccot x - inverse cotangent	acot(x)	>> acot(1) ans = 0.7854
arccotd x - inverse cotangent; result in degrees between -90° and 90°	acotd(x)	>> acotd(pi/6) ans = 62.3635
n! - factorial	factorial(n)	>> factorial(5) ans = 120

The result of entering the command is a variable with the name ans. The sign equal (=) is called the assignment operator and used to specify a value to a variable, *e.g.* to the ans. Entering a new value cancels its predecessor.

Arithmetic operations are performed in the following order: operations in parentheses (starting with the innermost), exponentiation, multiplication and division, addition and subtraction. If the expression contains operations of the same priority, they run from left to right.

Below are examples of arithmetic operations in the Command:

```
>> 6+2/5

ans =
6.4000
>> (6+2)/5
ans =
 1.6000
>> 6+2\5
ans =
8.5000
>> 6.203*10^23

ans =
 6.2030e+023
>> 2.3^2/3,2.3^(2/3)

ans =
 1.7633
ans =

 1.7424
>> 2^.1-1.72^(1/4)+log(15*.1005)/asin(pi/8)...
-sqrt(8.3)
ans =
-1.9373
```

First executed 2/5 and next 6+ executed

Left division: divide 5 by 2 (not the same as right division: divide 2 by 5) next

Result of exponentiation (10^23) and multiplication displayed here in scientific notations; 6.2030e+023 (means $6.2030 \cdot 10^{23}$)

First executed 2.3^2 and division by 3 executed next; after this 2.3^(2/3) computed in which division of 2 by 3 executed first and exponentiation executed next

Write three periods and press Enter to continue the expression on the next line

Note: the zero before the decimal point may be omitted

The outputted numbers are displayed here in short format (default format): – a fixed point followed by four decimal digits. The format can be changed to long, fourteen digits after the point, by typing the command: format long. To return to the default format, type format.

Other formats can be obtained by typing the help format command; the word after help appears in blue for easier viewing.

2.1.3. Help and Help Window

For information about the use of a command, type help with the command name after a space next to this word, *e.g.* help format as in the preceding subsection. Explanations will appear in the Command Window. To find a command concerning a topic of interest the lookfor command may be used. For example, for MATLAB® command/s on the subject of codons enter lookfor codon; after a long search, the commands with short explanations will appear on the screen, as shown below:

Type lookfor codon and press Enter

```
>> lookfor codon
codonbias - reports codon usage per amino acid for a DNA sequence.
codoncount - report codon counts for a sequence.
aminolookup - displays AA codes, integers, abbreviations, names, and codons.
>>
```

Click on codoncount for further information

For further information, click on the selected command or use the help command. To interrupt the search process, simultaneously the two abort keys Ctrl and c should be clicked; these keys should be used to interrupt of other processes, *e.g.*, that of program/command execution.

For more detailed information use the doc command, *e.g.* doc codoncount, this will open the Help window. The window can be opened in other ways, for example, by selecting the Product Help line in the Help options on the MATLAB® Desktop menu line (Fig. **2.4**).

The Help window comprises three panes: the Contents and Search Results on the left and the page containing information on the topic on the right. Information on any subject can be obtained by typing the relevant word/s into the search line in the upper left corner. The Search Results pane shows a preview of where the search words appear within the page, and the concrete information is displayed on the right.

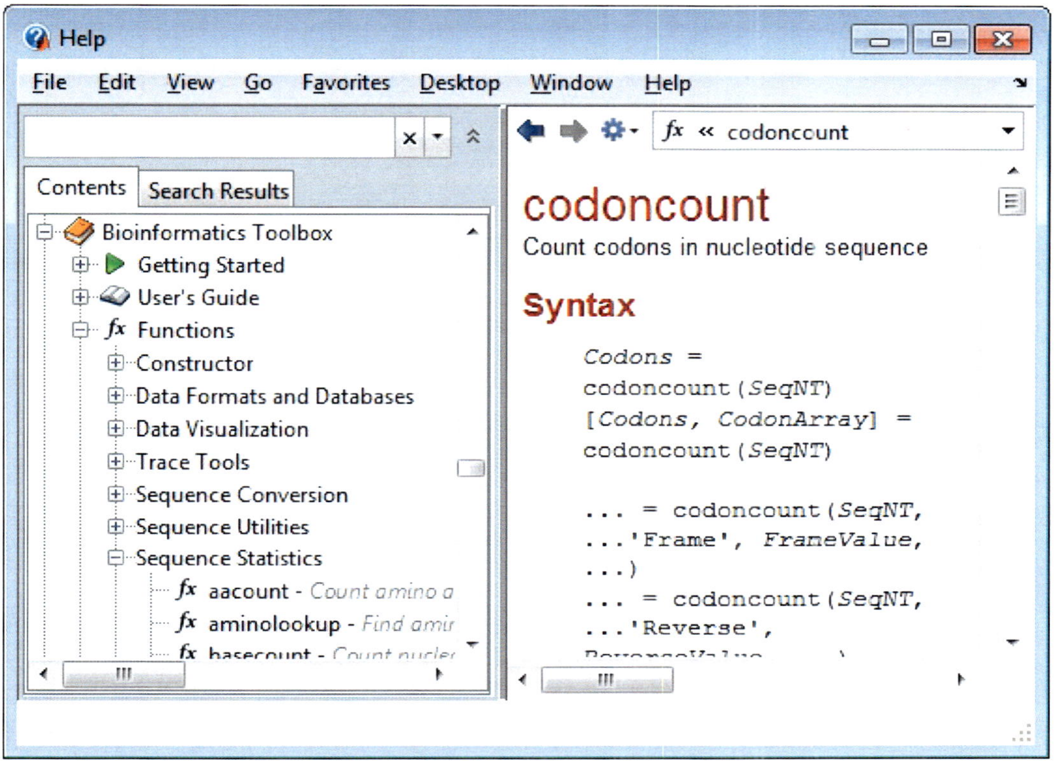

Figure 2.4: The Help Window with information about the codoncount command.

Note that information returned by the lookfor command can differ from computer to computer, as it is determined by the toolbox set installed with MATLAB®, *e.g.*, for the request shown about codon and codoncount - the Bioinformatics toolbox™ should be installed on your computer.

2.1.4. About toolboxes

While sin, cos, sqrt, log, and other MATLAB® functions are valid within a wide range of natural sciences from aeronautics to medicine, each area needs specialized commands to solve specific problems. For these purposes, basic and problem-oriented tools are assembled in so-termed toolboxes, *e.g.*, basic commands discussed thereafter are assembled in the MATLAB® toolbox, command related to statistics in Statistics toolbox, commands related to signal processing in the Signal Processing toolbox, commands for neural networks in the Neural Network toolbox, commands related to bioinformatics in the

Bioinformatics toolbox™, *etc.* To detect which toolboxes are available on your computer, use the ver command. After typing and entering this command in the Command Window, the header with product information and list of toolbox names, versions, and releases will be displayed as follows:

```
>> ver
-----------------------------------------------------------------
MATLAB Version: 7.14.0.739 (R2012a)
MATLAB License Number: 671014
Operating System: Microsoft Windows 7 Version 6.1 (Build 7601: Service Pack 1)
Java Version: Java 1.6.0_17-b04 with Sun Microsystems Inc. Java HotSpot(TM) 64-Bit Server VM mixed mode
-------------------------------------------------------------------------------
MATLAB                       Version 7.14     (R2012a)
Simulink                     Version 7.9      (R2012a)
Aerospace Toolbox            Version 2.9      (R2012a)
Bioinformatics Toolbox       Version 4.1      (R2012a)
...
```

This list was interrupted, as it can be quite long, depending on the installed toolboxes. Information about available toolboxes can also be obtained from the pop-up menu that appears after clicking the Start button on the bottom line of the MATLAB Desktop (Fig **2.2**).

2.1.5. Variables and Commands for Management of Variables

A variable is a symbol, namely, letter/s and number/s, to which a specific numerical value should be assigned. MATLAB® allocates space in the computer's memory for storage of the variable names and their values. A variable can be assigned a single number (a scalar) or a table of numbers (an array). The name can be as many as 63 characters long, and can contain letters, digits and underscores, the first character being a letter. Existing commands (sin, cos, sqrt, *etc.*) are not recommended to use as variable names, as their use could confuse the system.

The following screenshot demonstrates the assignment and usage of variables in algebraic calculations:

```
>> a=2
a =
 2
>> b=3
b =
3
>> c=sqrt(a^2+b^2)
c =
 3.6056
```

The value 2 is assigned to variable a

The value 3 is assigned to variable b

The value calculated by the expression on the right is assigned to variable c

MATLAB displays the variable and assigned value

Some variables are assigned by MATLAB, and are permanently stored; they can be used without a prior assignment. Such variables are termed 'predefined'. Besides previously mentioned pi and ans, these variables are inf (infinity), i or j (square root of -1), and NaN (not-a-number, used when a numerical value is moot, *e.g.*, 0/0).

The following commands, related to variable management, can be used: clear – for removing the memory or clear x y – for removing named variables x and y only; who for displaying the names of variables or whos for displaying variable names, matrix sizes, variable byte sizes and variable classes. Moreover, each variable that has the same information as in the case of whos and has some additional data is presented in the Workspace Window by the icon [icon]. To select or add desirable information about a variable, the right mouse's button should be clicked when the cursor is placed on the Workspace Window menu line; a popup menu appears with a list of additional info that can be shown.

2.1.6. Formats for Displaying Output

MATLAB displays output on the screen in a format specified by the format command in the following forms:

format or format *format_type*

The first command sets the short type of format, which is also the default format for numeric data. Four decimal digits are displayed in this format, *e.g.*, 3.1416. In cases when the real number is lesser than 0.001 or greater than 1000, the number is shown in the shortE format type, used scientific notations - a number between 1 and 10 multiplied by a power of 10 (*e.g.*, Boltzmann constant in scientific notations is presented as 1.3807e-023, in $m^2kg/(s^2K)$, and should be read as $1.3807 \cdot 10^{-23}$, and Avogadro constant 6.0221412927e023, in mol^{-1}, should be read as $6.0221412927 \cdot 10^{23}$). Thus, the number a=1000.1 is displayed in the short and shortE formats as 1.0001e+003 where e+003 is 10^3 and the whole number should be read as $1.0001 \cdot 10^3$. Note, that scientific notations can also be used for inputting variables, *e.g.*, A=6.0221e23.

The *format_type* parameter in the second of the format commands is a word that specifies the type of the displayed numbers. In addition to the short and shortE some others can be used. to show more decimal digits, the display output can be replaced by the long or longE format type. In this case 15 decimal digits are displayed. For example, setting the longE format type and inputting Avogadro' constant 6.0221412927, MATLAB® yields the following results:

```
>> format longE
>> A=6.0221412927e23
A =
6.022141292700000e+023
```

Note:

- The format commands, written with the format type, change the numbers on the display but do not change the numbers in the computer memory; nor do they affect the typing of the inputted numbers.

- Once a certain number format type is specified, all subsequent numbers are displayed in it.

- To return to the replaced short format, enter the format or format short command.

Details about additional format types used with the format command can be assessed by using the help format command.

2.1.7. Output Commands

MATLAB® automatically displays the result after entering a command and does not display the result if the semicolon follows the command. Additional commands are available for displaying the result; two of them are most frequently used: disp and fprintf.

The disp command displays texts or variable values without the name of the variable and the = (equal) sign. Every new disp command yields its result in a new line. The general form of the command reads

disp('Text string') or disp(Variable name)

The text between the quotes is displayed in blue.

For example:

The variable value displayed without the disp command

```
>> Bol=1.3807*10^-23
Bol =
1.3807e-023
>> disp('Boltzmann Const'),disp(Bol)
Boltzmann Const
1.3807e-023
```

The first disp command used to display string Boltzmann Const above the Boltzmann's constant value displayed by the second disp command

The fprintf command is used for displaying texts and data or saving them in a file. The command has various forms that present difficulties for beginners. Here, the simplest among them, are discussed for displaying calculation results.

The following form is used for formatted output of a text and a number on the same line:

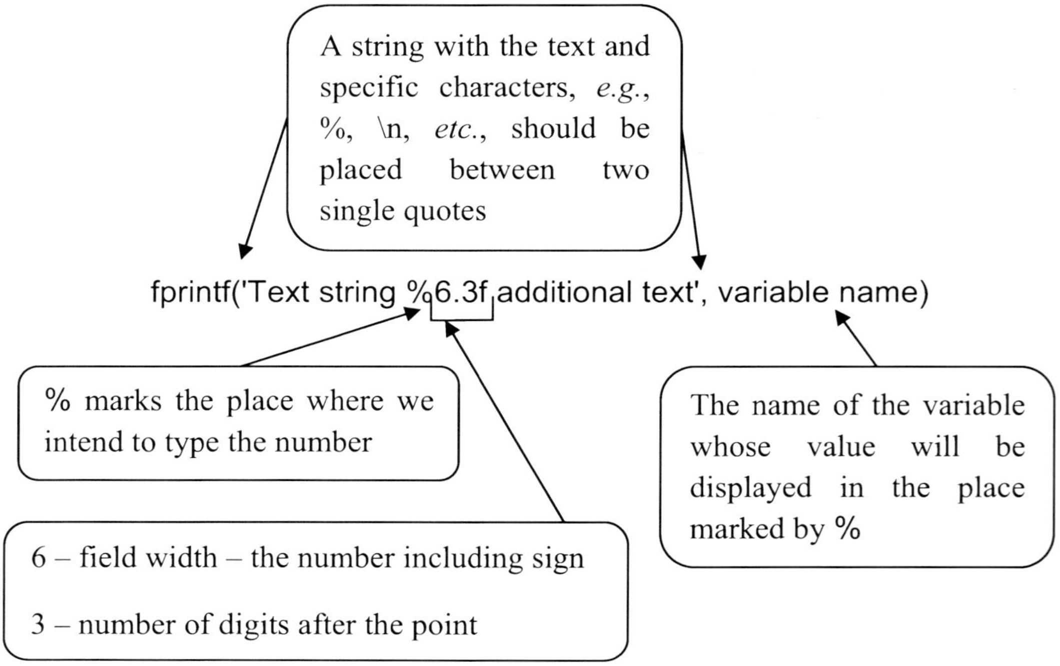

To display text with a new line, or to divide text into two or more lines the \n (slash n) characters should be written before the word that we want to see on the new line. The same characters should be written for appearance of the >> prompt on the new line after executing the fprintf command. The field width number and the number of digits after the decimal point (6.3 in the presented example) are optional; the sign % and the character f, called conversion character, are obligatory, *e.g.* if %f was written instead of % 6.3f the number will be displayed with 6 digits after the decimal point. The f specifies the fixed point notation in which the number is displayed. Additional notations that can be used are i (or d) - integer, e - exponential, *e.g.*, 2.309123e+001, and g - the more compact version of e or f, with no trailing zeros.

The addition of several %f units (or full formatting elements) permits the inclusion of multiple variable values in the text.

Below is an example of using the fprintf command:

Text for display in the first line

\n is for going to a new line

Text for display in the second line

```
>> mO2=15.9994;
>> mCH4=16.01313;
>> fprintf(' Mass of 0_2 is %7.3f g/mol\n Mass of CH_4 is %7.3f
g/mol\n',mO2,mCH4)

Mass of 0_2 is 15.999 g/mol
Mass of CH_4 is 16.013 g/mol
```

Variable name whose value is displayed

Note: % signs position for the number that should be displayed; 7 positions for the number value; 3 digits after the decimal point

The color of the text in the quotes is the same as that in disp (blue).

To display tables, described output commands can be used; they will be shown below, following study of the vectors, arrays and matrices (see 2.2.5).

2.1.8. Application Examples

2.1.8.1. Ribosomal RNA Volume

As shown in the figure:

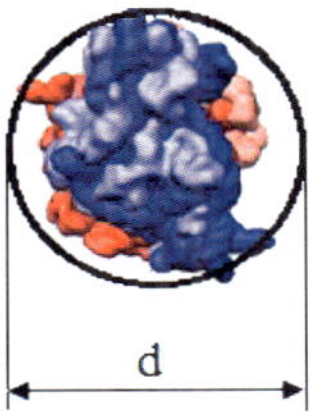

The volume of the ribosomal ribonucleic acid (rRNA) molecule, with some idealization, can be calculated using the expression for sphere volume:

$$V=4/3\pi(d/2)^3$$

where *d* is the rRNA diameter, about $2\cdot10^{-2}$ microns.

Problem: Calculate the rRNA volume.

The solution

Assign values to the d variable

```
>> d=0.02;
>> V_RNA=4/3*pi*(d/2)^3
V_RNA =
4.1888e-006
```

Calculate the rRNA volume

2.1.8.2. Distance Between Two Molecules

The distance d between the centers of two molecules shown in the figure (produced with MATLAB graphics commands) in a Cartesian coordinate system, is given by the expression

$$d=\sqrt{(x_1-x_2)^2+(y_1-y_2)^2+(z_1-z_2)^2}$$

where *x*, *y*, and *z* – are the coordinates, and the numbers 1 and 2 denote the first and second molecule, respectively. The dimensionless coordinates are: x_1=0.1, y_1=0.02, z_1=0.12, x_2=0.2, y_2=0.5 and z_2=0.4.

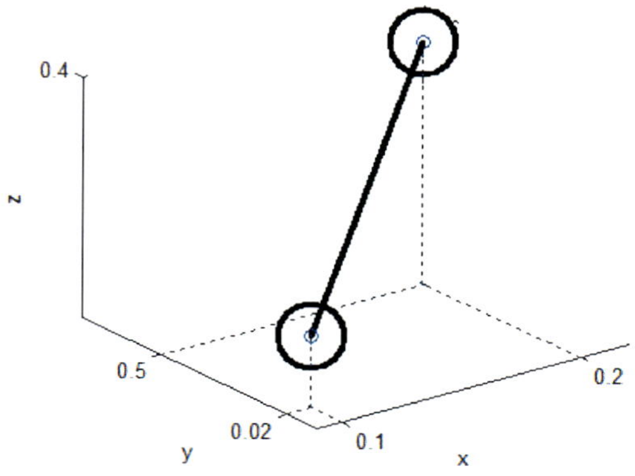

Problem: Calculate the distance for the given coordinates of the molecules.

The solution:

```
>> x1=0.1;y1=0.02;z1=0.12;
>> x2=0.2;y2=0.5;z2=0.11;
>> d=sqrt((x2-x1)^2+(y2-y1)^2+(z2-z1)^2)
d =
0.4904
```

Assign coordinate values to the variables x1, y1, z1, x2, y2, z2

Calculate the distance

2.1.8.3. Newton's Law of Cooling

A liquid (*e.g.* soup in a pot, coffee in a cup, *etc.*) is cooled during t time for the required temperature T (*e.g.* to be suitable to eat or to drink). According to Newton's law, the cooling time can be calculated by the expression

$$t = -\frac{1}{k}\ln\frac{T - T_s}{T_0 - T_s}$$

where T_s is the ambient temperature, T_0 is the initial temperature, k is a constant.

Problem: If the initial temperature of coffee in a cup is 73 C, the ambient temperature is 25 C, and k is 0.3 C/min, when will the coffee be cool enough to drink (T =29 C) ?

The solution:

```
>> To=73;
>> Ts=25;
>> T=29;
>> k=0.3;
>> t=-1/k*log((T-Ts)/(To-Ts))
t =
8.2830
```

2.1.8.4. Constant of a Chemical Reaction by the Arrhenius' Equation

The modified Arrhenius' equation represents the relationship between the chemical reaction rate constant k and the temperature T at where the reaction passes:

$$k = A\left(\frac{T}{T_0}\right)^n e^{-\frac{E_a}{RT}}$$

where E_a – the activation energy, A – the frequency of molecular collision, T_0 – reference temperature, R - the gas constant, n – dimensionless power.

Problem: Calculate the rate constant k for the reaction of interest with following parameters: E_a=75000 J/mol, $A=1\cdot10^{14}$ sec^{-1}, T=300 K, T_0 = 293 K, R=8.314 J/(K mol) and n=1/2.

Using specified parameters, the solution is:

```
>> Ea=75e3;
>> A=1e14;
>> T=300;
>> T0=293;
>> R=8.314;
>> n=1/2;
>> k=A*(T/T0)^2*exp(-Ea/(R*T))
k =
9.1490
```

2.2. VECTORS, MATRICES AND ARRAYS[3]

A normal table of numbers, which in natural sciences often represents data, is a matrix or array. The variables that were used heretofore were given in scalar form. Each of these variables is a 1x1 matrix in MATLAB®. Mathematical operations using matrices and arrays are more complicated than those using scalars: for matrices linear algebra operations should be applied [7], and for arrays - element-wise operations should be carried out.

2.2.1. Generation of Vectors and Matrices. Vector and Matrix Operators

Generation of Vectors

Vectors are presented as numbers written sequentially in a row or in a column, and termed respectively - row or column vectors. They can also be presented as

[3]Used pp. 15-28, 32; from the book cited in note 1; with permission of Biohealthcare Publishing (Oxford) Limited.

lists of words or equations. In MATLAB® a row vector is generated by typing the numbers in square brackets with spaces or comma between them, and a column vector - by typing semicolons or pressing Enter between numbers.

Say we have the data for an aerobic biomass process of wastewater biological treatment as in Table **2.2**.

Table 2.2: Biomass data

Time, minutes	0	25	50	75	100	125	150	200
Biomass, g/l	5.15	5.21	5.52	6.55	7.15	7.75	7.59	7.45

This data can be presented as two vectors; for example:

```
>> time=[0 25 50 75 100 125 150 200]
time =
0 25 50 75 100 125 150 200
>> b_mass=[5.15;5.21;5.5;6.55;7.15;7.75;7.59;7.45]
b_mass =
5.1500
5.2100
5.5000
6.5500
7.1500
7.7500
7.5900
7.4500
```

The data from the first line in Table **2.2** is assigned to the row vector named time

The data from the second line in Table **2.2** is assigned to the column vector named b_mass

Two frequently used operators for generating vectors with constant spacing are:

: (colon) and linspace.

The colon operator has the form

vector_name=i:j:k

where i and k are respectively the first and last term in the vector and j is the step between the terms within it. The last number cannot exceed the last number k. The step for j can be omitted, in which case it is equal to 1 by default, for example:

```
>> time=0:25:200
time =
0 25 50 75 100 125 150 175 200
```

First number 0, last number 200, step 25

```
>> x=-3:7
x =
-3 -2 -1 0 1 2 3 4 5 6 7
```

First number -3, last number 7, step by default is 1

```
>> y=0.2:0.12:1
y =
0.2000 0.3200 0.4400 0.5600 0.6800 0.8000 0.9200
```

First number 0.2, last number 1, step 0.12

```
>> z=15.2:-3.21:1.3
z =
15.2000 11.9900 8.7800 5.5700 2.3600
```

First number 15.2, last number is not less than 1.3, step -3. 21

The linspace operator has form

vector_name=linspace(a,b,n)

where a is the first number, b is the last number and n is the amount of numbers (this value is 100 by default when n is not specified).

For example:

```
>> x=linspace(0,28,8)
x =
0 4 8 12 16 20 24 28
```

8 numbers, first number 0, last number 28

```
>> y=linspace(-10,100,3)
y =
-10 45 100
```

3 numbers, first number -10, last number 100

```
>> z=linspace(15.2,1.3,5)
z =
15.2000 11.7250 8.2500 4.7750 1.3000
```

5 numbers, first number 15, last number 1.3

```
>> v=linspace(0,100)
v =
```

Amount of numbers is omitted, default is 100, first number 0, last number 100

Columns 1 through 8
0 1.0101 2.0202 3.0303 4.0404 5.0505 6.0606 7.0707

The position of an element in a vector is its address; for example, the fifth position in the eight element vector b_mass above (p.33) can be addressed as b_mass(5); the element located here is 7.15. The last position in a vector may be addressed with the end terminator, *e.g.* b_mass(end) is the last position in the b_mass vector and signs the number located here as 7.45; another means to address the last element is to give the position number, namely, b_mass(8).

Generation of Matrices and Arrays

A two-dimensional matrix or an array has rows and columns of numbers. It resembles a numeric table, the difference manifesting itself only in realization of certain mathematical operations. When the number of rows and columns is equal, the matrix is square; otherwise, it is rectangular. Like a vector, it is generated by typing the row of elements in square brackets with spaces or commas between them and with semicolons between the rows, or by pressing Enter between the rows; the amount of elements in every row should be equal.

The elements can also be variable names or mathematical expressions.

As an example, the Table **2.3** presents repeated tests on three batches of enzyme activity, units/mg:

Table 2.3: Enzyme activity (mg^{-1})

Batch 1	**Batch 2**	**Batch 3**
100.9	100.8	110.0
102.0	101.0	108.0
104.0	100.1	107.0

Matrix presentation of this table and some other examples are:

```
>> A=[100.9 100.8 110.0;102.0 101.0 108.0;104.0 100.1 107.0]
A =
100.9000 100.8000 110.0000
102.0000 101.0000 108.0000
 104.0000 100.1000 107.0000
>> B=[27 30
-13.4 7.25]
B =
27.0000 30.0000
 -13.4000 7.2500
>> c1=-4.21;c2=6.023;
>> C=[c1 c2;sin(2*pi*c1) log(c2)]
C =
-4.2100 6.0230
-0.9686 1.7956
```

A semicolon is placed before new line

Type Enter for inputting new line

Elements defined by variables

Elements defined by mathematical expressions

Manipulations with matrix elements use row-column addressing. For example, in matrix A in the previous example, set A(2,3) refers to the number 108.0000 and set A(3,2) to the number - 100.1000. Row or column numbering begins with 1, thus the first element in matrix A is A(1,1).

The semicolon can be used for sequential elements or an entire row or column, *e.g.*, A(2:3,2) refers to the second and the third numbers in column 2 of matrix A, A(:,n) refers to the elements of all rows in column n, and A(m,:) refers to those of all the columns in row m.

In addition to row-column addressing, linear addressing can be used. In this case, a single number is used instead of the row- and column- numbers, and the element's place within the matrix is indicated sequentially beginning from the first element of the first column and following along it, continuing along the second column and so forth, up to the last element in the last column. For example, A(6) refers to element A(3,2), A(8) refers to A(2,3), A(4:6) is the same as A(:,2), *etc.*

By using square brackets, it is possible to generate a new matrix by combining an existing matrix with a vector or with another matrix. Examples of matrix manipulations of this sort are presented below, using matrix A from the previous example (p.37).

```
>> V=linspace(127.1,252.3,3)
V =
 127.1000 189.7000 252.3000
>> B=[A;V]
B =
100.9000 100.8000 110.0000
102.0000 101.0000 108.0000
 104.0000 100.1000 107.0000
127.1000 189.7000 252.3000
>> B(3,2)
ans =
 100.1000
>> B(2:4,1)
ans =
102.0000
 104.0000
127.1000
>> B(2,1:3)
ans =
 102 101 108
>> B(3,:)
ans =
104.0000 100.1000 107.0000
>> B(2:4,1)=6.4321
B =
100.9000 100.8000 110.0000
6.4321 101.0000 108.0000
6.4321 100.1000 107.0000
6.4321 189.7000 252.3000
```

Produce vector V by the linspace

Create matrix B by joining matrix A and vector V, with V added to A as a new row

Refer to the element in row 3 and in column 2 of the matrix B

Refer to the element in column 1 and rows 2- 4 of the matrix B

Refer to the element in row 2 and columns 1 - 3 of the matrix B

Refer to the elements in row 3 and in column 1-3 in matrix B

Assign the value 6.4321 to the elements in column 1 and rows 2 - 4

To convert a row/column vector into a column/row vector and to exchange rows/columns in matrices, the transpose operator ' (quote) is applied, for example:

```
>> Aa=[3 1 2]
Aa =
 3 1 2
>> Bb=Aa'
Bb =
```

Produce the row vector Aa

Define the column vector Bb as transpose of row vector Aa

```
3
1
 2
>> B
B =
100.9000 100.8000 110.0000
 6.4321 101.0000 108.0000
6.4321 100.1000 107.0000
6.4321 189.7000 252.3000
>> C=B'
C =
100.9000 6.4321 6.4321 6.4321
100.8000 101.0000 100.1000 189.7000
110.0000 108.0000 107.0000 252.3000
```

Display previously defined matrix B with 4 rows and 3 columns

Change rows by columns in the matrix B with ' (quote) and assign results to the matrix C

2.2.2. Matrix Operations

Vectors, matrices, and arrays can be used in various mathematical operations in the same way as single variables, as illustrated below.

Addition and Subtraction

Addition and subtraction of two matrices are performed element by element, provided the matrices are equal in size, *e.g.* when A and B are two matrices each sized 3x2:

$$A = \begin{bmatrix} A_{11} & A_{12} \\ A_{21} & A_{22} \\ A_{31} & A_{32} \end{bmatrix} \text{ and } \quad B = \begin{bmatrix} B_{11} & B_{12} \\ B_{21} & B_{22} \\ B_{31} & B_{32} \end{bmatrix}$$

the sum of these matrices is

$$\begin{bmatrix} A_{11}+B_{11} & A_{12}+B_{12} \\ A_{21}+B_{21} & A_{22}+B_{22} \\ A_{31}+B_{31} & A_{32}+B_{32} \end{bmatrix}$$

In addition and subtraction the commutative law operations are valid, namely $A+B=B+A$.

Multiplication

Multiplication of matrices is more complicated, in accordance with the rules of linear algebra. It is feasible only when the number of row elements in the first matrix equals to that of column elements in the second; in other words, the inner dimensions of the matrices must be equal. Thus the above matrices A, 3×2, and B, 3x2, cannot be multiplied, but if B is replaced by another matrix with size 2×3, the inner matrices dimensions are equal and multiplication becomes possible.

$$\begin{bmatrix} A_{11}B_{11}+A_{12}B_{21} & A_{11}B_{12}+A_{12}B_{22} & A_{11}B_{13}+A_{12}B_{23} \\ A_{21}B_{11}+A_{22}B_{21} & A_{21}B_{12}+A_{22}B_{22} & A_{21}B_{13}+A_{22}B_{23} \\ A_{31}B_{11}+A_{32}B_{21} & A_{31}B_{12}+A_{32}B_{22} & A_{31}B_{11}+A_{32}B_{23} \end{bmatrix}$$

It is not difficult to verify that the product $B*A$ is not the same as $A*B$, the commutative law does not apply here.

Examples of matrix addition, subtraction and multiplication appear below, using the same A and B matrices as in the preceding section.

```
>> A=[100.9 100.8 110.0;102.0 101.0 108.0;104.0 100.1 107.0];
>> B=[100.9000 100.8000 110.0000; 102.0000 101.0000 108.0000;
104.0000 100.1000 107.0000; 127.1000 189.7000 252.3000];
>> A*B
??? Error using ==> mtimes
Inner matrix dimensions must agree.
```

The number of rows in the A-matrix is 3 and not equal to the number of columns in the B-matrix which is equal to 4; this generates the error message

```
>> C=B*A
C =
1.0e+004 *
 3.1902 3.1363 3.3755
3.1826 3.1293 3.3684
3.1832 3.1304 3.3700
 5.8413 5.7227 6.1465
```

Multiply B by A and assign resulting matrix to C

Produce row vector V1 from the first row of the A-matrix

```
>> V1=A(1,:),V2=A(:,3)
V1 =
100.9000 100.8000 110.0000
```

Produce row vector V1 from the first row of the A-matrix

```
V2 =
110
 108
107
>> V1*V2
ans =
 3.3755e+004
>> V2*V1
ans =
1.0e+004 *
1.1099 1.1088 1.2100
1.0897 1.0886 1.1880
1.0796 1.0786 1.1770
```

Multiply row vector V1 by column vector V2, the results is a scalar (number)

Note, the V1*V2 is scalar (size 1x1)

Multiply column vector V2 by row vector V1, the results is a 3×3 element matrix

An important application of matrix multiplication is the possibility to present a set of linear equations in matrix form, for example, a set of two equations with two variables

$$A_{11}x_1 + A_{12}x_2 = B_1$$
$$A_{21}x_1 + A_{22}x_2 = B_2$$

may be written in compact matrix form as $AX=B$ or in full matrix form as

$$\begin{bmatrix} A_{11} & A_{12} \\ A_{21} & A_{22} \end{bmatrix} \begin{bmatrix} x_1 \\ x_2 \end{bmatrix} = \begin{bmatrix} B_1 \\ B_2 \end{bmatrix}$$

Division

Division of matrices is even more complicated than their multiplication, becouse of the above-mentioned non-commutative properties of the matrix. A full explanation can be found in books on linear algebra. Here, the related operators are described in the context of their usage in MATLAB®.

Identity and inverse matrices are often used in dividing operations. An identity matrix I is a square matrix whose diagonal elements are 1's whose other elements are 0's; it can be generated with the eye command (see Table **1.4**). The commutative law applies for I - multiplication of A by I, or I by A, yields the same result: $AI=IA=A$.

The matrix B is called the inverse of A when left or right multiplication leads to the identity matrix: $AB=BA=I$. The inverse matrix can be written as A^{-1}. In MATLAB® this can be written in two ways: `B=A^-1` or with operator `inv` as `B=inv(A)`.

Where matrix products are involved, left, \, or right, /, division is used. For example, to solve the matrix equation $AX=B$, when A is a square matrix and X and B are column vectors, use left division: $X=A\backslash B$; to solve $XC=B$, when X and B row vectors and C is a transposed matrix of A, use right division $X=B/C$.

Use matrix division to solve the following set of equations.

$$x_1 - 2x_2 = 8$$
$$x_1 + 8x_2 = 12$$

Based on the above, this set of equations can be represented in two matrix forms:

$$AX=B \text{ with } A=\begin{bmatrix} 1 & -2 \\ 6 & 8 \end{bmatrix}, B=\begin{bmatrix} 8 \\ 12 \end{bmatrix}, \text{ and } X=\begin{bmatrix} x_1 \\ x_2 \end{bmatrix}$$

or

$$XC=D \text{ with } C=\begin{bmatrix} 1 & 6 \\ -2 & 8 \end{bmatrix}, D=[8\ 12], \text{ and } X=\begin{bmatrix} x_1 & x_2 \end{bmatrix}$$

The second form refers to the equation set rewritten with coefficients to the right of unknowns x_1 and x_2 as

$$x_1 - x_2 2 = 8$$
$$x_1 6 + x_2 8 = 12$$

The commands for solutions of both forms discussed above are:

```
>> A=[1 -2;6 8];
>> B=[8;12];
>> X_left=A\B
X_left =
4.4000
-1.8000
```

Equation form *AX=B*
Solution with left division *A\B*

Equation form *XC=D*
Solution with right division *D/C*

```
>> C=A';
>> D=B';
>> X_right=D/C
X_right =
4.4000 -1.8000
```

Note: In the latter case, *C* is the transposed *A* matrix, *D* is the transposed *B* vector and the solution *X* is a row vector

For an example with matrix division see Subsection 2.3.4.1.

2.2.3. Array Operations

All previously described operations concern matrices that obey the rules of linear algebra; however, many calculations (in particular in bioscience) call for the operations to be carried out by the so-called element-by-element procedure. In these cases, to avoid confusion, we use for them the term 'array'. These element-wise operations are carried out with the elements in identical positions in the arrays. In contrast to matrix operations, element-wise operations are confined to arrays of equal size; they are denoted by a point, typed preceding the arithmetic operator:.* (element-wise multiplication);./ (element-wise right division),.\ (element-wise left division), and.^ (element-wise exponentiation).

For example, if we have vectors $a=[a_1\ a_2\ a_3]$ and $b=[b_1\ b_2\ b_3]$ then element-by-element multiplication a.*b, division a./b, and exponentiation a.^b yields:

$$a.{*}b=[a_1b_1\ a_2b_2\ a_3b_3],\ a./b=[a_1/b_1\ a_2/b_2\ a_3/b_3],\text{ and } a.\hat{}\,b=[a_1^{\,b_1}\ a_2^{\,b_2}\ a_3^{\,b_3}]$$

The same manipulations for two matrices $A=\begin{bmatrix} A_{11} & A_{12} & A_{13} \\ A_{21} & A_{22} & A_{23} \end{bmatrix}$ and B= $\begin{bmatrix} B_{11} & B_{12} & B_{13} \\ B_{21} & B_{22} & B_{23} \end{bmatrix}$ leads to:

$$A.*B=\begin{bmatrix} A_{11}B_{11} & A_{12}B_{12} & A_{13}B_{13} \\ A_{21}B_{21} & A_{22}B_{22} & A_{23}B_{23} \end{bmatrix}, \quad A./B=\begin{bmatrix} A_{11}/B_{11} & A_{12}/B_{12} & A_{13}/B_{13} \\ A_{21}/B_{21} & A_{22}/B_{22} & A_{23}/B_{23} \end{bmatrix},$$

and

$$A.\wedge B=\begin{bmatrix} {A_{11}}^{B_{11}} & {A_{12}}^{B_{12}} & {A_{13}}^{B_{13}} \\ {A_{21}}^{B_{21}} & {A_{22}}^{B_{22}} & {A_{23}}^{B_{23}} \end{bmatrix}$$

Element-wise operators are frequently used for calculating a function in a series of values of its argument. Below are examples of array operations:

```
>> A=[3 6;11 4;5 7]          % Generate 3x2 array A
A =
3 6
11 4
 5 7
>> B=[1 2;3 10;1 4]          % Generate 3x2 array B
B =
1 2
3 10
 1 4
>> A.*B                      % Element-by-element multiplication of A by B
ans =
3 12
33 40
 5 28
>> A./B                      % Element-by-element division of A by B
ans =
3.0000 3.0000
3.6667 0.4000
 5.0000 1.7500
>> B.^2                      % Element-by-element exponentiation of B. As a result each term in B is a power of 3
ans =
1 4
```

```
9 100
 1 16
>> A*B
??? Error using ==> mtimes
Inner matrix dimensions must agree.
```

A and B have different inner dimensions: – the row number in A is not equal to the column number in B

```
>> x=1:4
x =
 1 2 3 4
```

Generate four-element vector x

```
>> y=4+x/2-x.^2./4
y =
4.2500 4.0000 3.2500 2.0000
```

Calculate vector $y=4+x/2-x^2/4$ at x previously given as a four-element vector using element-by-element operations

```
>> y=(x+5)./(3*x.^2-1)
y =
3.0000 0.6364 0.3077 0.1915
```

Calculate vector $y=(x+5)/(3x^2-1)$ at x previously given as four-element vector using element-by-element operations

2.2.4. Commands for Generation of Special Matrices and Additional Commands for Matrices and Arrays

There are commands for generating matrices with special values and those with random values. In particular, the ones(m,n) and zeros(m,n) commands are used for matrices of m rows and n columns with 1 and 0 as all elements. Various practical problems involve random numbers, for which the rand(m,n) or randn(m,n) command should be used, the former yielding a uniform distribution of elements between 0 and 1 and the latter, a normal distribution with mean 0 and standard deviation 1. For generating a square matrix (n × n), these commands can be abbreviated as rand(n) and randn(n). Below are examples:

```
>> ones(2,3)
ans =
1 1 1
1 1 1
```

Generate a 2×3 matrix, in which all elements are equal to 1

```
>> zeros(3,2)
ans =
0 0
0 0
0 0
```

Generate a 2×3 matrix, in which all elements are equal to 0

```
>> a=rand(2,3)
a =
0.9501 0.6068 0.8913
0.2311 0.4860 0.7621
>> v=rand(1,3)
v =
0.4565 0.0185 0.8214
>> b=randn(2,3)
b =
-0.4326 0.1253 -1.1465
-1.6656 0.2877 1.1909
>> w=randn(3,1)
w =
1.1892
-0.0376
0.3273
```

Generate a 2×3 matrix a with uniformly distributed random numbers between 0 and 1

Generate a row vector v with three uniformly distributed random numbers between 0 and 1

Generate a 2×3 matrix b with normally distributed random numbers

Generate a 3×1 column vector w with three normally distributed random numbers

To generate integer random numbers use the randi-command as shown in Table **2.4**.

Note: When the rand, randn, or randi command are used repeatedly, the new random numbers are generated each time; to restore the settings of the random number generator to produce the same random numbers as if restarting MATLAB®, type and enter the rng default command should in the Command Window.

In addition to the commands described in the previous sections, MATLAB® has many other commands that can be used for manipulation, generation and analysis of matrices and arrays; some of these are listed in Table **2.4**.

Table 2.4: Command for matrix manipulations, generation and analysis

Form of MATLAB® Presentation	Description	MATLAB® Example (Inputs and Outputs)
length(x)	Returns the length of vector x.	>> x=[3 7 1]; >>length(x) ans= 3

size(a)	Returns two-element row vector; the first element is the number of rows in matrix a and the second - the number of columns.	>>a=[1 2; 7 3; 9 6]; >>size(a) ans= 3 2
reshape(a,m,n)	Returns m-by-n matrix whose elements are taken column-wise from a. Matrix a must have m×n elements.	>>reshape(a,2,3) ans= 1 9 3 7 2 6
b = repmat(a,m,n)	Generates the large matrix b containing m×n copies of a	>> a=[0 1;1 0]; >> b =repmat(A,1,2) b = 0 1 0 1 1 0 1 0
strvcat(t1,t2,t3,...)	Generates the matrix containing the text strings t1,t2,t3,... as rows.	>> t1 = 'Alanine'; >> t2 = 'Arginine'; >> t3 = 'Asparagine'; >> strvcat(t1,t2,t3) ans= Alanine Arginine Asparagine
zeros(m,n)	Generates a m by n matrix of all zeros	>> zeros(2,3) ans = 0 0 0 0 0 0
diag(x)	Generates a matrix with elements of vector x placed in diagonal	>> x=1:3;diag(x) ans = 1 0 0 0 2 0 0 0 3
eye(n)	Generates square matrix with diagonal elements 1 and others 0	>> eye(4) ans = 1 0 0 0 0 1 0 0 0 0 1 0 0 0 0 1
randi(imax,m,n)	Returns m by n matrix of integer random numbers from value 1 up to	>> randi(10,1,3) ans =

	imax: the maximal integer value	9 10 2
b=min(a)	Returns row vector b with minimal numbers of each column in the matrix a. If a is vector, b is equal to the minimal number in a	>> a=[1 2; 7 3; 9 6]; >> b=min(a) b = 1 2 >> a=[1 2 7 3 9 6]; >> b=min(a) b = 1
b=max(a)	Analogously to min but for maximal element	>> a=[1 2 7 3 9 6]; >> b=max(a) b = 9
b=mean(a)	Returns row vector b with mean values calculated for each column of the matrix a. If a is a vector, returns average value of the vector a	>> a=[1 2; 7 3; 9 6]; >> b=mean(a) b = 5.6667 3.6667
sum(a)	Returns row vector b with column sums of matrix a. Returns vector sum if a is a vector	>> a=[1 2; 7 3; 9 6]; >> sum(a) ans = 17 11
std(a)	Analogously to sum but calculates standard deviation	>> a=[1 2; 7 3; 9 6]; >> std(a) ans = 4.1633 2.0817
det(a)	Calculates determinant of the square matrix a	>> a=[5 6;12 1]; >> det(a) ans = -67
sort(a)	For vector or matrix. Sorts elements of a vector or each column of a in ascending order.	>> a=[5 6;12 1;1 7]; >> sort(a) ans = 1 1 5 6 12 7
num2str(a)	Convert single numbers or numerical matrix elements into a string representation	>> a=12.4356; >> num2str(a) ans = 12.4356

All matrices described above, with the exception of some of those in Table **2.4**, have numerical elements, even if matrix elements written as expressions these expressions are translated to numbers.

A string also can be element of a matrix. A string is an array of characters: letters and/or symbols. A string is entered in MATLAB® between single quotes, *e.g.*

- 'Protein' or
- 'Human cells DNA <deoxyribonucleic acid> totals about 3 meters in length '.

Each character of the string is presented and stored as a number (thus the set of characters represents a vector or an array) and can be addressed as an element of vector or an array, *e.g.*, a(5) in the string 'Protein' is the letter 'e'. Below are examples of string manipulations:

```
>> a='Protein'
a =
Protein
```

Assign the string 'Protein' to the variable a; it comprise 7 letters and is a 7-element row vector

```
>> a(4)
ans =
t
```

The fourth element of the vector a is the letter t; thus a(4) is t

```
>> a(5:7)
ans =
ein
```

The fifth, sixth, and seventh elements of the vector a are the letters e, i, and n

```
>> a([1:4 3 7])
ans =
Proton
```

The 1st, 2nd, 3rd, 4th, 3rd, and 7th elements of the vector a are the letters P, r, o, t, o, and n

Strings can be placed as elements in a vector or a matrix. String rows are divided by a semicolon (;) similarly to numerical rows and strings within the rows are divided by a space or a comma. Rows should have the same number of elements, and each column element must be the same length as the longest of the elements. Spaces are added to shorter strings in order to achieve this alignment; for example,

```
>> Name=['RNA';'Guanine';'Uracil']
??? Error using ==> vertcat
CAT arguments dimensions are not consistent.
>> Name=['RNA    ';'Guanine';'Uracil ']
```

Error due to inequality in the length of the strings: number of the characters in the word RNA is 3, in Guanine is 7, and in Uracil 6

```
Name =
RNA
Guanine
Uracil
```

Four spaces were added after RNA and one space after Uracil; now the length of each of the strings is the same and the three strings are successfully written as a column vector

To avoid the calculation of the number of spaces to added to each string in the column use the strvcat command, as shown in Table **2.4**.

2.2.5. Output Table with the disp and fprintf Commands

The disp and fprintf commands can be used for displaying vectors, matrices and a caption. These commands allow output data to be presented as a table.

First we will show how it can be done with the disp command. For example, enzyme activity data with captions (see Table **2.3**) should be displayed with the following commands:

```
>> A=[100.9 100.8 110.0;102.0 101.0 108.0;104.0 100.1 107.0]
A =
100.9000 100.8000 110.0000
102.0000 101.0000 108.0000
104.0000 100.1000 107.0000
```

Generate matrix A with enzyme activity data (in Table **2.3**)

```
>> disp(' Table'),disp(' Batch 1 Batch2 Batch3'),disp(A)

Table
  Batch1    Batch2    Batch3
100.9000  100.8000  110.0000
102.0000  101.0000  108.0000
104.0000  100.1000  107.0000
```

The first two disp commands show the captions and the third outputs numbers from the A matrix. Note: To display the table in the presented view all disp commands should be written on the same command line

Now the fprintf command is used. This command permits a formatted output: for example, the same A-matrix with numbers displayed with one decimal digit can be presented as a table with the following commands:

```
>> fprintf(' Table\n Batch1 Batch2 Batch3\n'),fprintf('%7.1f %7.1f %7.1f\n', A')
                  Table
Batch1  Batch2  Batch3
 100.9   100.8   110.0
 102.0   101.0   108.0
 104.0   100.1   107.0
```

The first fprintf command shows two caption lines and the second outputs the numbers from the A matrix.
Note: To display the table in the presented view all fprintf commands should be written on the some command line

The fprintf command prints rows as columns, thus the A matrix should be transposed (A') before outputting; type the \n (back slash and letter n without space) to display each row on the new line at the end of the column format.

2.2.6. Application Examples

2.2.6.1. RNA Bases Table

Ribonucleic acid has four main bases: Adenine, Cytosine, Guanine, and Uracil.

Problem: Generate and display the matrix in which the first column is the serial number and the second column is the base name.

Execute the following steps:

- Generate a numerical column vector of values from 1 to 4;
- Generate a string column vector with the names Adenine, Cytosine, Guanine, and Uracil;
- Join these two column vectors into a matrix. In MATLAB®, all matrix elements should be of the same type, *e.g.*, if strings are written in one column, then strings must be written in another column or vise-versa. In our case we use the num2str command, which transforms numerical data into string data;
- Display the table title 'RNA bases';
- Display the resulting matrix.

The commands to solution are:

```
>> No=[1:4]';
```

Generate numerical column vector No

```
>> Name=strvcat(' Adenine',' Cytosine',' Guanine',' Uracil');
```

Generate string column vector Name; type each base by beginning with a space to separate the serial number from the base name in the next command

```
>> Table=[num2str(No) Name];
```

Generate the Table as a two column string matrix. The num2str command transforms numbers into strings

```
>> disp(' '),disp(' RNA bases'),disp(Table)

RNA bases
1 Adenine
2 Cytosine
3 Guanine
4 Uracil
```

The first disp displays a blank line; the second disp displays the title; the third disp displays the RNA bases table

2.2.6.2. Bacterial Growth Statistics

In a laboratory, the number of bacterial cells in two batches was checked at different times, and presented in two rows (batches) and ten columns (times) as follows

100 200 400 800 1600 3200 6400 12800

110 190 401 798 1610 3190 6390 12790

Problem: Find the mean, the difference between the maximal and minimal values (range), and the standard deviation for every row of the data, and display the results in two decimal places, using the fprintf command.

The steps are as follows:

- Assign the bacterial growth data to two-row matrix;
- Calculate the mean, range and standard deviation every row of data using the appropriate MATLAB commands;
- Display with the fprintf command the obtained statistics; show the mean values and range as fixed numbers without decimal digits, and the standard deviation as fixed numbers with two decimal digits.

The commands to be used follow:

Enter two bacterial data rows as columns of the bact matrix

```
>> bact=[27 27 35 28 32 33 31 35 28 30
 32 35 34 33 36 35 31 27 28 35]';
>> average=mean(bact);
>> range=max(bact)-min(bact);
>> st_dev=std(bact);
```

Calculate the mean, range and standard deviation

```
>> fprintf('\n Bacterial Statistics\n Mean %5d %5d\n Range %5d %5d\n St. dev.
%5.2f %5.2f\n',average,range,st_dev)
Bacterial  Statistics  dev.

Mean          31    33
Range          8     9
St.         3.10  3.10
```

Display the title and obtained bacterial growth statistics by the fprintf command

2.2.6.3. North-American Wind Chill Index

The wind chill w is the apparent temperature at wind velocity v and air temperature T. A formula used to calculate it in the United States is:

$$w = v^{0.16}(0.4275T - 35.75) + 0.6215T + 35.74$$

where T in degrees Fahrenheit, v in mph; v rises from 10 to 60 in steps of 10 and T decreases from 40 to -40 in steps of 20 [4].

Problem: Write the command for the wind chill matrix by giving vectors v and T and display it as a table, so that w is arranged in rows at a constant v and in columns at a constant T.

The steps to be used follow:

- Generate separately the column-vector v (size 5×1) and the row-vector T (size 1×5);

- Calculate the w-matrix according to the formula. The first multiplier of the w-expression, $v^{0.16}$ (after element-wise exponentiation of v) 5×1 in size, and the second multiplier (the terms in the parentheses) is the size 1×5. Thus, according to the linear algebra rule, their product would be the size 5×5 (the extreme values of the sizes of these vectors). The sum of $0.6215T$ and 35.74 on the right-hand side of the w-equation represents a column vector of size 5×1, and cannot be summarized with the initially defined matrix, which is of the size 5×5 (according to the rules of matrix addition, the matrices must be equal in size); thus, this column vector should be repeated 5 times (the number of columns in the matrix), which can be done by multiplication by the `ones(size(v))` terms;

- Display the title 'Wind chill' and the w-matrix with the digits preceding the decimal point only.

The commands for the solution are:

[4]The ranges and steps are taken arbitrarily and differ from those usually used, but the accepted range is saved.

Enter the velocity values in a column vector and the temperature values in a row vector

```
>> v=[10:10:60]';T=40:-20:-40;
>> w==v.^.16*(.4275*T-35.75)+ones(size(v))*.6215*T+35.74;
```

Calculate the wind chill index w

Display the title for the resulting table using disp

```
>> disp(' '),disp('Wind Chill'), fprintf('%5.0f %5.0f%5.0f%5.0f%5.0f\n',w')
Wind Chill
   34    9  -16  -41  -66
   30    4  -22  -48  -74
   28    1  -26  -53  -80
   27   -1  -29  -57  -84
   26   -3  -31  -60  -88
   25   -4  -33  -62  -91
```

Display calculated wind chill indices using fprintf

2.2.6.4. Weight Versus Height

Measurements of a weight *w* (in cm) and height *h* (in kg) in a group of students at an American college showed the following results:

Heights: 155 175 173 175 173 162 173 188 190 173 173 185 178 168 162 185 170 180 175 180 175 175 180 165;

Weights: - 54 66 66 71 68 53 61 86 92 57 59 80 70 59 50 145 68 78 67 90 75 74 84 53.

These data were fitted by the polynomial expression

$$w_f = 906.14 - 11.39h + 0.03780h^2$$

Problem: Write the commands for the input data in a two-row matrix, *w_h*, and calculate the weight by the expression and the percentage error, $100(w-w_f)/w$. Display the results as a three-column table listing every third value of the w, w_f, and the error.

The steps to be used follow:

- The height and weight values are assigned as above.
- The weights w_f and the errors are calculated by the above expressions.
- Every third value of the inputted and calculated values of weight and the calculated errors are written in a tree-row matrix tab and displayed as a three- column table.

```
>> w_h=[155,175,173,175,173,162,173,188,190,173,173,185,178,168,162,.
185,170,180,175,180,175,175,180,165;
54,66,66,71,68,53,61,86,92,57,59,80,70,59,50,145,68,78,67,90,75,74,84,53];
```

> Enter the values of height in the first row, and the values of weight in the second row of the matrix w_h.
> Note: To continue the data in the next line enter three periods (...)

```
>> w_f=906.14-11.39*w_h(1,:)+0.03780*w_h(1,:).^2;
```

> Calculate the weight by the w_f expression

```
>> error=100*(w_h(2,:)-w_f)./w_h(2,:);
```

> Calculate the percentage error

```
>> pr=1:3:length(w_f);
>> tab=[w_h(2,pr);w_f(pr);error(pr)];
>> fprintf('%8.0f %8.0f %8.0f\n',tab)

  54   49   10
  71   71    1
  61   67  -10
  57   67  -18
  70   76   -9
 145   93   36
  67   71   -5
  74   71    5
```

> Prepare three-row matrix with every third element of the imputed and calculated weights, and the error

> Print the resulting table.
> Note, the rows of the matrix tab are printed as columns by the fprintf command

2.3. FLOW CONTROL[5]

A calculating program represents a sequence of commands implemented in a given order. However, in many cases, the written order of single- or group-commands have to be altered, for example, when a calculation has to be repeated with new parameters or when one expression among several has to be chosen for calculating a variable. For instance, bacterial growth proceeds in four phases - lag, log, stationary, and death - for each of which a different expression is used according to the size of the population. Another example where single- or group commands to be altered is in sequence analysis of DNA-, RNA-, and protein sequences, where the process of comparison of two or more sequences (a procedure called alignment) is repeated until the best-matching scores are reached.

To realize such processes, flow control is applied. In MATLAB, special commands, usually called conditional statements, are used for these purposes; when these commands are used, the computer decides which command should be carried out next. The most frequent flow control commands are described below.

2.3.1. Relational and Logical Operators

Important operations of flow control are realized with relational and logical commands. Both groups of commands test the similarity between pairs of values or statements, but the first operates mostly with numerical values while the second with Boolean expressions.

Relational Operators

Operators matching a pair of values are called relational or comparison operators; the application result of such an operator is written as 1 (true value) or 0 (false value), *e.g.* the expression x<3 results in 1 if x is less than 3, and, otherwise, in 0.

The relational operators are:

< (less than);

[5]Used pp. 33-35, 38, 41-44 from the book cited in note 1; with the permission of Biohealthcare Publishing (Oxford) Limited

> (more than);

<= (less than or equal to);

>= (more than or equal to);

= = (equal to);

~= (not equal to).

Two-sign operators should be written without spaces.

When a relational operator is applied to a matrices or an array, it performs element-by-element comparisons. They return the array of 1's where the relation is true (the array has the same size as the size of the compared matrices), and the 0's where it is not. If one of the compared objects is scalar and the other a matrix, the scalar is matched against every element of the matrix. The 1's and 0's are logical data, which is not the same as numerical data, although they can be used in arithmetical operations.

Some examples follow:

```
>> 2*2==12/3
ans =
1
```

Since 2×2 is identical with 12/3 the result is true and the answer is 1

```
>> sin(2*pi)~=1
ans =
1
```

Since sin 2π=0 and not 1, the result is true and the answer is 1

```
>> M=[-7 8 -15;7 -8 4;-2 -15 -2]
M =
-7 8 -15
7 -8 4
 -2 -15 -2
```

Produces a 3×3 matrix M

```
>> B=M<=0
```

Checks whether each element in the matrix M is less than 0

B =
1 0 1
 0 1 0
1 1 1
>> M(B)
ans =
-7
 -2
-8
-15
-15
-2

Display the elements of M which are less than or equal to 0

Note: The displayed result is a vector that contains the elements of M that were taken from the positions where B is true (logical 1)

Logical Operators

Logical operators are designed for operations that contain the true or false values within the logical expressions. They can be used as addresses in another vector, matrix or array.

In MATLAB®, there are three logical operators: & (logical AND), | (logical OR), and ~ (logical NOT). Like relational operators, they can be used as arithmetical operators and with scalars, matrices, and arrays. Comparison is element-by-element, using logical 1 or 0 according to true or false results respectively. MATLAB® also has equivalent logical functions: and(A,B) - equivalent to A&B, or(A,B) - to A|B, not(A,B) - A~B. If the logical operators are performed on logical variables, then the results are according to Boolean algebra rules. In operations with logical and/or numerical variables the results are logical 1 or 0.

Some examples are:

>> x=-1.5;

Define variable x

>> -2<x<-1
ans =
0

The statement leads to an incorrect answer because it runs from left to right. Due to -2<x is true (1), then 1<-1 is false (0)

```
>> x>-2&x<-1
ans =
1
```

Here the logical & is used, leading to a correct result. First, the inequalities are run; both are true (1). Then the & leads to the answer 1

```
>> ~(x<3)
ans =
0
```

x<3 is stated in the parentheses and is run first, is true (1) and ~1 is 0

```
>> ~x<3
ans =
1
```

Here ~x is executed first: as x is nonzero then it is true (1), ~1 is 0, and 0<3 is true

Another of the MATLAB logical functions is find which in its simplest forms reads as

i=find(x) or i=find(A>c)

where i is a vector of the place addresses (indices) where are located non-zero elements of the x (first case) are located, or are elements of A larger than c (second case). In this case, any of the relational operators can also be used, *e.g.* <, >=, *etc.*); for example, vector T=[11 8.5 5.5 0 -1.5], thus

```
>> i=find(T)
i =
1 2 3 5
>> i=find(T<6)
i =
3 4 5
```

The order in which combinations of relational, logical, and conditional operators is executed (so-called precedence rules) can be obtained in advanced MATLAB courses. The necessary order of execution of such an operator can also be reached by the parentheses.

2.3.1.1. Application Example: Screening of the Amino Acid Molecular Weights

The molecular weights (g/mol) for ten amino acids appear in the following table:

Ala	Arg	Asn	Asp	Cys	Gln	Glu	Gly	His	Ile
89	174	132	133	121	146	147	75	155	131

Problem: Use the relational and logical operators to form a list of amino acids with molecular weights that are a) less than 100, b) between 100 and 150, and c) more than 150. Display the molecular weights together with amino names for each of these groups.

The steps are as follows:

- Assign the height and weight values, as they appear in the table.

- Input the names of the amino acids and their weights as a column vector each with names Name and Weight. Assemble the vectors in the Name_Weight matrix. Note that these vectors are of different types: the Name vector contains strings, and the Weight – numbers. Thus, the latter should be transformed to the string type using the num2str command.

- Find and save the row indices that designate the locations where the weights are less than 100; this can be done with the find logical command; assign defined indices to the m_less100 vector.

- Calculate the number of amino acids with weights of less than 100 by the sum command with the condition Weight >100 (relational operator).

- Display the name of the amino acid and its molecular weight with the Name_Weight matrix where the indices are the m_less100 vector and all column indices assigned by the column operator (:).

- The row indices, the number of amino acids with molar weights between 100 and 150 and above 150 g/mol, and their name-weight columns should be defined and displayed in the same way as it described for the less than 100 weights.

The commands used to solve this problem are:

```
>>Name=['Ala ';'Arg ';'Asn ';'Asp ';'Cys ';'Gln ';'Glu ';'Gly ';'His ';'Ile '];
>>Weight=[89174    132    133    121    146    147    75    155    131]';
>>Name_Weight=[Name num2str(Weight)];
>> m_less100=find(Weight<100);
```

Create the Name_Weight two columns matrix with the amino name and the molecular weight data

Define two column vectors: the Name and Weight with the amino name and the molecular weight data

Find addresses (indices) where the molecular weight is less than 100

```
>> n_m_less100=sum(Weight<100)
n_m_less100 =
2
```

Calculate the number of amino acids with weights less than 100

```
>> Name_Weight (m_less100,:)
ans =
Ala 89
Gly 75
```

Display the names and weights of those less than 100

```
>> m_between100and150=find(Weight>=100&Weight<=150);
```

Find addresses with molecular weights between 100 and 150

```
>> n_m_between100and150=sum(Weight>=100&Weight<=150)
n_m_between100and150 =

 6
```

Calculate the number of sequences with weights between 100 and 150

Display the weights between 100 and 150

```
>> Name_Weight (m_between100and150,:)
```

```
ans =
Asn 132
Asp 133
Cys 121
Gln 146
Glu 147
Ile 131
```

```
>> m_above150=find(Weight>150);
>> n_m_above150=sum(Weight>150)

n_m_above150 =
2
>> Name_Weight (m_above150,:)
ans =
Arg 174
His 155
```

Find addresses with molecular weights larger than 150

Calculate the number of sequences with weights larger than 150

List the names of aminoacids with weights larger than 150

2.3.2. The If Statements

To manage an order of command execution, various conditional statements are used. The first of these is the if statement, which has three forms: if … end, if … else … end, and if … elseif … else … end. Each if construction should terminate with the word end; its words appear on the screen in blue. The if statement forms and their constructions are shown in Table **2.5**:

Table 2.5: If Statement Forms

The Form	How Commands Should be Designed
if … end	if conditional expression MATLAB command/s end
if … else … end	if conditional expression MATLAB command/s else MATLAB command/s end
	if conditional expression

if … elseif … else… end	MATLAB command/s elseif conditional expression MATLAB command/s else MATLAB command/s end

In Table **2.5**, the conditional expression is an expression that uses the relational and/or logical operators, for example a<=v1&a>=v2 or b ~ = c.

When the if conditional statement is typed and entered in the Command Window next to the prompt >>, the new line (and additional lines, after entering) appears without the prompt until the word end is typed and entered.

An application example of the if statement is presented at the end of sub-section 2.3.4.2.

2.3.3. Loops in MATLAB

A loop is another method of program flow control. It permits a single command or a group of commands to be repeated several times. Each cycle of commands is termed a pass. There are two loop commands in MATLAB: for … end and while … end. These words appear on the screen in blue. Similar to the if statement case, each for or while construction should terminate with the word end.

The loop statements are written in general form in Table **2.6**:

Table 2.6: Loops

for … end loop	while … end loop
for k=[initial: step: final] MATLAB command/s end	While conditional expression MATLAB command/s end.

In for … end loops, the commands written between for and end are repeated k times, a number that increases every pass by the addition of the step-value; this process is continued until k reaches or exceeds the final value.

The square brackets in the expression for k (Table **2.6**) mean that k can be assigned as a vector, for example k=[3.5 -1.06 1:2:6]. The brackets can be omitted if there are only colons in k, *e.g.* k=1:3:10. The last pass is followed by the command next to the loop.

For some calculations realized with for...end loops, matrix operations can also serve. In such cases, matrix operators are actually a superior method, because the for...end loops work slowly. The advantage of using matrix operators is negligible for short loops with a small number of commands, but appreciable for large loops with numerous commands.

The while ... end loop is used where the number of passes is not known in advance and loop terminates only when the conditional expression is false. In each pass, MATLAB® executes the commands written between the while and end; the passes are repeated until the conditional expression is true. An incorrectly written loop may continue indefinitely, for example,

```
>>a=2;
>>while a >0
a=1.5*a
end
```

in this case, after a becomes greater than $1.7977 \cdot 10^{308}$ (the maximum possible positive real number), the expression a = inf appears repeatedly on the screen. Press the Ctrl and C keys at the same time to interrupt the loop.

Examples of for ... end and while ... end loops used for calculating sin(x) *via* the series $\sum_{k=0}^{n}(-1)^k \frac{x^{1+2k}}{(1+2k)!}$ at x=pi/6, are:

```
>> x=pi/6;
```

Defining variable x

```
>> s=0;n=5;
```

Setting the s sum to zero and the n to 5. Note: the number of terms in the series is counted from 0 and is n+1=6

```
>> for k=0:n
s=s+(-1)^k*x^(1+2*k)/factorial(1+2*k);
end
>> s
s =
0.5000
```

For … end loop. New element of the series is calculated each pass and is added to the sum s

Calculating sin(x) as series with the for … end loop

Setting the first element of the sum to 1 and terms counter k to 1

```
>> s=0;k=0;

>> while x^(1+2*k)/factorial(1+2*k)>=.000
s=s+(-1)^k*x^(1+2*k)/factorial(1+2*k);
k=k+1;
end
>> fprintf('sin(x)=%f n=%i\n',s,k)
sin(x)=0.500002 n=3
```

Displays results with the fprintf; i - integer

while … end loop. New element of series is calculated k times and added to sum s until he is greater than 0.0001

Calculating sin(x) as series with the while … end loop

In the first example, the sum *s* is calculated within the for … end loop. At the beginning of the first pass the *s* value equals zero; during this pass the first term (*k*=0) is calculated and added to the s. On the second pass *k*=*k*+1=1, the second term of the series is calculated and added to the previous *s* value. This procedure is repeated up to *k*=5 (n=5 in this example). After which the loop ends and the obtained value is displayed by typing and entering the variable name *s*. In case of for ... end loop, the number of passes is fixed. Situation that is more complex is presented by the second example, the while ... end loop. In this instance, a condition of some kind should be given for ending the loop. The value of the *k*th term is larger than 0.0001 is used for this purpose. Similarly to the previous example, in the first pass the s value is equal to zero and k=0 (k is called counter in this case), thise values are assigned before the loop. In this pass, the first term of the series is calculated and added to the sum s, after which the k value is increased by 1. The new term (without a sign) is calculated and checked if it is greater than 0.0001. If this condition is true, the next pass is started to calculate the next term. If it is false, the loop ends and the fprintf command displays the obtained s value and the number of the term used. The latter value is an integer; the conversion character i then used for displaying the value of k.

Note: the for ... end and while ... end loops and if statements can incorporate additional loops and/or if-statements; the order and number of such inclusions is not restricted and predetermined solely by calculation purposes.

2.3.4. Application Examples

2.3.4.1. Mosquito Population and Rainfall

Weather conditions have a strong influence on the mosquito population. For example, an experiment show that at a monthly rainfall q of 2, 7, 11, 18, and 23 mm, the mosquito density d (average monthly number of mosquitoes by all mosquito-monitoring stations) was 0.8, 2.1, 4, 4.9, and 5.7 respectively. These data can be described by the linear equation $d=a_1+a_2q$ in which the coefficients a_1 and a_2 are obtainable from the following set of equations

$$a_1 n + a_2 \sum_{i=1}^{n} q_i = \sum_{i=1}^{n} d_i$$

$$a_1 \sum_{i=1}^{n} q_i + a_2 \sum_{i=1}^{n} q_i^2 = \sum_{i=1}^{n} d_i q_i$$

where n – the number of observed values.

This set can be represented in matrix forms $AX=B$ or $XA=B$, in our case:

$$\begin{bmatrix} n & \sum_{i=1}^{n} q_i \\ \sum_{i=1}^{n} q_i & \sum_{i=1}^{n} q_i^2 \end{bmatrix} \begin{bmatrix} a_1 \\ a_2 \end{bmatrix} = \begin{bmatrix} \sum_{i=1}^{n} d_i \\ \sum_{i=1}^{n} d_i q_i \end{bmatrix}$$

or

$$\begin{bmatrix} a_1 & a_2 \end{bmatrix} \begin{bmatrix} n & \sum_{i=1}^{n} q_i \\ \sum_{i=1}^{n} q_i & \sum_{i=1}^{n} q_i^2 \end{bmatrix} = \begin{bmatrix} \sum_{i=1}^{n} d_i & \sum_{i=1}^{n} d_i q_i \end{bmatrix}$$

Problem: Define the a-coefficients with left- and right- divisions; print the result as a linear equation with the relevant coefficients a_1 and a_2.

The steps to be taken are as follows:

- Generate two row vectors with the given d and q values;
- Generate a 2×2 matrix A with the sums on the right-hand side of the first matrix forms; use the `sum` command for calculating sums;
- Generate a column vector B with the sums on the right-hand side of the first matrix equation;
- Use the left division $A\backslash B$ to calculate the a-coefficients;
- Use the `fprintf` command to display the coefficients in the written linear equation;
- Use right division A/B. For execution of this division, A should be written as per the second matrix equation, using the quote operator ('). The letter serves to transform the column vector B into the row vector; the right division in this case is a verification of the previous solution;

- Use the fprintf command to display the coefficients directly in the written linear equation.

The commands for the solution are:

```
>> d=[2, 7, 11, 18, 23];
```

Generate vectors d and q of the response and concentration data

```
>> q=[0.8, 2.1, 4, 4.9, 5.7];
>> A=[length(q) sum(q);sum(q) sum(q.^2)];
```

Generate the matrix A and vector B for solving the first matrix form: AX=B

```
>> B=[sum(d);sum(d.*q)];
>> a=A\B
a =

-1.9933
4.0552
```

Solution *via* the left division: X=A\B

Using fprintf for displaying results with 2 digits after decimal point

```
>> fprintf('\n The equation is d=%5.2f+%5.2f*q\n',a(1),a(2))
The equation is d=-1.99+ 4.06*q
```

The solution *via* the right division: X=B/A

```
>> aa=B'/A'
aa =
 -1.9933 4.0552
>> fprintf('\n The equation is d=%5.2f+%5.2f*q\n',aa(1),aa(2))
The equation is d=-1.99+ 4.06*q
```

Note: To solve the second matrix form: XA=B, the matrix A and the vector B should be transposed by the quote operator (')

2.3.4.2. Population Growth of Bacteria

Changes in a bacteria population size N in cell/mL were measured from t_0= 1.5 for up to 14 (hours). Obtained results were fitted by the following expressions:

$$N = \begin{cases} \text{floor}\left[N_0 e^{\mu(t-1.5)}\right], & 1.5 \le t < 8.5 \\ N_c, & 8.5 \le t \le 12 \\ \text{floor}\left[N_c e^{-2.338(t-12)}\right], & 12 < t \le 14 \end{cases}$$

where t is time in hours, N_0 is the initial bacteria population at time t_0, N_c is the population in the stationary phase; μ is the growth rate constant in h^{-1}; floor connotes that the bacteria number should be an integer; the necessary parameters are: N_0=84, N_c =35.6·10^8, μ=2.18.

<u>Problem</u>: Calculate bacteria populations at 1.5, 2, 3, …, 14 hours.

The required steps are:

- Determine the variables N_0, N_c, and μ, and a 1x14 vector with the t values;

- Use the `for… end` loop in which every pass runs for the new t value defined by its index (address), *t(i)*;

- Introduce the loop statement `if … elseif … else … end`, where the conditions and expressions on the right-hand side of the N equation should be written in the blank spaces; the N values should be indexed for generating the vector of calculated N-values for each t.

- Use the `fprintf` command to display the vector of calculated N-values.

The commands for calculating N are:

```
>> No=84;Nc=35.6e8;mu=2.18;

>> t=[1.5 2:14];

>> for i=1:length(t)
 if t(i)>=1.5&t(i)<8.5
N(i)=floor(No*exp(mu*(t(i)-1.5)));
elseif t(i)>=8.5&t(i)<=12
 N(i)=Nc;
else
 N(i)=floor(Nc*exp(-2.338*(t(i)-12)));
end
end
>> fprintf('N=\n'), fprintf('%10.0f\n',N)
N=
        84
       249
      2210
     19551
    172960
   1530058
  13535369
 119738026
3560000000
3560000000
3560000000
3560000000
 343612931
  33165687
```

Define the N_o, N_c, μ

Define the time values

for…elseif… end loop

if…else…end statement

Display results with the two fprintf commands

2.3.4.3. Dilution

The resulting molar concentration of a solution, M_2, is calculated by the following expression

$$M_2 = \frac{M_1 V_1}{V_2}$$

where V_2 is the final solution volume, M_1 and V_1 are respectively the initial concentration and the solution volume.

A series of standard solutions were prepared with the M_1 values 0.5, 1, 1.5 and 2 mole/L and common V_1 values 0.1L.

Problem: Calculate the table of molar concentrations M_2 if each of the prepared series of standard solutions had beed diluted by 0.1, 0.3, 0.6, and 0.9 L of water.

The calculation can be made using two methods: with for… end loops; and without the loops, using only the vectors for V_2 and M_1.

The required steps follow:

- Enter the value of V_1 and generate vectors for M_1 and V_2;
- Generate a matrix with the number of rows equal to the length of the M_1 vector and the number of columns equal to the length of the V_2 vector; this step pre-allocates the matrix and reduce operation time when using the `for… end` construction (a minor consideration for small matrices but quite significant for large ones);
- Calculate M_2 (using the expression above) in the two `for… end` loops: the external one for M_1 and the internal one for V_2; such a construction yields all values M_2 for each V_2;
- Display the calculated matrix M_2 using the `fprintf` command, in which the obtained values are presented with three digits after the decimal point.
- Repeat the same calculations but without loops; for this calculation, rewrite the expression in the form $M_1V_1(1/\ V_2)$ so that the element-wise division in brackets is first and followed by the multiplication; $(1/\ V_2)$ produce row vector with 1×5 in size; for the inner dimension identity transform the vector M_1 using the quote operation (') to a column vector of 4×1 in size; the next multiplication by the scalar V_1 does not change the vector size, and the product of the [4×1]*[1×5] matrices is the final 4×5 matrix with the calculated M_2 values.

```
>> V1=1;
>> M1=.5:.5:2;
>> V2=.1:.2:.9;
```

Define the scalar V1 and the two vectors M1 and V2 with the initial solution volume and molarity, and the final solution volumes

Generate a 4×5 zero matrix for the future calculated values of the solute concentrations M2

```
>> M2=zeros(length(M1),length(V2));
>> for k=1:length(M1)
for j=1:length(V2)
M2(k,j)=M1(k)*V1/V2(j);
end
end
```

The two for ... end loops for final solute concentrations

The final molarity calculations in the loops

```
>> fprintf('\n Concentration table\n'),fprintf('%5.3f %5.3f %5.3f %5.3f %5.3f\n',
M2')
Concentration table
 5.000  1.667  1.000  0.714  0.556
10.000  3.333  2.000  1.429  1.111
15.000  5.000  3.000  2.143  1.667
20.000  6.667  4.000  2.857  2.222
```

Use two fprintf for displaying the title and results with 3 digits after the decimal point

Molarity calculations without loops

```
>> M2v=M1'*V1*(1./V2);
>> fprintf('\n Concentration table\n'),fprintf('%5.3f %5.3f %5.3f %5.3f
%5.3f\n',M2v')
Concentration table
 5.000  1.667  1.000  0.714  0.556
10.000  3.333  2.000  1.429  1.111
15.000  5.000  3.000  2.143  1.667
20.000  6.667  4.000  2.857  2.222
```

Title,legnd, xlabel, ylabel, and text
Use two fprintf command for displaying the title and results with 3 digits after the decimal point

2.4. QUESTIONS AND EXERCISES[6]

1. Use the following command to list the variables located in the workspace together with their byte size, and some other: a) lookfor, b) whos, c) who. Choose the correct answer.

[6]Used pp. 45, problems 11-15 from the book cited in note 1; with the permission of Biohealthcare Publishing (Oxford) Limited

2. In the shortE format, the predefined variable π is displayed as: a) 3.1416, b) 3.14, c) 3.1416e+000, d) 3.141592653589793, e) 3.141592653589793e+000. Choose the correct answer.

3. In the MATLAB form, the $y = \dfrac{\ln 2.303}{\log 10}$ expression should be written as follows: a) y=ln(2.303)/log(10), b) y=ln(2.303)/log(10), c) y=ln(2.303)/log10(10), d) y=log(2.303)/log(10).

Which of the forms presented is correct ?

4. The V=[1 2;3 4] command produces: a) a row vector V with four numbers; b) a column vector V with four numbers; c) a square matrix V with four numbers.

5. The matrix $\begin{bmatrix} 1 & 0 & 0 \\ 0 & 1 & 0 \\ 0 & 0 & 1 \end{bmatrix}$ can be generated with: a) diag(1:3), b) eye(3), c) ones(3), d) zeros(3,4). Choose the correct answer.

6. Normally distributed random numbers can be generated with the following command: a) randi, b) randn, c) rand. Choose the correct answer.

7. Check which of the answers below is the correct result of the division [3 6;9 12]/[1 2;3 4]:

a) ans = 3 3 3 3	b) ans = 3 0 0 3

8. A row vector E of numerical values can be transformed into a column vector with the following MATLAB expression: a) E^{-1}, b) inv(E), c) 1/E, d) E'. Choose the correct answer.

9. An element located in the second row and the third column of the 4×4 matrix A should be addressed by the following MATLAB® expression: a) A(3,2), b) A(10), A(32), c) A(6), d) A(2,3).

Note: There may be more than one correct answer.

10. With a degree of simplification, the DNA molecule can be represented as a cylinder and its volume can be described by the expression

$$V = \pi \left(\frac{d}{2} \right)^2 h$$

where d, the diameter of the DNA molecule, is approximately $1.58 \cdot 10^3$ μm, and h, its length, is $3.34 \cdot 10^{-3}$ μm. Calculate the DNA volume.

11. The mass flow rate (in L/min) of blood in the human circulatory system can be calculated by the empirical expression

$$\psi = 0.707 m^{0.425} h^{0.725} + 0.625$$

where m = mass in kg and h = height in m. Calculate the mass flow rate for men with the parameters m=80 kg and h=1.8 m.

12. The temperature distribution in a biological system containing blood vessels is described by the expression

$$T = T_b + (T_a - T_b) \frac{\ln \frac{b}{r}}{\ln \frac{b}{a}}$$

Calculate the temperature at $r=(a+b)/2$ when a=0.5, b=0.65, T_a=315, T_b=310.

13. The velocity v of molecules in the Cartesian coordinate system is represented *via* its coordinate components v_x, v_y, and v_z by the equation

$$v = \sqrt{v_x^2 + v_y^2 + v_z^2}$$

Calculate the velocity for v_x, v_y, and v_z 2.1, -3.1, and 0.72 respectively.

14. The decay process over time of radioactive substances is described by the equation

$$N = N_0 \left(\frac{1}{2}\right)^t$$

where t is the number of elapsed half-live periods (the half-live being the time it takes for a decaying substance to disintegrate by half), N_0 the initial amount and N the residual amount.

a) Calculate N for t = 0,8,16, and 24 days for substances with N_0=500 μCi (microCuries).

b) Display the data as a two-column table, with the first column t and the second column N.

15. The Fourier series is one of the best instruments for describing complex biological shapes; the first terms in these series can be obtained as

$$F=a_1\cos(x+\varphi_1)+b_1\sin(x+\varphi_2)$$

Calculate F for coefficients a_1 and b_1 1.2 and 0.7 respectively; phase angles φ_1 and φ_2 0.1 and 0.2 respectively; and x = π/7.

16. The molecular weights of 15 randomly generated amino sequences are 1558, 1758, 1794, 1480, 1712, 1738, 1636, 1546, 688, 1648, 1654, 1676, 1616, 1726, 1760. The sequences were named Seq_1, Seq_2 and so on, up to Seq_15.

a) Generate a Weight vector with the molecular weight values;

b) Generate a Name vector with the acid name notations; use the `strvcat` command;

c) Generate a 15×2 matrix in which the first column contains the sequence names and the second column - the sequence weights; use the `num2str` command for the string representation of the values of the matrix columns;

d) Display the matrix with the disp commands.

17. Use the data in Exercise 16 for listing sequences with the molecular weights: a) less than 1650, b) between 1650 and 1700, c) more than 1700. Display the results so that the title appears for each group and then, each row shows the amino acid name and molecular weight; use the disp commands. Create an empty line between displayed groups; use the disp command with a space inside quotes (' ').

18. Wind speed and air temperature are combined in the U.S. wind chill index that can be calculated by the so-called 'old' expression

$$w = 91.4 + 0.0817\left(3.71\sqrt{v} + 5.81 - 0.25 * v\right)\left(T - 91.4\right)$$

where the wind velocity v (m/s) is 4, 5, 10, 15, 20, 25, 35, 40, 45 and the air temperature T (F) descends from 35 to -35 with step 10.

a) Calculate w for each of the given values of v and T using the for...end statements;

b) Display the results with the fprintf command, showing only integer values (the digits preceding the decimal point only).

19. Calculate the wind chill index by the expression from the preceding exercise without for.0...end statements, using v- and T-vectors only.

20. Below are the blossom yield data for ten trees, checked twice at different times:

27 27 35 28 32 33 31 35 28 30

32 35 34 33 36 35 31 27 28 35

a) Generate a vector blossom_1 with the first row of the table data;

b) Generate a vector blossom_2 with the second row of the table data;

c) Joint the generated vectors within a 10×2 matrix and display it (without using the disp or fprintf commands) as two columns in which the first column presents blossom_1 and the second column - blossom_2;

d) Determine the minimal and maximal values for each row of the blossom data matrix;

e) Determine the integer mean value for each row of the blossom data; use the round command;

f) Calculate the range *r* as the difference between the maximal and minimal values;

g) Display all results with a single fprintf command so that the two values appears on a new line with its nomenclature (*e.g.*, Average = 30.00 32.C0).

21. An instrument used in biotech laboratory has a response *R* with the values 0.31, 0.43, 0.70, 1.1, 1.5, 1.79, and 2.2 to the following compcund concentrations *c*: 100,150,200, 250, 400, 550, 650, and 850 mg/mL. The best linear fit for these data is the equation $c=a_1+a_2R$; the a_1 and a_2 coefficients can be defined by solving the set of the following equations

$$a_1 n + a_2\sum_{i=1}^{n} R_i = \sum_{i=1}^{n} c_i$$

$$a_1\sum_{i=1}^{n} R_i + a_2\sum_{i=1}^{n} R_i^2 = \sum_{i=1}^{n} R_i c_i$$

where *n* is the number of (*R,c*) points.

a) Find the coefficients by solving the set with the left division rule;

b) Find the coefficients by solving the set with the right division rule;

c) Show the results in the form of a linear equation with the obtained coefficient values displayed with three digits after the decimal point.

2.5. ANSWERS TO SELECTED QUESTIONS AND EXERCISES

2. c) 3.1416e+000

3. c) y=ln(2.303)/log10(10)

6. b) randn

8. d) E'

11. ψ=7.5962

13. v=3.8129

15. F=1.3889

18.

Wind chill index

```
   35    32    22    16     11      8      6      4
    3     2    25    22     10      2     -3     -7
  -10   -12   -13   -14     15     11     -2    -11
  -17   -22   -25   -27    -29    -30      5      1
  -15   -25   -31   -36    -40    -43    -45    -46
   -5   -10   -27   -38    -46    -51    -55    -58
  -60   -62   -15   -20    -39    -51    -60    -66
  -71   -74   -76   -78    -25    -31    -52    -65
  -74   -81   -86   -89    -92    -94    -35    -41
  -64   -78   -88   -96   -101   -105   -108   -109
```

19. Same answer as in Exercise 18.

21. The equation is c=-53.682+358.129*R

Send Orders for Reprints to reprints@benthamscience.net
Primary MATLAB® for Life Sciences: Guide for Beginners, 2013, 73-129

CHAPTER 3

MATLAB® Graphics

Abstract: Available two and three dimensional graphic commands are described in the chapter. The line, bar, histogram, and many other plots are generated with the MATLAB® plotting tool. The appropriate commands with their graphical possibilities are presented by examples of bio-data, equilibrium reaction, microorganism population growth, Ponderal index, *etc*. The questions and life-science problems together with answers to some of them are given in conclusion.

Keywords: 2D and 3D plot commands; lines, meshes, surfaces; life science examples; microorganism population; Ponderal index.

INTRODUCTION

In the sciences and technological fields in general and in life sciences in particular, observational data or results of calculations are often presented graphically. The ability to plot various graphs is a necessity for all specialists that works in bioscience, biotechnology, and bioengineering. MATLAB has a wide selection of available commands that facilitate the generation of two- (sometimes called XY or 2D) and three-dimensional (XYZ or 3D) plots.

Using two-dimensional graphics it is possible to draw linear, semi- or logarithmic plots, bars or histograms, pies, polar, and many others. In the separate Figure Window several curves can be plotted in a plot and several plots can be presented. A plot can be formatted for the desired line stile or marker form, and the desired thickness or color; it is possible also to add a new line, grid, texts, captions, or a legend to the plot.

To present data involving more than two variables, plots having three axes can be used. MATLAB provides a variety of means to visualize three-dimensional data, which allow the building of spatial lines, mesh- and surface- plots, and various geometric figures and images. Generated plots can be formatted using commands or interactively *via* the Figure Window.

This chapter will present the most important commands for two- and three-dimensional plotting. It is assumed that the reader has thoroughly studied the

Leonid Burstein

preceding chapter; therefore, in the following description, explanations to commands are written, in most cases, as inline MATLAB comments - next to the percentage (%) and not in special frames (as in the preceding chapter).

3.1. GENERATION OF XY PLOTS

The plot command is the basic command used for XY plotting. In its simplest forms, it can be written as:

plot(y) or plot(x,y)

where x and y are two vectors of equal length, the first being used for horizontal axis and the second, – for vertical axes.

In the first form of the plot command the y values are plotted *versus* their indices.

After running the plot command with the given values of x and y, the curve y(x) is created in the MATLAB Figure Window with a linear axis scale (by default).

For example, a biotechnology company is using bacteria broth to produce an antibiotic; the acidity level (pH) of the broth was measured for five hours every half hour. The result: 5.52, 5.73, 5.84, 6.26, 6.32, 6.3, 6.04, 6.09, 5.94, 6.03, 6.12. To present these data, generate a plot with the *x*-axis as time and the *y*-axis as pH by the following commands that should be typed in the Command Window:

```
>> t=0:.5:5;
>> pH=[5.52, 5.73, 5.84, 6.26, 6.32, 6.3, 6.04, 6.09, 5.94, 6.03, 6.12];
>> plot(t, pH)
```

After entering these commands, the Figure Window opens with the pH-time plot as shown in Fig. **3.1**.

To change the line style and/or marker type, its thickness or its color use the plot command with additional optional arguments written just after the x and y identifiers:

plot(x,y, 'Line Specifiers','Property Name','Property Value') where the Line Specifiers determines the line type, the marker symbol and the color of the plotted lines (see Table **3.1**), the Property Name assigns properties to be specified by the Property Value. For some of the possible properties and required values, see Table **3.2**.

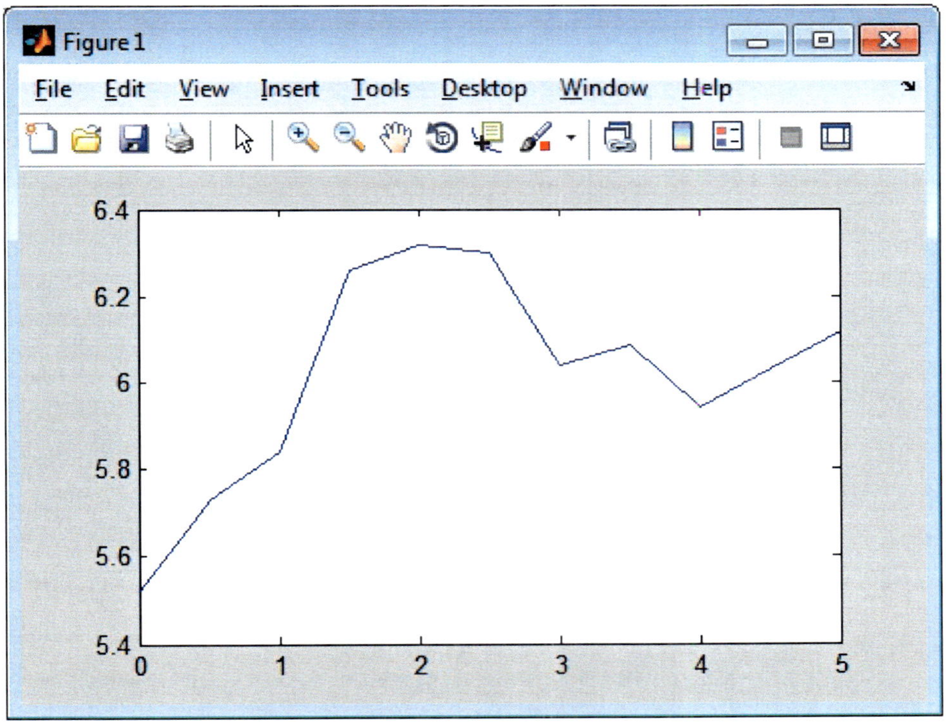

Figure 3.1: Acidity level data plotted in Figure Window with default settings.

Line specifiers, property names and property values are typed in the plot commands as character strings in inverted commas. The specifiers and property names with their values can be written in any order, and one or more of them can be omitted altogether. The omitted properties would be taken by default.

Table 3.1: Specifiers for the 'Line Specifiers' character string*

Line Style	**Specifier**	**Line Color**	**Specifier**	**Marker Type**	**Specifier**
Solid(default)	-	Blue (single line)	b	Circle	o
Dotted	:	Green	g	Asterisk	*
Dash-dot	-.	Red	r	Point	.

Dashed	- -	Black	k	Square	s
(none)	no line	Yellow	y	Diamond	d
		Cyan	c	Plus	+
		Magenta	m	Triangle (inverted)	v
		White	w	Triangle (upright)	^
				Five-pointed asterisk	p or pentagram
				Six-pointed asterisk	h or hexagram

*incomplete

Table 3.2: Available property names, its values and purposes*

Property Name (Spelling)	What it Specifies	Property Value
LineWidth or linewidth	The width of the line	A number in points (1 point = 1/72 inch). The default line width is one-half point
MarkerSize or markersize	The size of the marker (by the symbol)	A number in points. The default value is 6. For '.' marker – 1/3 of specified size
MarkerEdgeColor or markeredgecolor	The color of the marker or the edge color for filled markers	A character based on the color specifiers in Table **3.1**
MarkerFaceColor or markerfacecolor	The fill color for markers that have closed area (*e.g.* circle or square)	A character based on the color specifiers in Table **3.1**

*Incomplete.

The following is the some examples of the plot command with specifiers and properties:

plot(y,'-m') generates the magenta solid line with *x*-equidistant y points.

plot(x,y,'o') generates the points with x,y coordinates marked by the circle.

plot(x,y,'y') generates the yellow solid (default) line that connects the points.

plot(x,y,'--p') generates the blue (default) dashed line and points marked with five-pointed asterisks.

plot(x,y,'k:h') generates the black dotted line and points marked with six-pointed asterisks.

plot(t,pH,'-mo','LineWidth',4,'MarkerSize',10,'markeredgecolor','k', 'MarkerFace Color','y') plots the magenta 3-points solid line (1 point equals 1/72 inches) and *x*,*y*-values marked with 10 points black-edged yellow circles.

By entering the last command with previously used biomass-time data, we can obtain the plot shown in Fig. **3.2**.

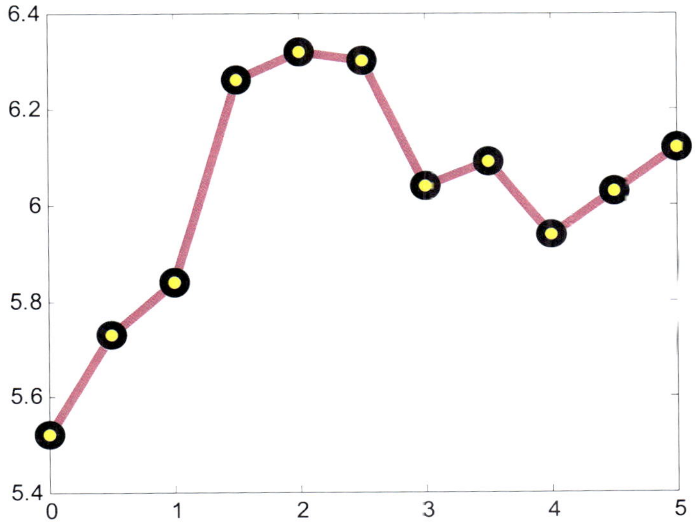

Figure 3.2: Acidity levels, pH, generated by the plot command with specifiers and property settings.

In the examples above, the plots were presented by the *x*,*y*-points obtained by the measurements: in this case the data is given as a table. In many instances the function can be given as an *y*(*x*) expression. In this case the vector of the *y* values should be calculated at given vector of *x*-values (see the example in the subsections below).

Note:

- Type and enter the close command in the Command Window for closing one Figure Window; use the close all command to close more than one Figure Window.

- Each input of the plot command deletes the previous plot.

3.1.1. Single Plot with More Than One Curve

Two or more curves in the same plot can be graphed with at least two options: by typing the pairs of *x,y*-vectors into the plot command and by using the hold on /hold off commands.

The plot Command Option

Commands for creating two or three curves in a single plot have forms:

plot(x1,y1,x2,y2) or plot(x1,y1,x2,y2,x3,y3)

where x1 and y1, x2 and y2, x3 and y3 are pairs of equal-length vectors containing the *x,y* data. These commands create graphs with two and three curves, respectively. To create graph with more than three curves the new *x,y*-pairs should be added in the plot command. For example, plot (in the same plot) two different series of shrub heights: 10, 20, 28, 39, 42 and 15, 25, 32, 36, 41 (in inches), measured at aged 1, 5, 10, 15, and 20 months. To execute this, enter the following commands (without comments) in the Command Window:

```
>> x=[1 5:5:20];        %creates vector x
>> y1=[10 20 29 37 42];y2=[15 25 32 36.6 41];      %creates vectors y1 and y2
>> plot(x,y1,x,y2,'--k') % generates two lines: solid and dashed, the latter in black
```

The resulting two-curve plot is shown in Fig. **3.3**.

The hold Command Option

When one plot already exists and it is desired to add a new curve in it, type the hold on command; the new curve is created by entering a new plot command. To complete the hold on process, we can enter the hold off command; this terminates the hold process and shows the next graph in the new Figure Window.

For example, at new series of heights: 19, 23, 26, 32, 36 that measures the same shrub's ages can be added to an existing graph (see Fig. **3.3**) by entering the additional commands:

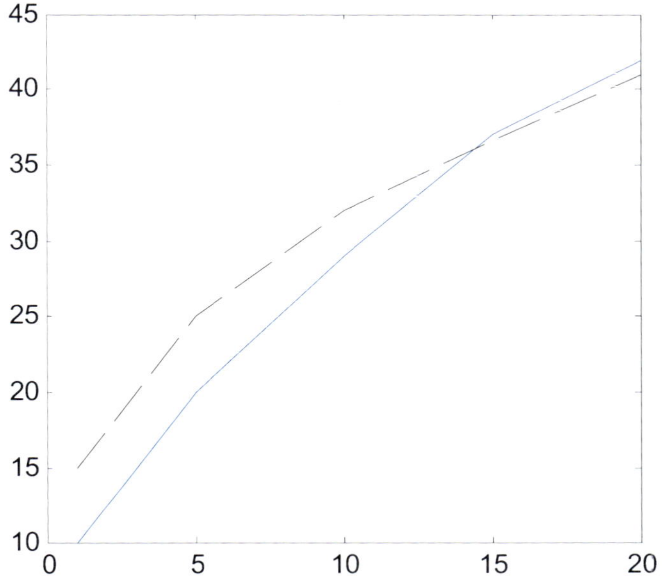

Figure 3.3: Two curves presenting two series of shrub heights in a single plot.

```
>> y3=[17, 22, 27, 32, 36];    % create new vector y
>> hold on
>> plot(x,y3,':r')        % add vector y to the same plot
>> hold off
```

The resulting plot is shown in Fig. **3.4**.

3.1.2.3. Several Plots on the Same Page

It is often desirable to place several plots on the same page, or, in other words, to multiply graphs in the same Figure Window. For this purpose, the subplot command is used, in this form:

subplot(m,n,p) or subplot mnp

where m and n are the rows and columns of the panes into which the page is divided; p is the plot number made current by this command (see Fig. **3.5, a**); the p can be a vector with two or more non-intervening spanned panes. This means that the plots can be arranged asymmetrically so that one of the plots can be placed into two or more columns or rows (see Fig. **2.5, b**).

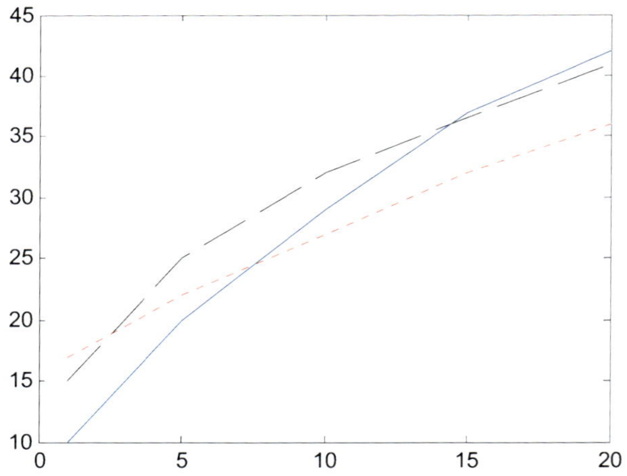

Figure 3.4: Three series of shrub heights in a single plot produced using the hold command option.

For example:

subplot(2,2,4) or subplot 224	creates 4 panes arranged in 2 rows and 2 columns and makes subplot 4 current.
subplot(2,2,[3,4])	creates 4 panes on the page and spans the 3rd and 4th panes for the third plot (the bottom of the current page); makes the last subplot current.
subplot(2,3,2) or subplot 232	creates 6 panes arranged in 2 rows and 3 columns and makes subplot 2 current.
subplot(2,1,2) or subplot 212	creates 2 panes in the same column and makes the last subplot current.
subplot(1,2,1) or subplot 121	creates 2 panes in the same row and makes the first subplot current.

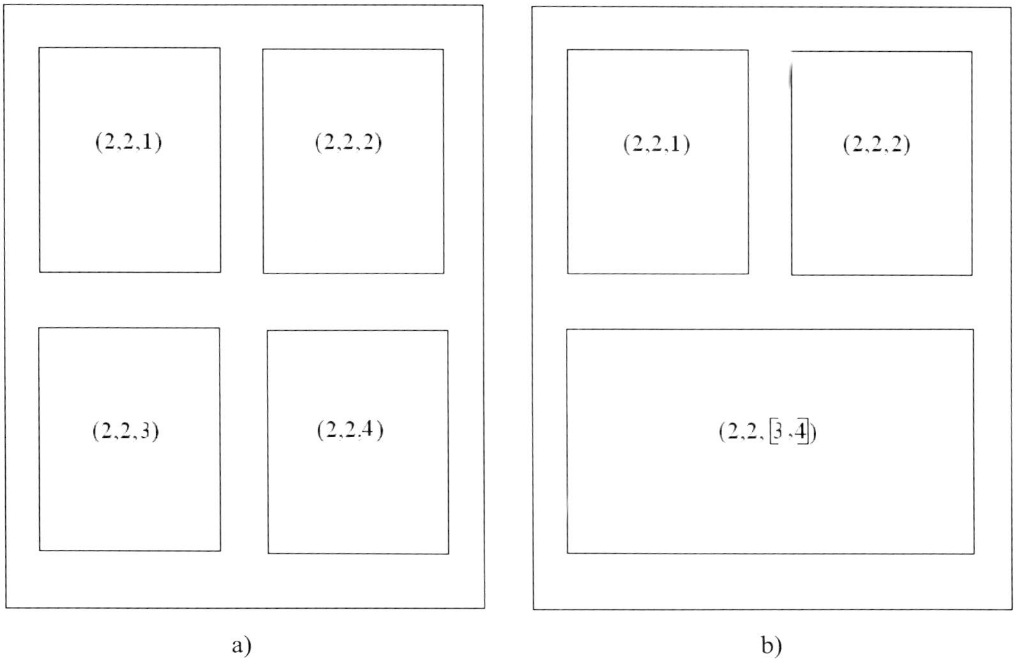

Figure 3.5: Arrangements of the page in four (a) and three (b) panes.

As an example, generate on one page three plots aranging the panes as per Fig. **3.5, b**: a one-point plot, the pH data plot as per Fig. **3.2**, and an ellipse in parametric form x=3sin(t) and y=5cos(t). The MATLAB® commands for generating and arranging the plots in such way are:

```
>>subplot(2,2,1)                 % makes pane 1 current
>> plot(0.1,'p','MarkerSize',10)  % plots a five-points asterisk of tenth size
>> subplot(2,2,2)                % makes pane 2 current
>> t_pH=0:.5:5;                  % creates the t_pH vector
>> pH=[5.52, 5.73, 5.84, 6.26, 6.32, 6.3, 6.04, 6.09, 5.94, 6.03, 6.12]; %pH vector
>>plot(t_pH,pH,'-mo','LineWidth',2,'MarkerSize',5,'markeredgecolor','k',...
'MarkerFaceColor','y') % plots the circle
>> t=0:pi/100:2*pi;              % creates the t vector
>> subplot(2,2,[3,4])            % makes pane 4 current
>> plot(5*sin(t),4*cos(t));      % plots the ellipse
```

The resulting plot is shown in Fig. **3.6**.

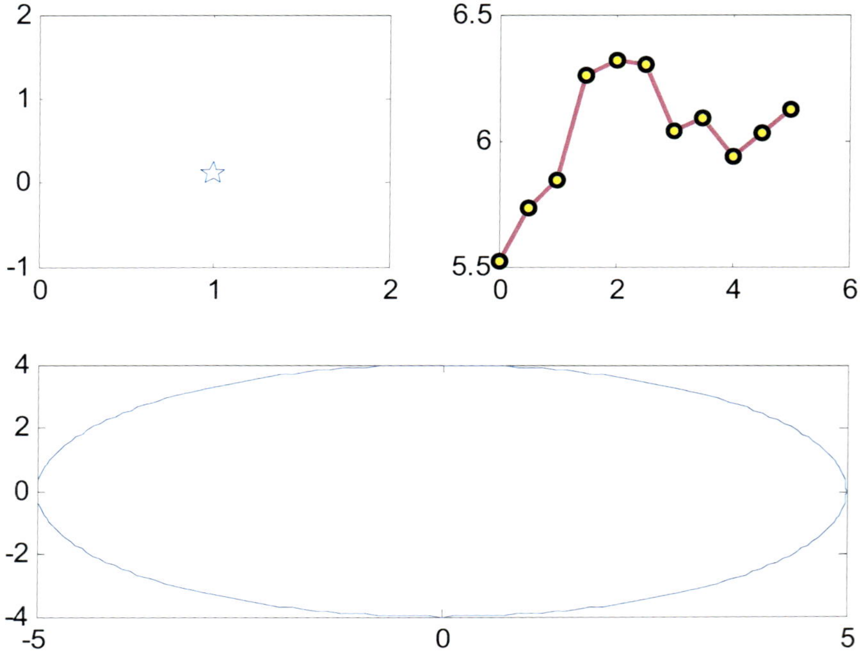

Figure 3.6: Three plots on the same page.

3.1.3. Formatting 2D Plots

In practice, a figure must have a title, a grid, axis labels, suitable axes ranges, and text, while the plotting commands described above produce bare plots only. Explanations, captions, or other additions can be introduced into the plot by including the specifying commands in the created program or by interactively using the Plot Tools editor, available in the Figure Window. The first method is preferable when the intention is to use the written program repeatedly with different *x*,*y* values and the second method can be used when a created figure is intended to be saved, *e.g.*, for use in a demonstration.

3.1.3.1. Commands for 2D Plot Formatting

Commands for formatting a plot should be entered after the plot command. Some of these commands are described below.

The grid *Command*

Use the grid or grid on commands to add a grid to the created plot. The grid off command removes the grid lines from the latticed plot, *e.g.*, typing grid in the Command Window immediately after the commands used to produce Fig. **3.3** will add the grid to the figure.

The axis *Command*

This command has a number of forms, some of them are:

```
axis([xmin xmax ymin ymax])

axis equal

axis square

axis tight

axis off
```

In the first command, the *x* and *y* axes can be adjusted to the limits written in the brackets; the second command sets the same scale for *x*, shape width, and *y,* shape height, (*x*/*y* - width-to-height ratio, called the aspect ratio); the third sets the axes region as a square; the fourth sets the axis limits to the range of the data to be performed on the plot; and the last removes the axis from the plot.

As an example, enter the sequence commands that calculate *sine* and *cosine*, plot them, and set axis limits with the axis tight command:

```
>> x=0:pi/100:pi;        % pi is the maximal values of x
>> y1=sin(2*x);y2=cos(2*x); % note: 1 is the maximal value of y1 and y2
>> plot(x,y1,x,y2,'--k')          % creates the plot with maximal x-axis limits 3.5
>> axis tight   % sets the xmax and ymax to pi and 1 respectively
```

Fig. **3.7**, a was produced using these commands.

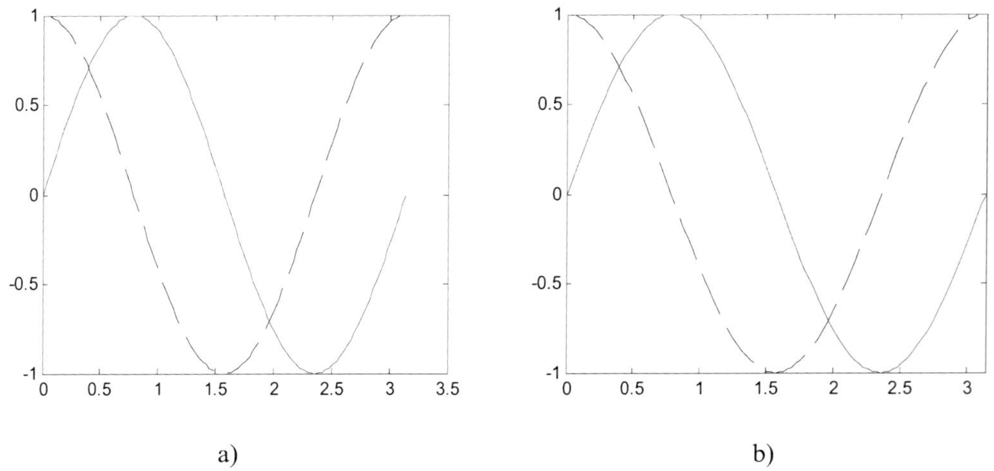

Figure 3.7: A sine2x and cosine2x plot, constructed without (a) and with (b) the axis tight command

Fig. **3.7** shows (a) the *x*-axis limit is set 3.5 and the maximal *x* value is about 3.14 before the axis tight command can be inputted; (b) the *x* limit and the maximal *x* value are equal, after inputting the axis tight command.

The xlabel, ylabel *and* title *Commands*

This group of commands provides text for the *x* and *y* axes and for the top of the plot. The text should be written in string form, between single quotes. The commands take the forms:

xlabel('text string')

ylabel('text string')

title('text string')

In the text string, Greek letters can be include with Latin letters; the font size, name, color, and style, text angle, and some other property options can be written after the text (see below, Formatting of text strings).

The text *and* gtext *Commands*

These commands have the following form:

text(x,y,‘text string’)

gtext(‘text string’)

The text command produces the text starting from the point of the *x* and *y* coordinates. The gtext command places the text at the location chosen by the user. After the gtext command is entered, the Figure Window appears with two crossed lines; the user can move these lines by shifting the mouse to the proper point and then enter the text by clicking on the left mouse button.

As an example, add the title, xlabel, ylabel, text and grid commands to the commands that constructed the plot in Fig. **3.2**:

>> title(‘ Acidity level *vs*. Time')
>> xlabel('Time, min'),ylabel(' Acidity level, pH)
>> text(2.5,6.3,' Acidity level’) % display the Acidity level words at x=2.5 and y=6.3
>> grid

The resulting plot is shown below in Fig. **3.8**.

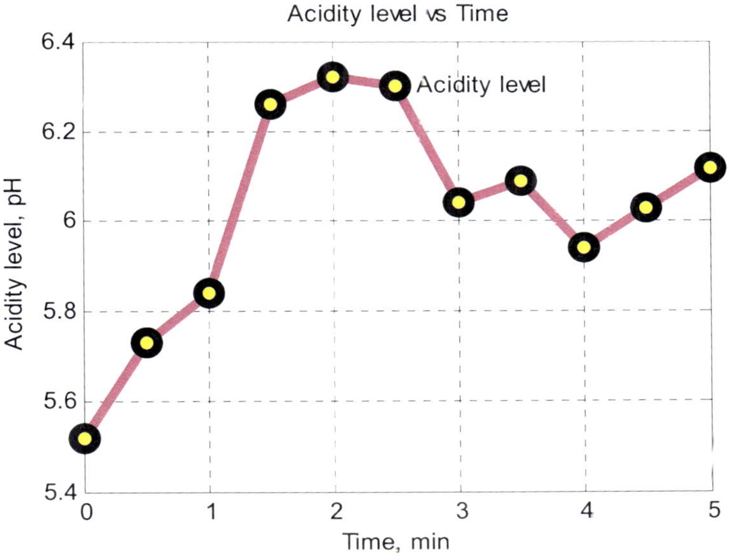

Figure 3.8: Acidity level plot formatted with xlabel, ylabel, title, text, and grid commands.

The legend *Command*

This command should be written as:

legend('text string1','text string2',...,'Location', location)

The command is used to explain each of the plotted curves and prints explanations written in 'text string1',' text string2',.... The 'Location' property is optional; it specifies the location area where the legend explanations should be placed. For example:

location = 'NorthEastOutside' places the legend outside the plot frames, to the right; location = 'Best' places the legend inside the plot at a location where there is less conflict with data in plot.

The default location for the legend is in the upper-right corner of the plot.

Thus, the legend in Fig. **3.7** may be generated by inputting the command: legend('Sin2x','Cos2x','Location','best')

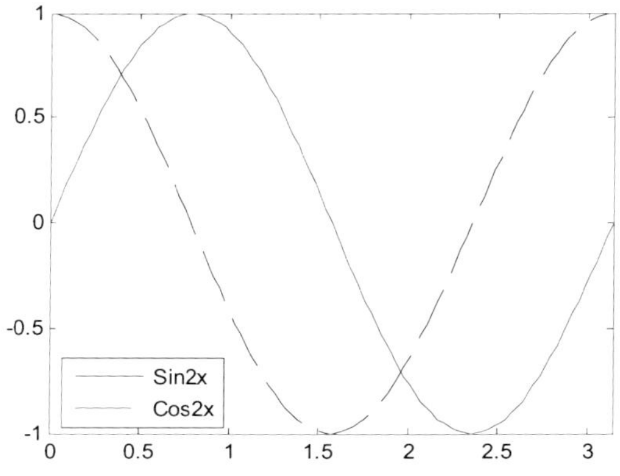

Figure 3.9: Plot of the sin2x and cos2x functions with legend.

Formatting Text Strings

Text in the text string-s in the commands described above can be formatted by writing special characters (called modifiers) inside the string or by including the options PropertyName with PropertyValue in the command after the text string.

Some useful modifiers used for setting the font name, style, size, color, Greek letters, or sub- and superscripts are:

\b \it \rm	Sets the bold, italic, or normal fonts respectively.
\fontsize{number}	Specifies the size of the letters, for example, \fontsize{12} sets letter size 12.
\fontname{name}	Specifies the name of the used font, for example, \fontname{Arial} sets Arial font.
\name of the Greek letter	Sets a Greek letter, for example \sigma sets σ and \Sigma sets Σ.
_ ^	Sets subscripts and superscripts respectively, for example, '^oC' sets the superscript for 'o'; the resulting text is displayed as ^{o}C.

The text color or its background can be regulated by including the property (the name and the value) in the command. Some property names and their values are:

'Color', 'color specifiers from Tab.3.1'	sets the text color; for example 'Color', 'r' sets the color red for the text string.
'BackgroundColor', 'color specifiers from Tab.3.1'	sets the background color (rectangular area); for example 'BackgroundColor','y' sets the color yellow for the background area.

A detailed explanation is available from the Text Properties section of the MATLAB documentation (in the MATLAB Help Window).

3.1.3.2. Formatting 2D Plots with the Plot Editor

The Figure Window contains an assortment of formatting buttons and menu items for interactively formatting the plot. Click the Edit Plot button, , on the bar under the menu to start the Plot Edit mode. The Figure Window menu line, with the bar containing the buttons used most frequently is shown in Fig. **3.10.** The properties of the axes and lines, as well as the entire figure can be changed by using the pop-up menu, summoned by clicking the Edit option in the Figure menu. The title, axis labels, texts and legend are activated by using the pop-up menu summoned by clicking the Insert option in the menu.

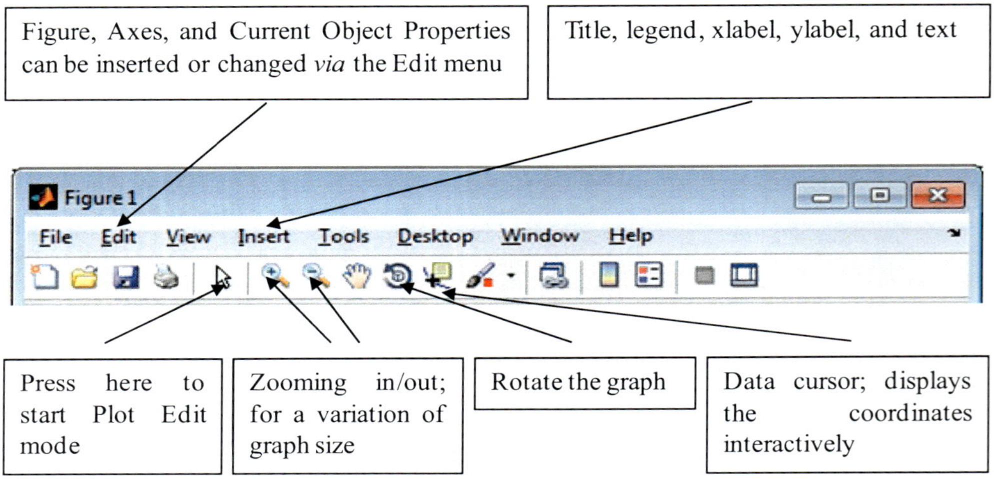

Figure 3.10: Plot Editor buttons in Figure Window.

After activating the 'Plot Edit' mode the text, legend and objects in the plot can be shifted by clicking on each of them. The special Property Editor is opened by double clicking on the shifted curve, plotted point, or axes; the editor has the means to change or edit the various characteristics of the clicked object. Detailed information is available in the Help Window by calling the Editing Plot section.

3.2. GENERATING *XYZ* PLOTS

MATLAB® has three main groups of commands for the tree-dimensional presentation of lines, meshes and surfaces. These, some other commands, and various formatting commands are described below.

3.2.1. Generating Lines in Three Dimensional Plots

Points in three-dimensional space are described by three coordinates each and the lines that connect these points. Similar to the plot command used for two-dimensional line plotting, the plot3 command is used for plotting a three-dimensional line. The simplest form of this command is:

plot3 (x,y,z),

This is a more complicated form:

plot3(x,y,z, 'Line Specifiers','Property Name','Property Value')

In these commands, *x, y,* and *z* are the equivalent vectors, with coordinates for each of the points; the Line Specifiers, Property Name and Property Value are properties and they have the same significance as in the two-dimensional case.

The grid, xlabel, and ylabel commands are also used in three-dimensional plots; in addition, the zlabel command can be used.

For example, a three-dimensional plot is produced by writing the commands as follows:

```
>> t=-4*pi:pi/100:4*pi;
>> x=t.*cos(2*t);
>> y=t.*sin(2*t);
>> z=t;
>> plot3(x,y,z,'k','LineWidth',4)
>> grid
>> xlabel('x'),ylabel('y'),zlabel('z')
```

These commands compute the parametrically given coordinates $x=t\cdot cos(2t)$, $y=t\cdot sin(2t)$, and $z=t$ with t changed from -4π up to 4π with step $\pi/100$. The plot3 command is used here with the property name LineWidth and their values are 4, which increases the width of the line by four times; other commands generate grids and captions to the axis.

The plot appears in the Figure Window after the commands are inputted. The line has the attributes shown in Fig. **3.11**.

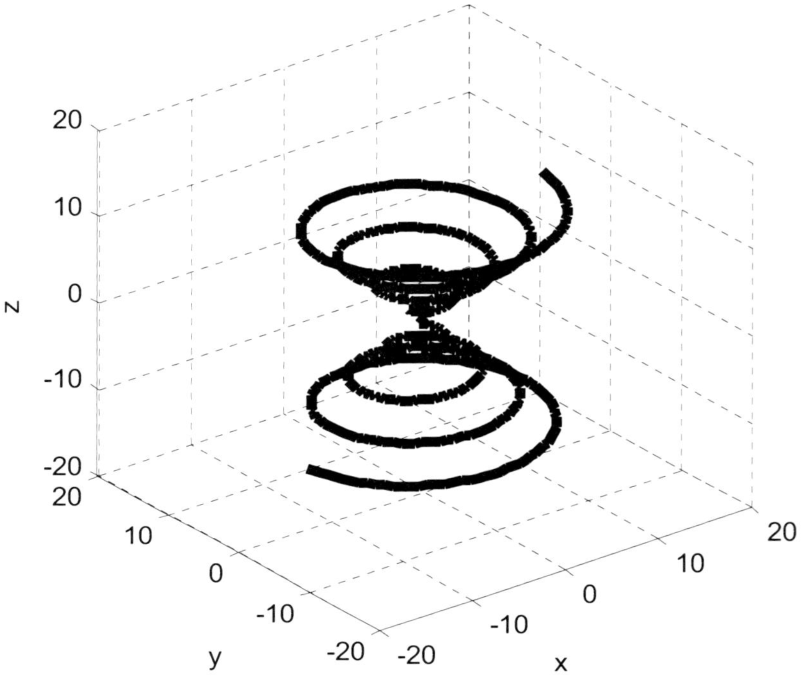

Figure 3.11: A line in three-dimensional coordinates.

3.2.2. Mesh Plots

The main commands used in the three-dimensional plotting are mesh and surf. In order to understand them it is necessary to understand mesh construction in MATLAB®. Since every point in three-dimensional space has three coordinates *x*, *y* and *z*, it is necessary to use them in order to reconstruct a surface. In other words, when z is a function of two variables *x* and *y* we must generate two two-dimensional matrices with the *x*- and *y*- coordinate values respectively and calculate the matrix of the *z*-coordinates for every (*x*,*y*)-pair. The area of the *x* and *y* coordinates for which the *z*-coordinates must be obtained is called the domain. An example of point representation in three-dimensional space is shown in Fig. **3.12**.

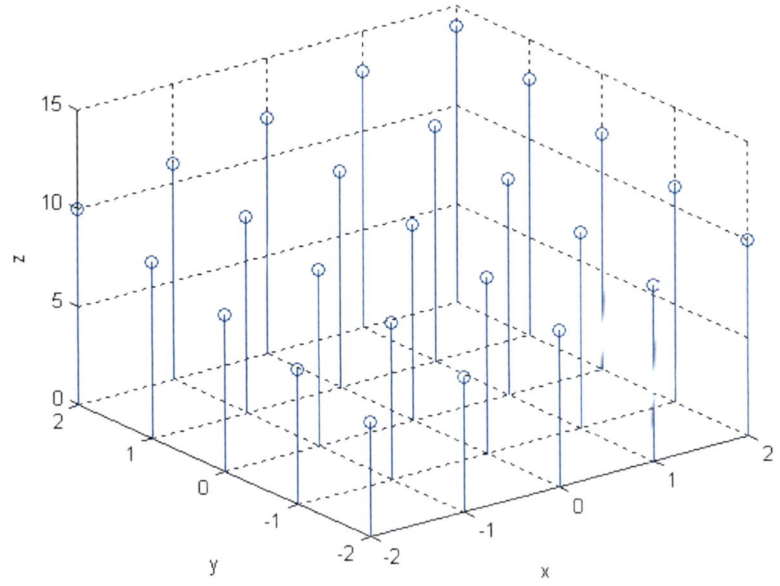

Figure 3.12: Three-dimensional points and their *x*,*y*- projection[1].

In this figure, the domain is represented in the orthogonal grid, in the *x*,*y* plane and constructed with the axis tick vectors *x* =-2…2 and *y*=-2…2. Each node in the *x*,*y* plane has a pair of *x*,*y* values. We obtain the *X*-matrix by writing all the *x*-values, ordered by rows (along each iso-*y* line); the same procedure yields the *Y*-matrix:

$$X = \begin{pmatrix} -2 & -1 & 0 & 1 & 2 \\ -2 & -1 & 0 & 1 & 2 \\ -2 & -1 & 0 & 1 & 2 \\ -2 & -1 & 0 & 1 & 2 \\ -2 & -1 & 0 & 1 & 2 \end{pmatrix} \qquad Y = \begin{pmatrix} -2 & -2 & -2 & -2 & -2 \\ -1 & -1 & -1 & -1 & -1 \\ 0 & 0 & 0 & 0 & 0 \\ 1 & 1 & 1 & 1 & 1 \\ 2 & 2 & 2 & 2 & 2 \end{pmatrix}$$

When the *X* and *Y* matrices were defined, the *z*-coordinates should be obtained for every grid point; the element-by-element calculations are used for this. When the *X*, *Y*, and *Z* matrices were generated, the whole surface can be plotted.

[1]Generated with the `stem3(x,y,z)` command; the expression used is: $z=8+x+y$

A special command, meshgrid, creates the *X* and *Y* matrices from the given vectors of *x* and *y*. The command takes the following form:

[X,Y]= meshgrid(x,y)

X and Y here are the matrices of the grid coordinates that determine the dividing of the domain produced by the command based on the given x and y vectors. When the x and y vectors are equal, this command may be simplified to

[X,Y]= meshgrid(x)

For the particular case illustrated in Fig. **3.12** the *X* and *Y* matrices presented above can be created as follows:

```
>> x=-2:2;
>> [X,Y]=meshgrid(x)
X =
    -2  -1   0   1   2
    -2  -1   0   1   2
    -2  -1   0   1   2
    -2  -1   0   1   2
    -2  -1   0   1   2
Y =
    -2  -2  -2  -2  -2
    -1  -1  -1  -1  -1
     0   0   0   0   0
     1   1   1   1   1
     2   2   2   2   2
```

Plot the 3-D mesh graph for the expression:

$$z = \frac{xy}{x+y}$$

with the x and y coordinates given between 0.1 and 2 with the step 0.1.

The following command generates the mesh with colored lines:

mesh(X,Y,Z)

where X, Y, and Z are coordinate matrices, and two of them, X and Y are defined with the meshgrid command for the given vectors x and y, and the third matrix, Z, is calculated with these matrices by using the above expression.

Thus the program that plots the mesh surface reads as follows:

```
>>x=0.1:0.1:2;
>> [X,Y]=meshgrid(x);
>> Z=(X.*Y)./(X+Y);
>>mesh(X,Y,Z)
>>xlabel('x'),ylabel('y'),zlabel('z')
>>grid on
```

The resulting plot is shown below in Fig. **3.13**.

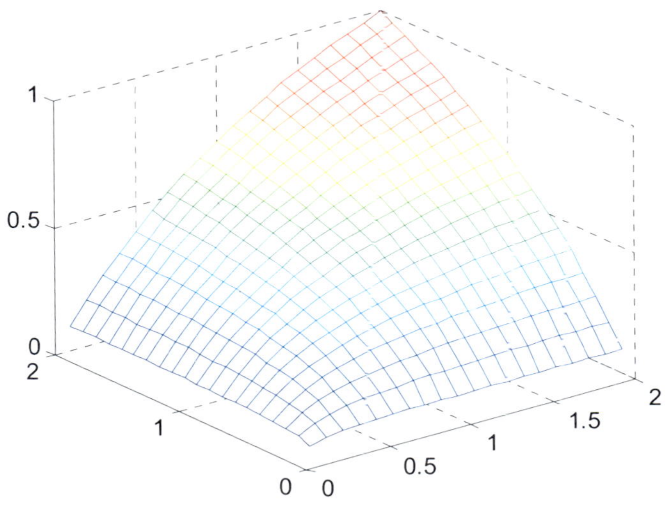

Figure 3.13: Mesh Plot

3.2.3. Surface Plots

The surf command is used to generate the plot with colored surfaces between the mesh lines. This command takes the following form:

surf(X,Y,Z)

where X, Y, and Z are the same matrices as in the mesh command.

By using this command for the function in the example above, can enter commands as follows:

```
>>x=0.1:0.1:2;
>> [X,Y]=meshgrid(x);
>> Z=(X.*Y)./(X+Y);
>>surf(X,Y,Z)
>>xlabel('x'),ylabel('y'),zlabel('z')
>>grid on
```

The resulting plot is shown in Fig. **3.14**.

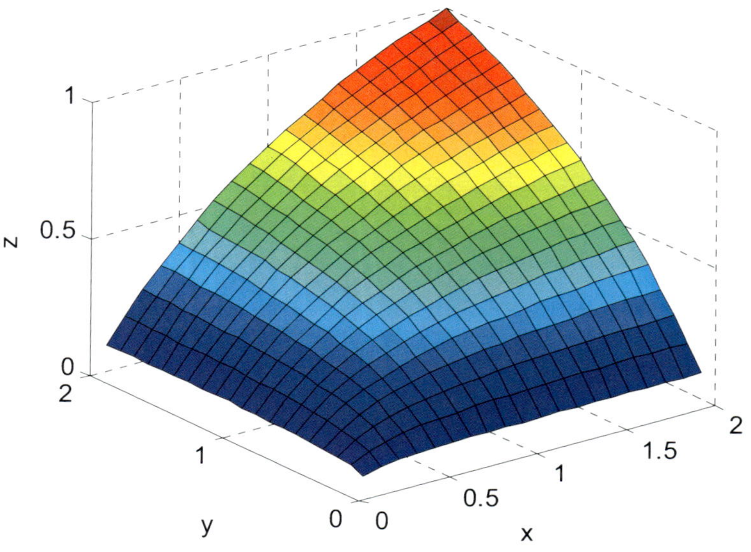

Figure 3.14: Surface plot.

The surf and the mesh commands can be used in the surf(Z) or mesh(Z) forms. They plot Z values *versus* the indices of the Z-matrix.

3.2.4. Formatting and Rotation of 3D Plots

Many 2D commands, such as grid, title, xlabel, ylabel, and axis, described in section 3.1.3 are suitable for 3D plot formatting. There are many additional commands for formatting three-dimensional plot. Some of them are described below.

3.2.4.1. The colormap Command

Surfaces or meshes have colors. Color plays important role in plots, particularly in the generation of three-dimensional plots. After entering the mesh or surf commands, colors are automatically generated according to the *z*-values. Another option is the colormap command, in wich the colors can be set by the user. The command takes the following form:

colormap(c)

where c is a row vector with three elements: the first specifies red color intensity, the second, green color intensity and the third, specifies blue color intensity (RGB); intensities are graded from 0 to 1, as follows:

c=[0 0 0] - black c=[1 1 1] - white c=[1 0 0] - red	c=[0 1 0] - green c=[0 0 1] - blue c=[0 1 1] - cyan	c=[1 1 0] - yellow c=[1 0 1] - magenta c=[0.5 0.5 0.5] - gray	c=[1 0.62 0.4] - copper c=[0.49 1 0.83] - Aquamarine

If the colormap([0 0 1]) command is entered after entering the commands that produced the mesh plot in Fig. **3.13**, the mesh lines change in color to blue.

Another form of this command is

colormap name

This form is intended for use with built-in colormaps: the name can be jet, cool, winter, spring, or some others. For example the colormap winter changes colors to shades of blue and green.

3.2.4.2. The view Command

Each 3D plot is shown in MATLAB from a certain viewpoint. The plot orientation relative to the viewer is regulated by the view command, which takes the form view(az,el)

where az and el are the angles, azimuth and elevation respectively; the azimuth is the horizontal (*x,y*-plane) angle relative to the negative direction of the *x*-axes; the elevation angle is the vertical angle that defines the geometric height above the *x,y*-plane.

An az angle oriented in a counter-clockwise direction is defined as positive; the el angle counted as positive when it is taken in the direction of the *z*-axes. Both angles must be given in degrees, its default values are az=-37.5°, and el=30°.

The observation point and view angles used in a 3D plot are shown in Fig. **3.15**.

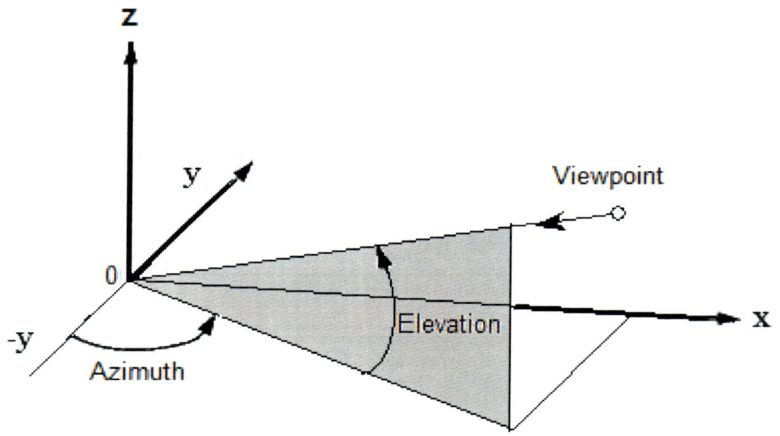

Figure 3.15: An observation point and its azimuth and elevation angles in 3D plots.

Different surface plans can be viewed, depending on of the view angles, *e.g.*,

- The *x,y*-projection of the 3D plot can be obtained with az=0 and el=90, a top view, which can be entered simply as view(2);
- The *x,z*-projection of the 3D plot can be obtained with az=el=0, front view;
- The *y,z*- projection of the 3D plot can be obtained with az=90 and el=0, side view.

It is possible, for example, to plot four different views in the same Figure Window:

- angles az=-37.5°, and el=30°, the default view;
- angles az=37.5° and el=30 °, mirroring the default view;
- angles az=0 and el=90, the top view;
- az=el=0, the front view.

The function to be blotted is Maxwell-Boltzmann velocity distribution for gaseous helium $f_v = 4\pi\left(\frac{M}{2\pi RT}\right)^{\frac{3}{2}} v^2 e^{-\frac{Mv2}{2RT}}$, where the molecular weight M is 0.004 kg/mol, the gas constant R=8.314 J/(mol K), v and T are changed within the ranges 0 … 2500 m/s and 50 … 500 K respectively. The commands are:

```
>> M=4e-3;R=8.314;
>> v=0:100:1300;T= 50:50:500;
>> [X,Y]=meshgrid(v,T);
>> fv=4*pi*(M./(2*pi*R*Y)).^(3/2).*X.^2.*exp(-M.*X.^2./(2*R*Y));
>> subplot(2,2,1), surf(X,Y,fv)
>> xlabel('v'), ylabel('T'),zlabel('f'),title('Default view'),
>> axis tight   % sets axis limits to the data range
>> subplot(2,2,2), surf(X,Y,fv)
>> view(37.5,30)      % az=37.5° and el=30 °
>> xlabel('v'), ylabel('T'),zlabel('f'),title('az=37.5^o, el=30^o')
>> axis tight   % sets axis limits to the data range
>> subplot(2,2,3), surf(X,Y,fv)
>> view(2)     % az=0° and el=90° – top view
>> xlabel('v'), ylabel('T'),title(' az =0^o, el =90^o')
>> axis tight   % sets axis limits to the data range
>> subplot(2,2,4), surf(X,Y,fv)
>> view(0,0)  % az=0° and el=0° – front view
>> xlabel('v'),zlabel('f'), title(' az =0^o, el =0^o')
```

```
>> axis tight   % sets axis limits to the data range
```

The results appear in Fig. **3.16**, below:

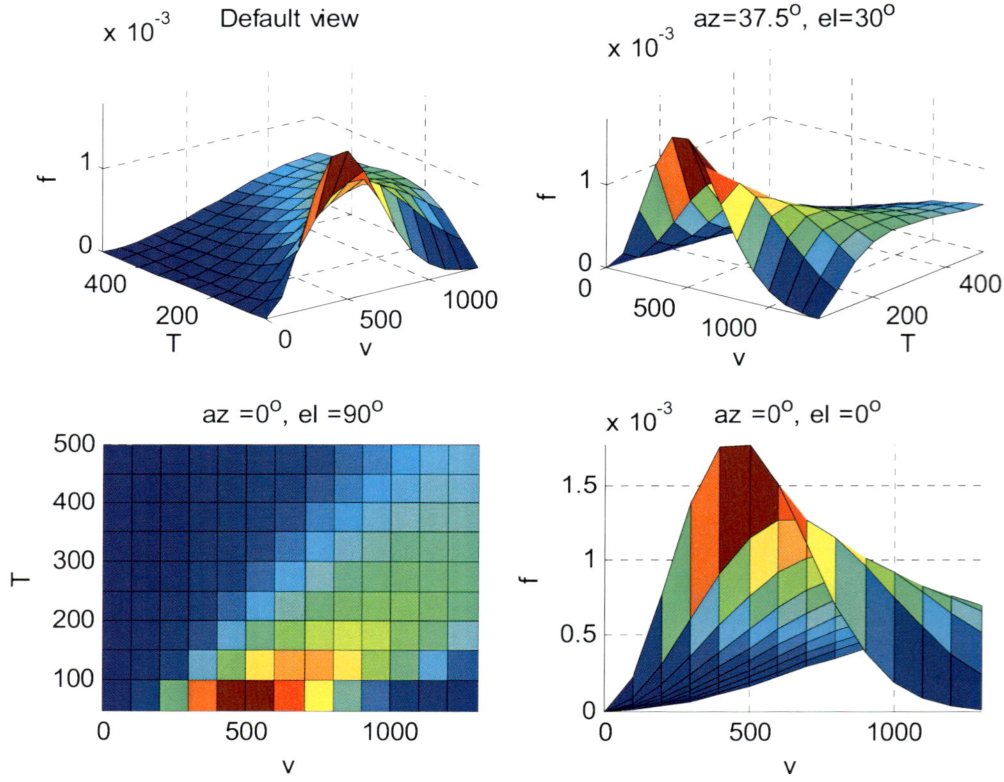

Figure 3.16: The Maxwell-Boltzmann distribution function plotted with different view angles az and el.

The commands above correspond to the following steps;

- Assign the *M* and *R* values;
- Create vectors *v* and *T*;
- Create *X* and *Y* grid matrices in the range of the *v* and *T* vectors respectively using the meshgrid command;

- Calculate the Maxwell-Boltzmann function, *f*, for each pair of the *X* and *Y* values;
- Divide the page (Figure Window) into four panes and select the first pane for the first plot using the subplot command;
- Generate the first plot with the surf command at default viewpoint;
- Set the axis limits to the data range with the axis tight command;
- Select the second pane for the second plot using the subplot command;
- Generate the second plot with the surf command;
- Set the plot viewpoint to the angles to be mirrored to the default angle values using view command;
- Set the axis limits to the data range with the axis tight command;
- Select the third pane for the third plot using the subplot command;
- Generate the third plot using the surf command;
- Set the top view angles using the view(2) command;
- Set the axis limits to the data range with the axis tight command;
- Select the fourth pane for the fourth plot using the subplot command;
- Generate the fourth plot using the surf command;
- Set the front view angles using the view(3) command;
- Set axis limits to the data range using the axis tight command.

3.2.4.3. Rotation Mode for the Plot

To rotate the plot with the mouth press the  button on the toolbar in the Figure Window; the azimuth and elevation angle values appear simultaneously in the bottom- left corner of the Figure Window. A plot view in the Figure Window using rotation mode is shown below in Fig. **3.17**.

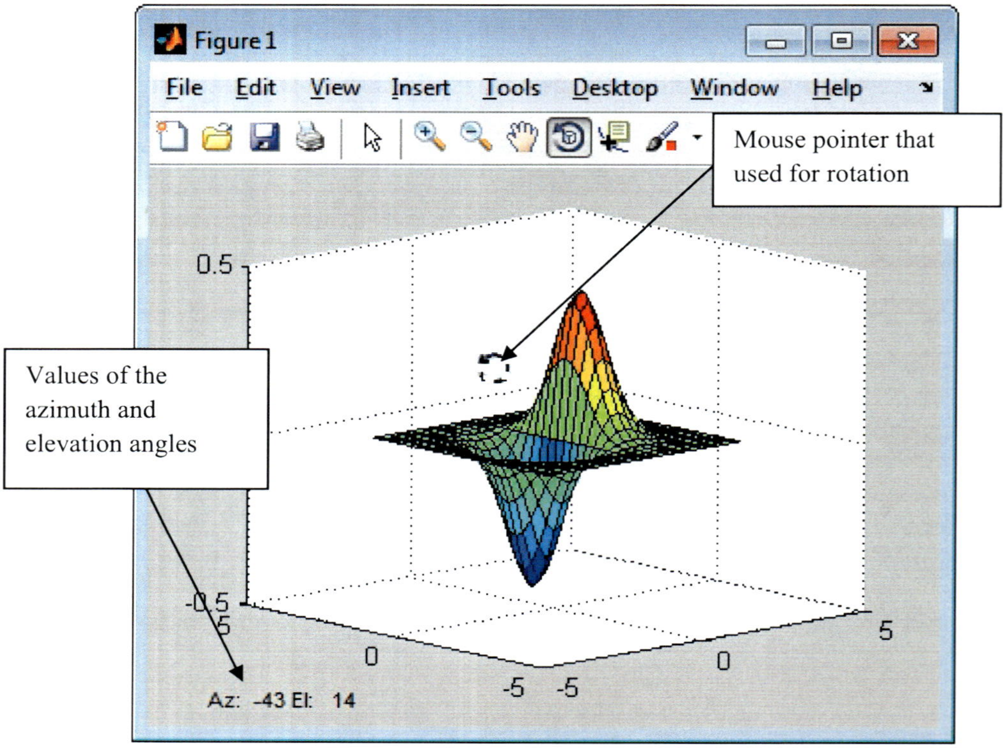

Figure 3.17: The Figure Window with the plot in rotation mode, including the rotate cursor and the values of the azimuth and elevation angles.

Rotation mode can also be introduced by inputting the rotate3d on command. This can be accomplished by entering this command in the Command Window and then doing the following:

- Proceed to the Figure Window;
- By pressing on the mouse button and moving the mouse, we can rotate the plot and simultaneously view the az and el values, which change together as the mouse moves.

Entering the rotate3d off command interrupts this mode.

3.3. SPECIALIZED TWO- AND THREE-DMENSIONAL PLOTS

Among the 2D and 3D graphs used by life science specialists are plots that have error boundaries for each of the *x*,*y* points, histograms, logarithmical plots and other objects. These graphs can be constructed by using specialized commands. Some of these graphs together with a list of additional graphic commands are briefly described below.

3.3.1. Plot with Error Bars

Frequently, bio-data is observed with a degree of uncertainty. Thus it is desirable to show recorded values with error limits in each data point. This can be accomplished by using the errorbar command, which plots observed points with error limits. The two simplest forms of this command are

errorbar(x,y,l,u) or errorbar(x,y,e)

where *x* and *y* are the data vectors, l, u, and e are vectors with lower, upper and symmetrical (two-sided equal) errors, respectively.

For an example, generate the Figure Window with two plots showing the acidity level data used in Section 3.1. The first plot shows this data with the side-asymmetric errors: the upper one is 0.15 pH and the lower is 0.75 pH. The second plot shows this data with symmetric errors of ± 0.15 pH at each point, yielded by entering the commands (see Fig. **3.18**).

```
>> t=0:.5:5;     % vector with the time data
>> pH=[5.52, 5.73, 5.84, 6.26, 6.32, 6.3, 6.04, 6.09, 5.94, 6.03, 6.12]; % pH data
>> u= 0.15+zeros(1,length(pH)); % creates vector with upper errors
>> l=u/2;        % creates vector with lower errors
>> e=u;          % creates vector of two-side equal errors
>> subplot(1,2,1),
>> errorbar(t,pH,l,u) % plot data with different lower and upper errors
>> xlabel('Time, hour'),ylabel('Acidity level, pH')
>> title('Asymmetric Error'),grid
>> subplot(1,2,2),
```

```
>> errorbar(t,pH,e)     % plot data with two-side equal error
>> xlabel('Time, hour'),ylabel('Acidity level, pH')
>> title('Symmetric Error'),grid
```

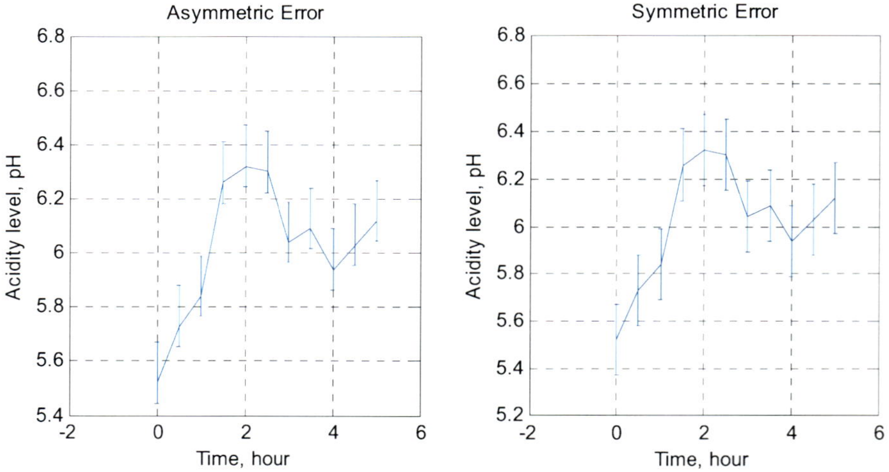

Figure 3.18: Plot of acidity level data with error bars.

To format the line color and style, and marker include line style and/or marker specifiers in the errorbar command, *e.g.*, inputting the errorbar(t,pH,e,'--o') command changes the line to a dashed line and assigns the data points with circles into the previous plot.

3.3.2. Plotting a Histogram

The histogram is one of the popular graphs for representing data in statistical analysis in the life sciences. The values in a histogram are divided according to certain intervals (called bins) and are plotted in the form of vertical bars whose heights represents the number of data in each of them. Histograms are plotted using the hist command. The simplest form of this command follows:

hist(y)

where y is the vector containing the data points; the command generates a graph of bins that presents the numbers of data points in each of the 10 (default) equally spaced bins.

For example, the weights (in grams) of 29 mushrooms from an experimental plant site were 57, 48, 42, 44, 50, 38, 57, 62, 63, 39, 32, 83, 63, 47, 48, 47, 54, 41, 36, 69, 75, 53, 71, 33, 23, 42, 29, 75, 60. To plot a histogram by these data enter the following commands:

```
>> y=[57, 48, 42, 44, 50, 38, 57, 62, 63, 39, 32, 83, 63, 47, 48, 47, 54, 41, 36, ...
69, 75, 53, 71, 33, 23, 42, 29, 75, 60];
>> hist(y)
>> xlabel('Mushroom weight, g'),ylabel('Number of weights per one bin')
```

The resulting plot is shown below in Fig. **3.19**.

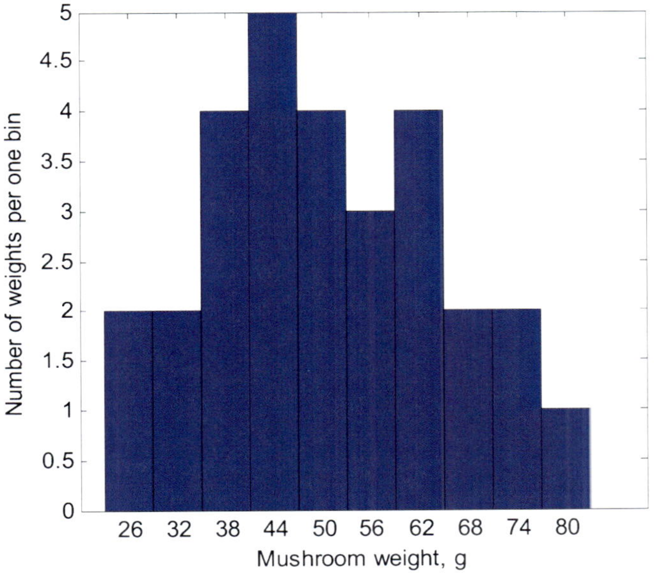

Figure 3.19: Histogram plot of the mushroom weight data.

The form:

```
n=hist(y)
```

allows the generation of the `n` vector containing the numbers of data points in each of the bins; the command yields a numerical output but does not plot a histogram.

Using the n=hist(y) command for the example cited above, the following frequencies can be displayed in the Command Window:

```
>> n=hist(y)
n =
2 2 4 5 4 3 4 2 2 1
```

Note, the n=hist(y) command does not plot a histogram but returns the number of elements in each bin.

There are additional forms of the hist command that can be applied in order to define frequency numbers in each of the bins or when the various numbers of the bins and their locations have to be plotted. Enter the help hist command in the Command Window for more detailed information.

3.3.3. Plots with Semi-Logarithmic Axes

When generating graphs in the life sciences and technology, one of the coordinates is frequently represented on a logarithmic scale. This allows the display of values in a wider range than can be shown using a linear axis; in addition, exponential relationships become linear in form in a semi-logarithmic scale. Use of these relations is widespread in biotechnology, for example, expressions for first-, second- or higher order reactions, population growth rates, radioactive decay, sterilization processes, *etc.* The semilogy or semilogx commands should to be used for this purpose. Following is the commands in its simplest form:

semilogy(x,y,' Line Specifiers') and semilogx(x,y,' Line Specifiers')

The first command generates a plot with a log-scaled (base 10) *y*-axis and a linear *x* –scale; the second command generates a plot with a linear *y*-axis and a log-scaled *x*-axis; the Line Specifiers property specifies the line type, point symbol, and color for the lines drawn in the semi-log plot.

For example, bio-oil viscosity data are 120.14, 55.45, 19.92, 8.95 cP (centipoise) at 298.15, 306.15, 318.15, 328.15 °K respectively. A semi-logarithmic plot can be plotted using the following commands:

```
>> Vis=[120.14 55.45 19.92 8.95]; T=[298.15 306.15 318.15 328.15];
>> semilogy(T, Vis,'-o')        %plots N on a semi log y axis and a lineal x-axis
>> xlabel('Temperature, ^oK'), ylabel('Bio-oil viscosity, cP')
>> axis tight, grid
```

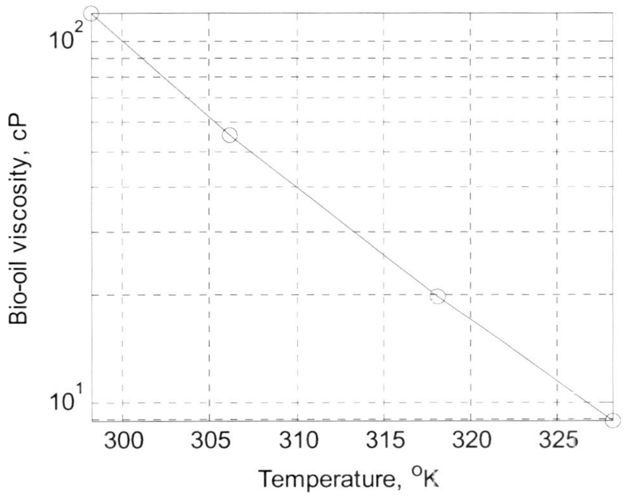

Figure 3.20: The semi-log graph for the temperature-viscosity relationship of bio-oil.

In the example above, the semilogy command was used together with the axis tight command (described above in the subsection 3.1.3.1) to set the axis limits for the range of the viscosity and temperature data.

The data on the semi-log graph in Fig. **3.20** is nearly linear; on a normal graph produced by the plot command these data generate an exponential-like curve.

3.3.4. Supplementary Commands for Two- and Three- Dimensional Graphics

MATLAB® provides additional commands for 2D and 3D plotting. A complete list of 2D, 3D, and specialized plotting functions can be obtained by entering the following commands in the Command Window: help graph2d, help graph3d, or help specgraph. Table **3.3** presents some additional commands for two- and three-dimensional plotting that can be useful for the graphic presentation of bio-data; the table provides the format of the corresponding basic command with short explanations, examples, and the resulting plots.

Table 3.3: Additional Commands and Plots for 2D and 3D Graphics*[2].

Commands	Examples	Plots
figure generates a new Figure Window; figure(h) generates a Figure Window with a number h or calls up the existing Figure Window with number h	>>figure(2)	
fplot('function',limits) plots a function y=f(x) with specified x-limits (the limits of the y-axis may be added)	>>fplot('exp(.1*x)',[10,60])	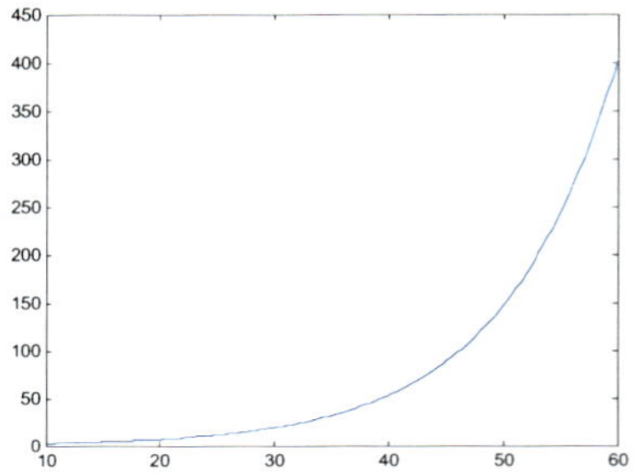
polar(theta,rho) generates a plot with polar coordinates in which theta and rho are the angle and radius respectively.	>>th=linspace(0,2*pi,150); >> r=4*cos(3*th); >> polar(th,r)	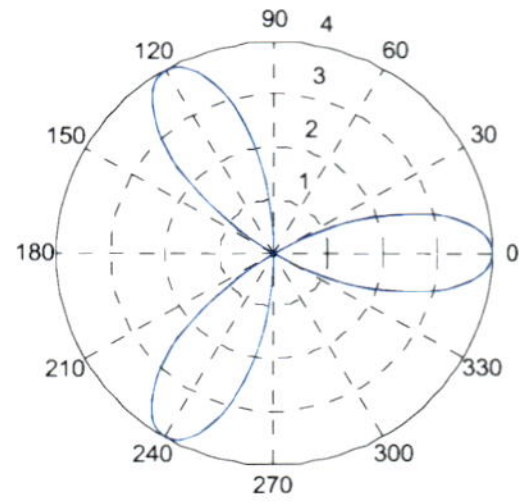
loglog(x,y) generates a plot with both the x- and the y- axes log scaled (base 10)	>>x=linspace(0.1,20,100); >> y=5+exp(-0.5*x); >> loglog(x,y)	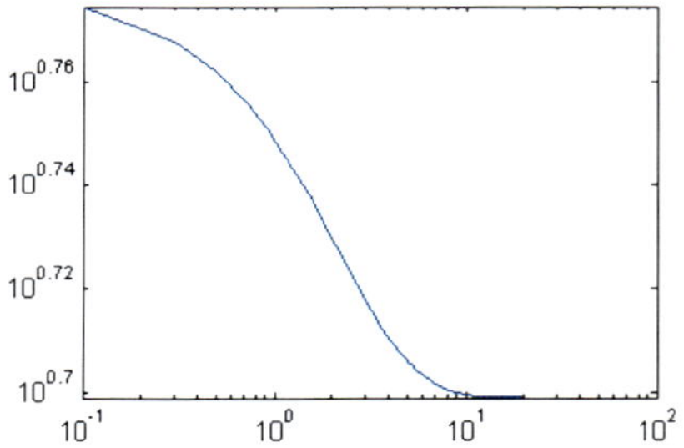

[2]The table with minor changes/additions is taken from the author's book [2]. With the permission of Biohealthcare Publishing (Oxford) Limited.

sphere or sphere(n) plots a sphere with 20 or n mesh cells respectively	>> sphere(40)	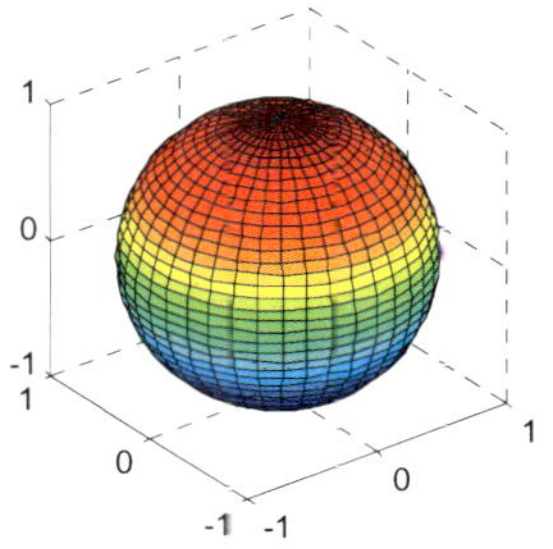
box on draws a box around the plot; box off removes a drawn box from the plot	>> box on	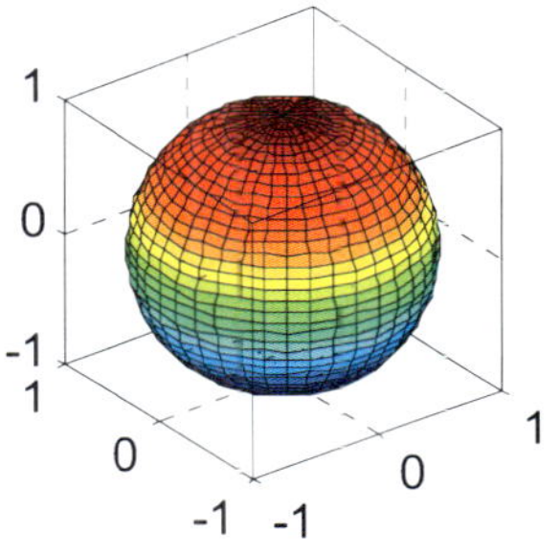
cylinder or cylinder(r) draws an ordinary and a profiled cylinder with the profile given by the r expression	>> t = 0:pi/10:2*pi; >>r=atan(t); >> cylinder(r)	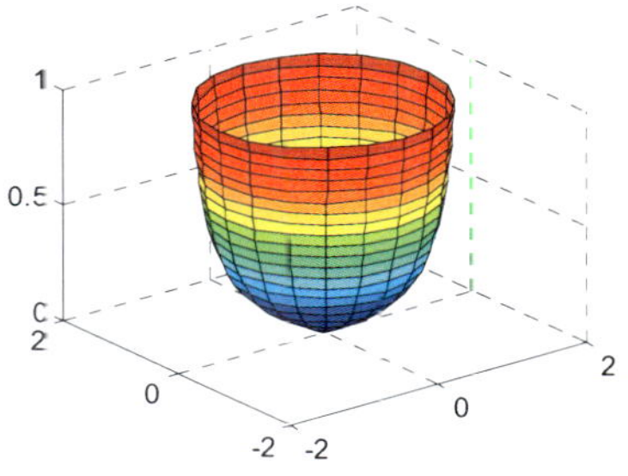
contour(X,Y,Z,v) displays in the *x,y*-plane isolines of matrix Z; Z is interpreted as the height with respect to the x,y-plane; v is the number of contour lines or the vector- specified contour lines. The form c=contour(X,Y,Z,n) with clabel(c) displays the c level	>> x=-2:.2:2; >> [X,Y] = meshgrid(x); >> Z=X.*exp(-X.^2-Y.^2); >> contour(X,Y,Z,7); >>% Or with level values >> c = contour(X,Y,Z,7); >> clabel(c)	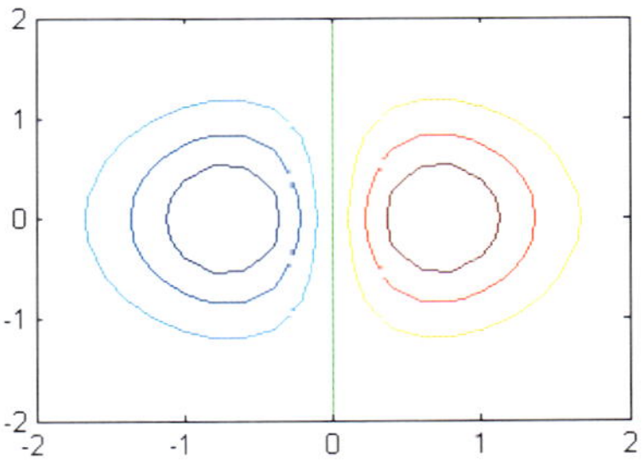

values of the isolines		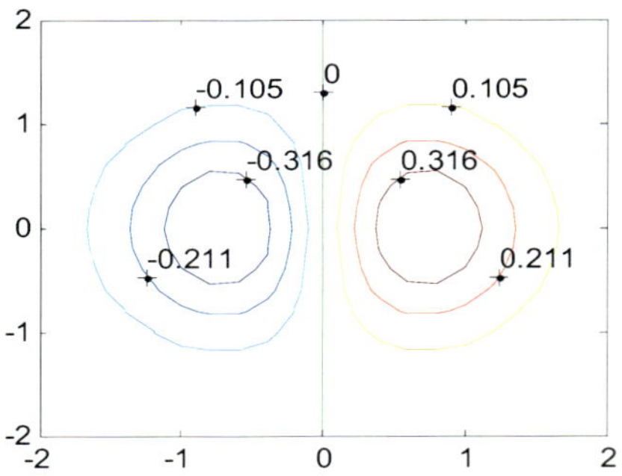
contour3(X,Y,Z,n) displays isolines of matrix Z in the *x*,*y*-plane; Z is interpreted as the height with respect to the *x*,*y* -plane; n is the number of contour lines	>> x=-2:.2:2; >> [X,Y] = meshgrid(x); >> Z=X.*exp(-X.^2-Y.^2); >> contour3(X,Y,Z,7);	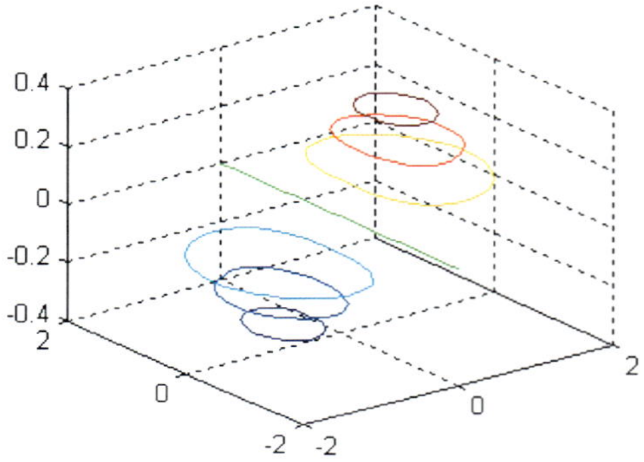
surfc(X,Y,Z) generates surface and contour plots	>> x=-2:.2:2; >> [X,Y] = meshgrid(x); >> Z=X.*exp(-X.^2-Y.^2); >> surfc(Z);	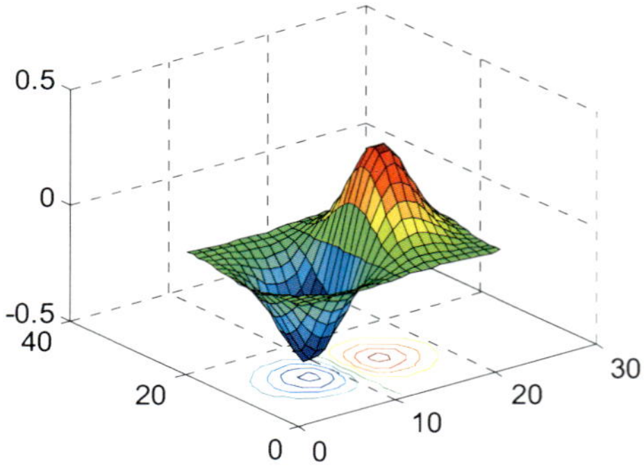
bar(x,y) displays the values in a vector or matrix as vertical bars	>> x=55:5:100; >> y=[1,2,1,0,1,4,3,3,5,5]; >> bar(x,y) >> xlabel('Grades'), >> ylabel('Number of Grades per Bin')	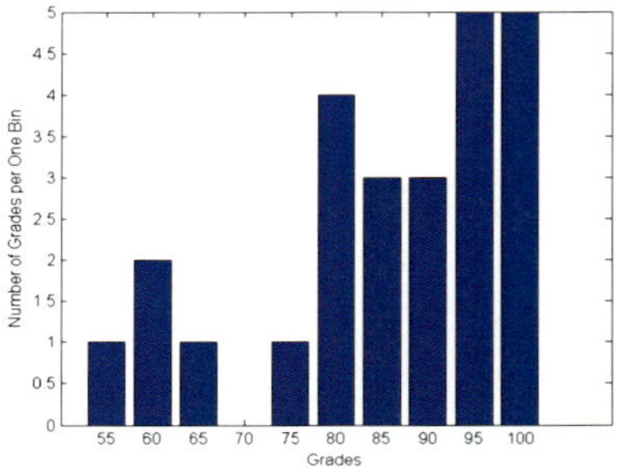

bar3(Y) generates 3D-bar plot data grouped in columns	>> Y=[2 3.4 7.1 2.2 1; 3 6 4.1 3 2; 0.3 5 6.3 4 2]; >> bar3(Y)	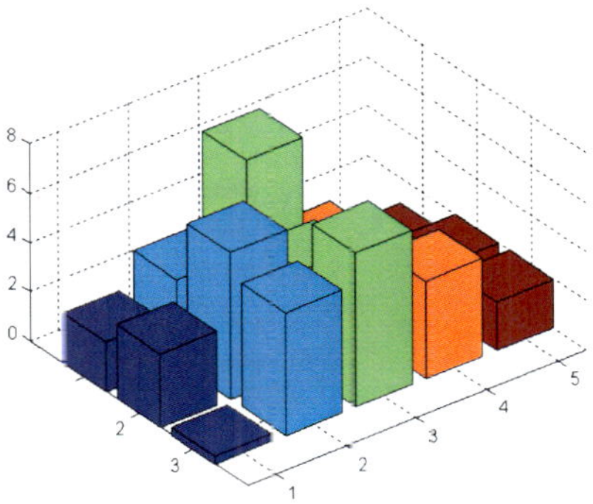
stem(x,y) displays data as lines extending from a baseline along the x-axis; a circle (default) terminates each stem	>> x=55:5:100; >> y=[1,2,1,0,1,4,3,3,5,5]; >> stem(x,y) >> xlabel('Grades'), >> ylabel('Number of Grades per Bin')	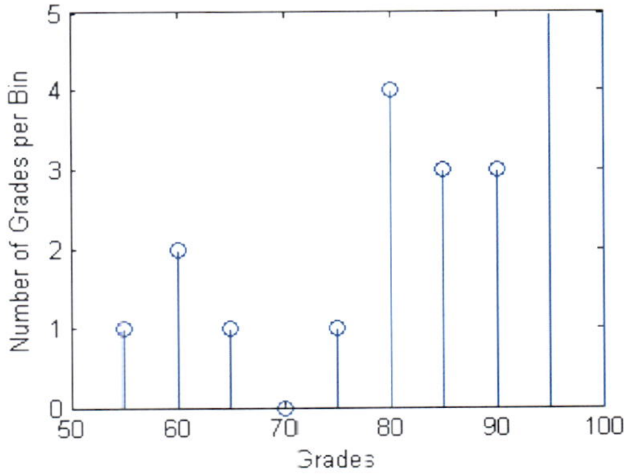
stem3(x,y,z) generates 3D boxed plot with lines from the x,y - plane to the z value that terminates by the circle (default). The x, y, and z coordinates must be vectors or matrices of the same size	>> x=0:0.5:2; >> [X,Y]=meshgrid(x); >> z= X.*Y./(X+Y); >> stem3(X,Y,z)	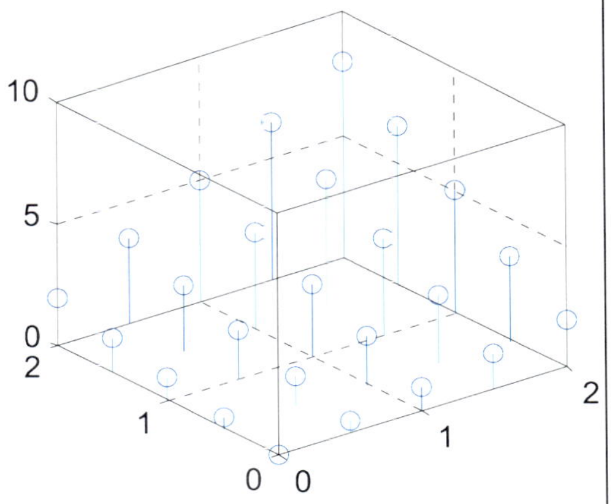

stairs(x,y) generates step-like plot of the discrete y data given at the specified x points.	>> x=1900:20:2000; >> y=[76 106 132 179 227 249]; >> stairs(x,y) >> xlabel('Year'), >> ylabel('People, mln')	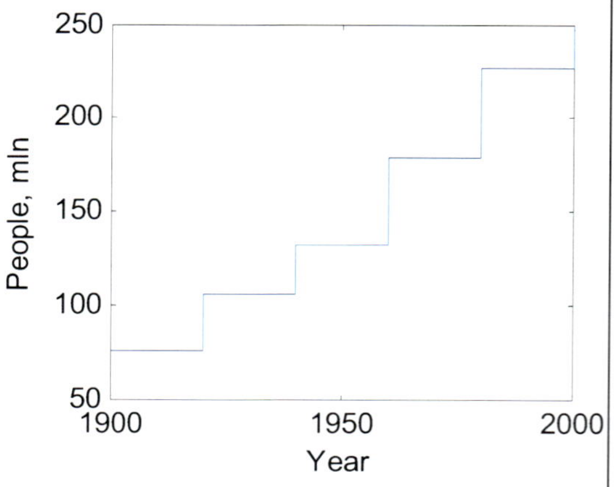
pie(x) draws a pie chart using the data in x; each element in x is represented as a slice	>> x=[56 68 42 91 100]; >> pie(x) >> title('Group Grades')	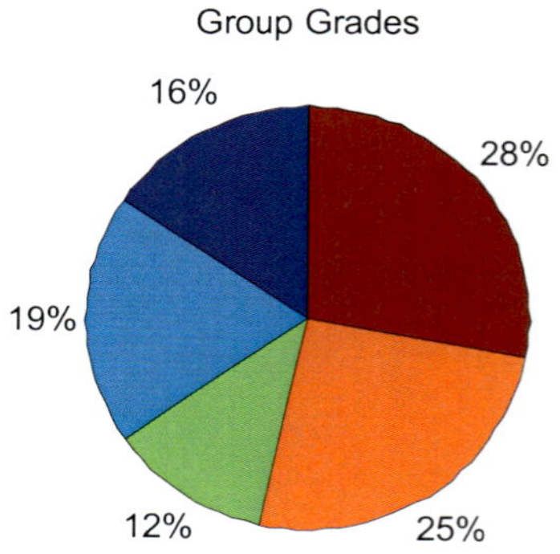
pie3(x,explode) generates a pie chart; explode specifies an offset of a slice from the center of the chart; explode is a vector of the same length as X, in which 1 denotes an offsetted slice and 0 a plain slice	>> x=[56 68 42 91 100]; >> explode=[0 1 0 0 0]; >> pie3(x,explode) >> title('Group Grades')	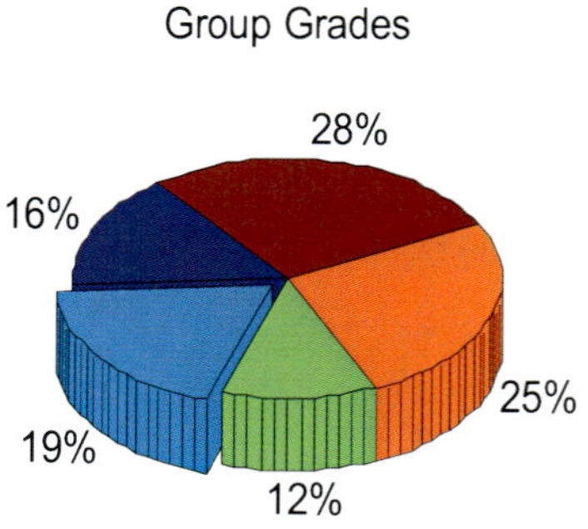

* The commands are described in their simplest form.

3.4. APPLICATION EXAMPLES

3.4.1. Simple Equilibrium Reaction: Species Concentrations

Suppose two species are in equilibrium A⇌B with initial concentrations $[A]_0$ and $[B]_0$ equal 0.25 and 0.1 mole/L respectively; the concentrations at time t=0, 0.1, …, 1 can be determined using the following equations

$$[A]=[A]_0\frac{1}{k_f+k_b}\left(k_b+k_f e^{-(k_f+k_b)t}\right)+[B]_0\frac{k_f}{k_f+k_b}\left(1-e^{-(k_f+k_b)t}\right)$$

$$[B]=[A]_0\frac{k_f}{k_f+k_b}\left(1-e^{-(k_f+k_b)t}\right)+[B]_0\frac{1}{k_f+k_b}\left(k_b+k_f e^{-(k_f+k_b)t}\right)$$

The forward and backward reaction rate constants k_f and k_b equal 2 and 1 min^{-1} respectively.

<u>Problem</u>: Calculate and plot results in three concentration-time subplots on the same page divided into four panes; the first plot presents $[A]$ - t and $[B]$ - t curves, has a grid and is located in the first and second panes on the page; the second plot presents the sole $[A]$ - t curve in the third pane; and the third - $[B]$ - t curve is in the fourth pane. The two latter plots have no grid; add captions to the plots.

The commands for this presentation follow:

```
>> A o=.25;Bo=0.1;kf=2;kb=1;%determine the initial concentration and reaction rates
>> t=0:.1:1;                                    % create time vector
>> r1=1/(kf+kb)*(kb+kf*exp(-(kf+kb)*t));  % addend in the A and B expressions
>> r2= kf /(kf+kb)*(1-exp(-(kf+kb)*t));  % addend in the A and B expressions
>> A=A o*r1+Bo*r2;                              %calculate A concentrations
>> B=A o*r2+Bo*r1;                              %calculate B concentrations
>> % == commands for current plot generation and it formatting ==
>> subplot(2,2,[1 2])                           %for placing plot at 1 and 3 positions
>> plot(t,A,t,B,'--')                           %plot A and B vs. t; A - solid
                                                line(default),B – dashed
>> xlabel('Time, min'),
```

```
>> ylabel('Concentration,g/l'), grid
>> title('Two species concentration vs. time')
>> legend('The species A', 'The species B')
>> subplot 223
>> plot(t,A)                          %plot A vs. t
>> xlabel('Time, min'),ylabel('Concentration, g/l'),
>> title('Concentration of the A-species vs. time')%, grid
>> subplot 224
>> plot(t,B)                          %plot B vs. t
>> xlabel('Time, min'),ylabel('Concentration, g/l'),
>> title('Concentration of the B-species vs. time')%,grid
```

The plot created by these commands follows:

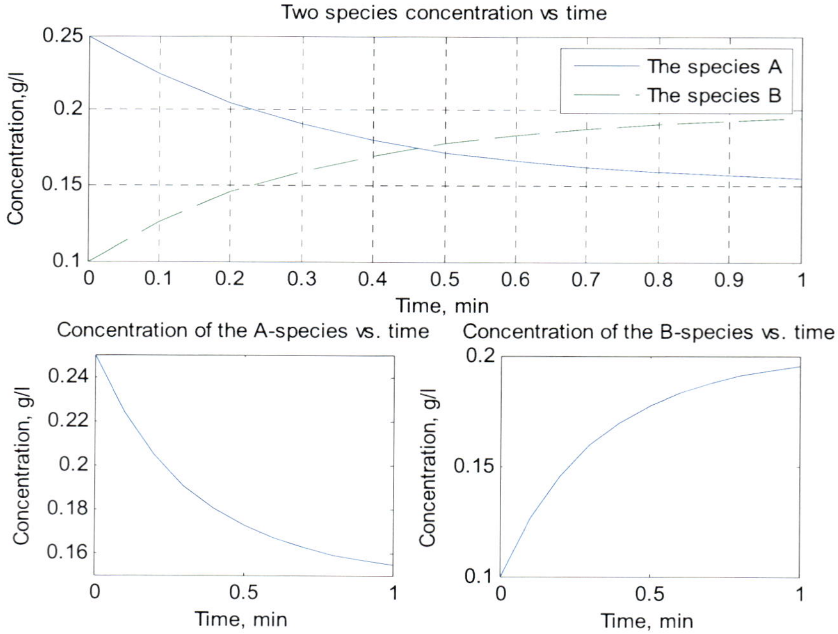

3.4.2. Microorganism Growth Curve

The general equation for microorganism (microbes, bacteria, *etc.*) population growth is:

$$N = N_0(1+r)^n$$

where N and N_0 are respectively the current and initial number of microorganisms; n is the number of generations that have elapsed; and r is the growth rate in parts shown with percentages.

If for example a type of microorganisms has a growth rate of r=.5 units per half hour; the initial number N_0 of bacteria in a flask is 150; the elapsed generation time is a half hour and a whole observation period is 4 hours; then n is equal to 0, 1,…, 8.

Problem: Calculate and plot bacteria growth during a period of 4 hours in three plots on one page: (a) N *versus* time t in discrete, step form, (b) N *versus* time t in regular, continuous form, and (c) logarithm N *versus* t; mark calculation points by a circle (the letter 'o') and add a grid and captions to the plots.

The commands for solving this problem follow:

```
>> No=150;r=.5;
>> x=0:8;       % number of generations elapsed
>> N=round(No*(1+r).^x);   % round to the nearest integer of microorganisms
>> t=x/2;       % elapsed time
>> subplot(3,1,1)
>> stairs(t,N)  % the command for stairs-like plot
>> title('Stairs plot for bacterial growth')
>> xlabel('Time elapsed, hours'), ylabel('Number of bacteria, cell')
>> grid
>> subplot(3,1,2)
>> plot(t,N,'-o')          %the command for regular plot
>> title('Bacterial growth during 4 hours')
>> xlabel('Time elapsed, hours'), ylabel('Number of bacteria, cell')
>> grid
>> subplot(3,1,3)
>> semilogy(t, N,'-o') %the command for semi log plot
>> title('A log plot of bacterial growth during 4 hours')
```

```
>> xlabel('Time elapsed, hours'), ylabel('Log of number of cells'),grid
```

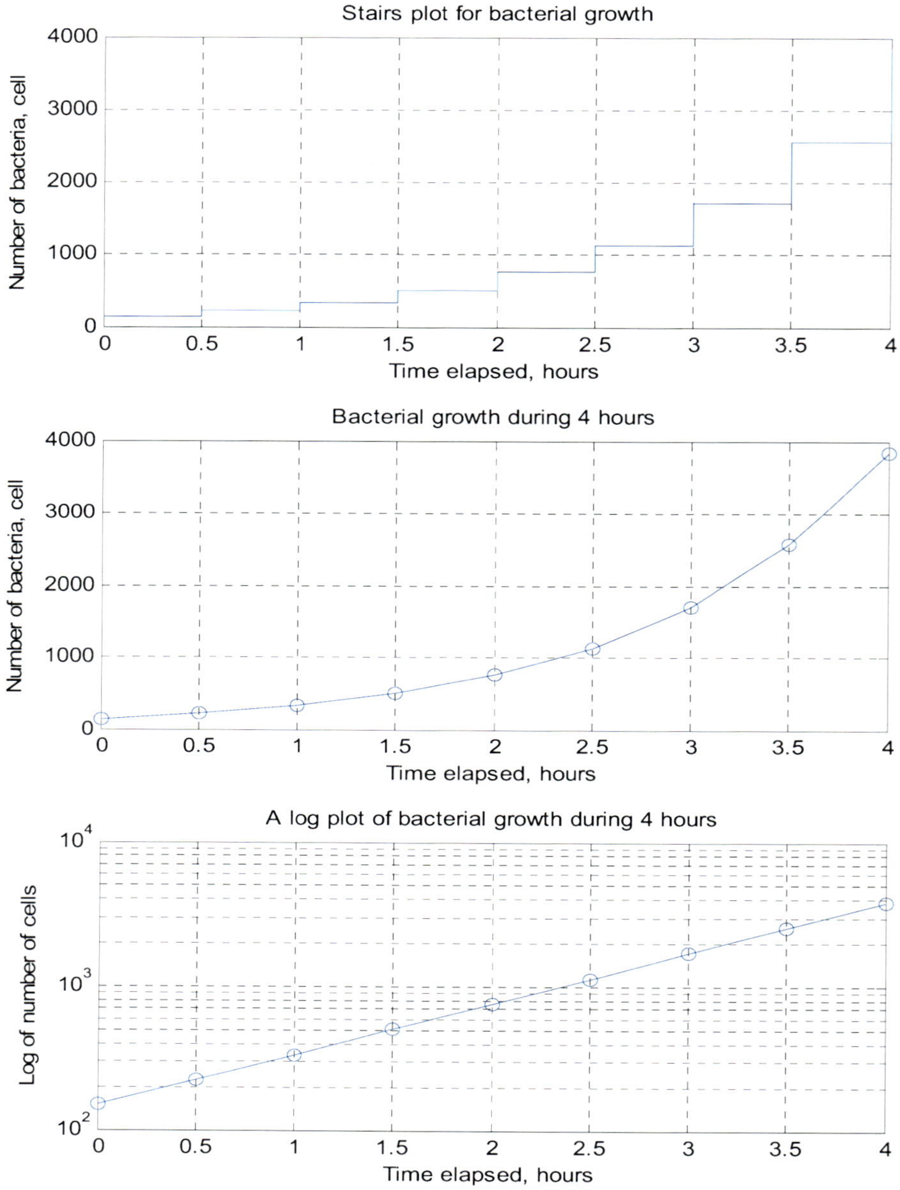

3.4.3. Specific Volume of Air

The specific volume, v, of air at atmospheric pressure, p, and different temperatures, T, can be calculated with the ideal gas equation of state as:

$$v = \frac{RT}{p}$$

with p=101.3 kN/m^3, R=0.286 kJ/(kg°K), and T in degrees of K.

The experimental air density values measured at temperatures 0, 20, 40, ..., 100 °C (or 273.15, 293.15, 313.15, ..., 373.15 °K) with mean two-sided error $\delta v = \pm 0.1\%$ are 0.7734 0.8288 0.8873 0.9372 1 1.0571 m^3/kg.

Problem: Calculate and plot the air density as determined theoretically (using the equation of state) and experimentally (using measured data with data errors at each point).

The commands that calculate the theoretical specific volumes and plot both theoretical and experimental specific volumes of air at atmospheric pressure and temperatures 273.15 ... 373.15 °K are given below

```
>> T=273.15:20:373.15;        % in °K
>> v_exp=[0.7734 0.8288 0.8873 0.9372 1 1.0571]; % in kg/m^3
>> p=101.3;   % in atmospheric pressure in kN/m^2
>> R=.286;    % in kJ/(kg°K)
>> v_theor= R*T/ p;
>> error=0.001* v_theor;
>> errorbar(T, v_exp,error,'.b'),hold on        % plots exper. points with error bars
>> plot(T, v_theor), grid      %plots theoretically calculated curve
>> xlabel('Temperature, ^oK'),ylabel('Specific volume, m^3/ kg')
>> title('Specific volume of air'),
>> legend('experimental points', 'theoretical curve'), hold off
```

The resulting plot is:

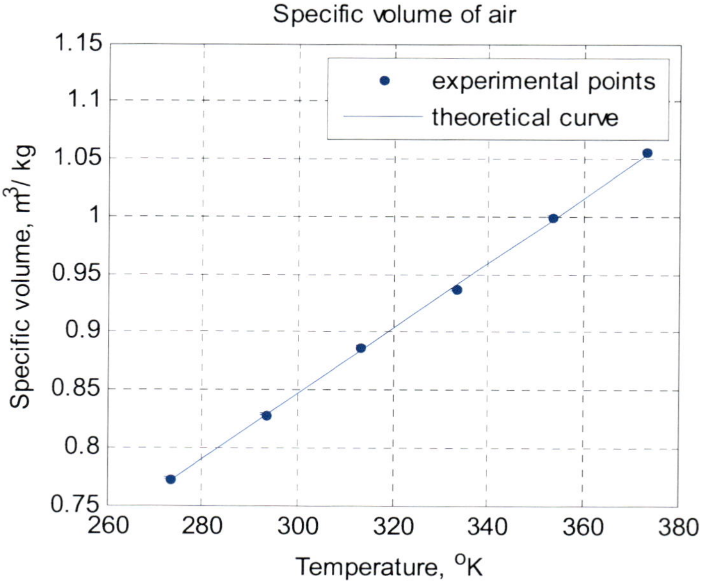

3.4.4. Bivariate Normal Distribution

The single and bivariate normal (Gaussian) distributions are widely used in life-science statistics bioinformatics, biophysics, biomathematics and other disciplines where data analysis is necessary. In general, a two-dimensional probability density function, $f(x, y)$, of the bivariate normal distribution of the X (*e.g.* species weight) and Y (*e.g.* species volume) variates with the correlation coefficient ρ is given by

$$f(x,y)=\frac{1}{2\pi\sigma_x\sigma_y\sqrt{1-\rho^2}}e^{-\left[\frac{(x-\mu_x)^2}{2\sigma_x^2}+\frac{(y-\mu_y)^2}{2\sigma_y^2}-\frac{\rho(x-\mu_x)(y-\mu_y)}{\sigma_x\sigma_y}\right]}$$

where μ_x and μ_y are the mean values of the x and y variates respectively, and σ_x and σ_y are those of the variate deviations.

Problem: Calculate and plot the distribution function for μ_x=60, μ_y=90, σ_x =4, σ_y=6, ρ=0.1 in x-axis limits $\mu_x \pm 3\sigma_x$ and y-axis limits $\mu_y \pm 3\sigma_y$.

To solve this problem the following steps must be taken:

- Assign values of the μ_x, μ_y, σ_x, σ_y, and ρ;

- Calculate boundaries for x and y as $x = \mu_x \pm 3\sigma_x$ and $y = \mu_y \pm 3\sigma_y$;

- Define 40-point vectors x and y with the linspace command;

- Create an X,Y grid in the ranges of the x, y vectors by using the meshgrid command;

- Calculate f by the above expression;

- Generate a X,Y,f plot with the surf command

- Set plot axes to the previously calculated boundaries with the axis tight command.

The commands are:

```
>> muX=60; muY=90;
>> sigmaX=4; sigmaY=6;ro=.1;
>> xlim=3*sigmaX; ylim=3*sigmaY; % setting limits for x, y
>> xmin=muX-xlim;xmax=muX+xlim;
>> ymin=muY-ylim;ymax=muY+ylim;
>> x=linspace(xmin,xmax,40); % defining vector x
>> y=linspace(ymin,ymax,40);        % defining vector y
>> [X,Y]=meshgrid(x,y);       % create X,Y grid from the x,y vectors
>> r1= (X-muX).^2/(2*sigmaX^2);
>> r2= (Y-muY).^2/(2*sigmaY^2);
>> r3=(X-muX).* (Y-muY)/(sigmaX*sigmaY);
>> f=1/(2*pi*sigmaX*sigmaY*sqrt(1-ro^2))*exp(-(r1+r2-ro*r3)/(1-ro^2));%f(x,y)
>> surf(X,Y,f)% plot surface graph
>> xlabel('x'),ylabel('y'),zlabel('f(x,y)')
>> axis tight   % set plot to the x and y variate limites
```

Below is the figure generated by these commands:

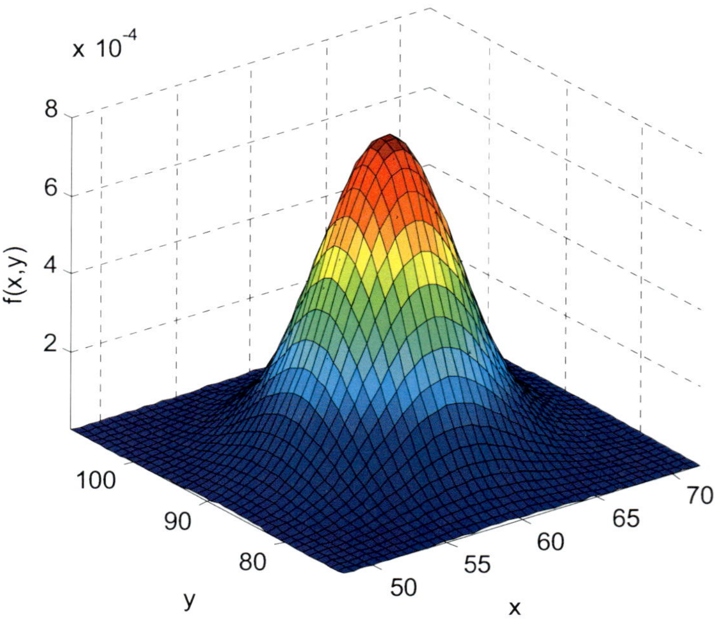

3.4.5. The Ponderal Index

The Ponderal Index, PI, characterizes the relations between body weight and individual volume, when the latter is defined by body height. The expression is:

$$\mathrm{PI} = \frac{m}{h^3}$$

where m is weight in kg and h is height in m, and PI is in kg/m^3.

Problem: Calculate and generate a three dimensional surface plot in which m and h are on the horizontal plane and the z-axis is the Ponderal index; take x=40, 50, …, 160 kg, and h=1.45, 1.55, …, 2 m. Present the plot with the azimuth and elevation angles equal to -138 and 26 degrees respectively.

To solve the problem the follows steps must be taken:

- Create the vectors of the m and h values;

- Create *X*,*Y* grid matrices in the ranges of the *m* and *h* vectors respectively by using the meshgrid command;
- Calculate PI for each pair of m and h values using the above expression;
- Generate 3D plot by the determined *X*,*Y*,PI-values;
- Set the required view point for generated plot.

The commands are:

```
>> m=40:10:160;h=1.45:0.05:2;
>> [X,Y]=meshgrid(m,h);                 % creates X,Y grid from the x,t vectors
>> PI=X./Y.^3;                          % calculate element-wise the PI
>> surf(X,Y,PI);                        % plot surface graph
>> xlabel('Weight, kg');ylabel('Height, m');zlabel('Ponderal Index, kg/m^3')
>> view(-138,38)                        % az=-138° el=38
```

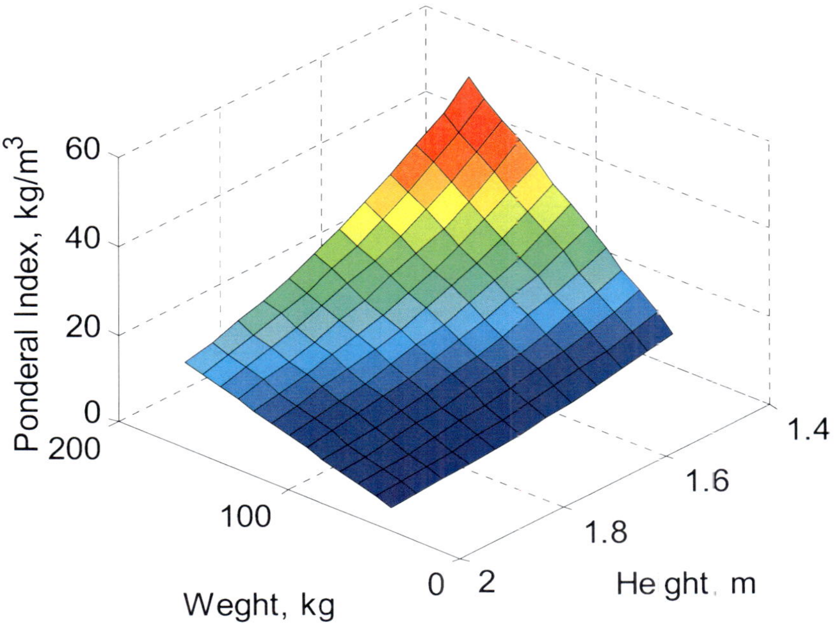

3.4.6. Partial Pressure in a Generic First Order Reaction

For the various gaseous reaction of type A→B, A→B+C, 2A→B, *etc.* the partial pressure, P_A, can be calculated by the expression:

$$P_A = P_0 e^{-kt}$$

where P_0 is the initial partial pressure of the A component, k is reaction rate constant and t- time. The rate constant k changes with the temperature in accordance with the Arrhenius equation:

$$k = ae^{-\frac{E_a}{RT}}$$

in which a is the frequency factor, E_a is activation energy, T is temperature and R is the gas constant.

Problem: Calculate and generate a three dimensional surface plot of the partial pressures (z-axis) as a function of time (x-axis) and temperature (y-axis). The values of the parameters in the above equations are P_0 =55 Torr, $a = 10^{14}$ min^{-1}, E_a=77000 J/mol, T=293,294,..., 303 K, R=8.314 j/(K mol), t=1,1.25,..., 5 min. Present the plot with the azimuth and elevation angles 123 and 26 degrees respectively. Change the colors to the color combination autumn. Add axis labels, a grid and a caption to the graph.

To solve this problem the following steps must be taken:

- Assign values to the parameters P_0, a, E_a, R, and create the vectors of the t and T values;

- Create a X,Y grid in the ranges of the t and T vectors respectively using the meshgrid command;

- Calculate k and P_A for each pair of X and Y values using the above expressions;

- Generate a 3D plot using defined X, Y, P_0-values;
- Set the required view point and color combination.

The commands are:

```
>> Po=55; ea=77e3;a=1e14;R=8.314;a0=.25;
>> t=1:.25:4; T=293:303;
>> [X,Y]=meshgrid(t,T);
>> k=a*exp(-ea./(R*Y));
>> Pa=Po*exp(-k.*X);
>> surf(X,Y,Pa),grid on
>> xlabel('Time, min'), ylabel('Temperature, K'), zlabel('Pressure, Torr')
>> view(67,22)
>> colormap spring
```

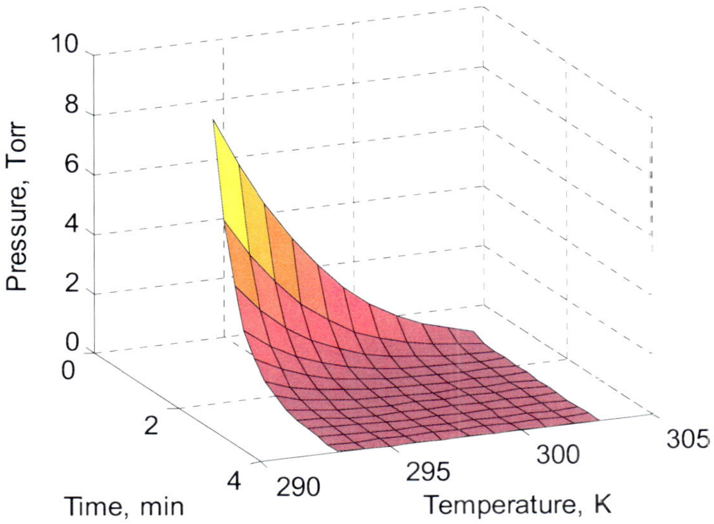

3.5. QUESTIONS AND EXERCISES

1. Choose the correct answer. Which sign or word specifies an upright triangular marker that designates a point on the plot? Choose from: (a) +, (b) the word 'circle', (c) ^, (d) *t*.

2. In a three-dimensional graph the `mesh` command generates: (a) a surface, (b) a surface mesh, (c) a line.

3. To place several plots on the same page (in the same Figure Window), it is necessary to divide this page using the following command: (a) `hold on`, (b) `plot(x1, y1, x2, y2, …)`, (c) `subplot`.

4. To produce a plot without an axis it is necessery to use the following command: (a) `hold off`, (b) `grid off`, (c) `axis off`.

5. In an aerobic biomass process the mass/time data are: m=5.15, 5.21, 5.5, 6.55, 7.15, 7.75, 7.59, 7.45 g/l at t=0, 25, 50, 75, 100, 125, 150, 200 min. Plot the graph in which the x-axis is time and the y-axis is the biomass and data points, marked by a diamond with a solid line between the data points. Add axis labels, a grid and a caption to the plot.

6. Generate three plots on one page for the following geometrical figures.

Hypocycloid:

$$x = 1.1\cos\varphi + \cos(1.1\varphi)$$
$$y = 1.1\sin\varphi - \sin(1.1\varphi)$$

with 200 equally spaced φ values in the range $0 \le \varphi \le 4\pi$.

Polar rose:

$$x = 2\sin 4\varphi\cos\varphi$$
$$y = 2\sin 4\varphi\sin\varphi$$

with 100 equally spaced φ values in the range $0 \le \varphi \le 2\pi$.

Fermat's spiral:

$$x = \sqrt{\varphi}\cos\varphi$$
$$y = \sqrt{\varphi}\sin\varphi$$

with 100 equally spaced φ values in the range $0\le \varphi \le 8\pi$.

Place all geometrical figures on the same page (Figure Window) so that the hypocycloid and polar rose are located in the first graph lines and the Fermat's spiral in the second line. Make the figure width and figure height equal and add a captions and a grid to each of the plots.

7. Plot the reagent concentration changes in a second order reaction

$$x = \frac{2\cdot 10^{-5}\left(e^{-0.0256t}-1\right)}{0.002e^{-0.0256t}-0.01}$$

where t is the time that changes from 0 to 23 min, and x is the reagent concentration in gmol.

Add a curve of this reaction velocity to the graph:

$$v = 319.45(0.01-x)(0.002-x)$$

where v in gmol/min.

Add axis labels, a grid, and a legend to the graph.

8. The experimental kinematic viscosity η - temperature T data are 120.14, 81.78, 58,.48, and 43.30 cP at 298.15, 308.15, 318.15, and 328.15 K respectively. There is ±0.5% uncertainty for these data.

The experimental data was described and can be calculated by the Andrade-type expression:

$$\eta = Ae^{\frac{B}{T}}$$

where A=0.00142, B=3382.

Plot the calculated and measured viscosity values. Provide the error bars at each measured point; add axis labels, a caption, a grid, and a legend.

9. Plot the surfaces of the two following bodies on one page. Make the width and height equal in size to the first body and make the axis squared for the second body; add titles and remove the axis from each body plot:

a) Toroid

$$x = (R + r \cdot \cos v) \cdot \cos u$$
$$y = (R + r \cdot \cos v) \cdot \sin u$$
$$z = r \cdot \sin v$$

where R=6, r=2, u=0,.,2π, v=0,…, 2π, take the number of the u and v values equal 30.

b) Möbius' strip:

$$x = \left(1 + \frac{1}{2} v \cdot \cos \frac{u}{2}\right) \cos u$$
$$y = \left(1 + \frac{1}{2} v \cdot \cos \frac{u}{2}\right) \sin u$$
$$z = \frac{1}{2} v \cdot \sin \frac{u}{2}$$

where u is ranged between 0 to 2π and v between -1 to 1; take the same number for the u and v values as for the first body.

10. The radioactive substance decay data, N, are: 400, 200, 100, 50, and 25 disintegrations per minute at 0, 1, 2, 3, and 4 hours respectively. Plot these data in semi-logarithmical coordinates in which x is time and y is log(N). Add axis labels, a grid, and a caption.

11. The weights (in mg) of 33 vials from a lot are: 65, 80, 95, 93, 67, 81, 90, 93, 92, 83, 86, 83, 90, 94, 93, 96, 96, 98, 96, 59, 75, 81, 65, 88, 81, 65, 88, 81, 60, 57, 61, 68, 77, 75, 76, 70. Plot a histogram for these data and add a title to the graph. Calculate the average and standard deviation and write the determined values into

the graph using the text commands (take the initial text coordinates as follows: x=60 and y=5.5 for the average, and x=60 and y=5.0 for the standard deviation).

12. The doubling time of a bacterium is a half hour. The initial number N_0 of bacteria in a flask was 100. The general equation for bacterial population growth is $N = N_0 2^n$, where n is the number of generations that have elapsed and equals 6. Calculate and plot bacteria growth during 3 hours in two plots on one page: (a) N *versus* time t, and (b) logarithm N *versus* t; mark the calculation points with a circle (the letter 'o'); add axis labels, a grid, and captions to each plot.

13. The V_2 volume of a solute in water is calculated by the expression $V_2 = V_1 M_1/M_2$ (see Subsection 2.2.5.4), in which M_1 is the final molar concentration of the solution, and M_1 and V_1 are the initial solute concentration and the solution volume respectively. Given the initial solute concentration M_1= 1mol/L, plot the three dimensional graph $V_2(M_2, V_1)$ in which M_2 changes in the range 0.1 … 2 mol/L and V_1 changes in the range 0.1. 0.9 L. Show the three-dimensional graph with the azimuth and elevation angles -135 and 35 degrees respectively. Add axis labels, a grid, and a caption to the graph.

14. In a first-order reaction the concentration $[A]$ changes with time t by the law $[A] = [A]_0 e^{-kt}$, where $[A]_0$ is the initial concentration of the A-species; k is the reaction rate constant that changes with temperature by the Arrhenius equation $k = ae^{-E_a/(RT)}$, where a is frequency factor, E_a - is activation energy, T – is temperature, and R – is the gas constant. The values of the parameters in these equations are $a=10^{14}$ sec^{-1}, E_a=77000 J/mol, T=293, 294, …, 303 K, R=8.314 J/(K mol), $[A]_0$ = 0.25 mol/L, t=1, 1.2, …, 4 sec. Generate a three-dimensional surface plot of the concentration (z-axis) as a function of time (x-axis) and temperature (y-axis). Present the plot with azimuth and elevation angles 123 and 26 degrees respectively. Change the colors to the autumn color combination.

15. A rigid body motion, studied in fluid biomechanics, is described by time-dependent coordinate equations. Plot the trajectory of the body that was described by the following set of the coordinate equations:

$$x = \sin(2\pi t)$$
$$y = \cos(2\pi t)$$
$$z = t^3$$

Use the LineWidth property equals 5. The time t is given in 0 ... 1 dimensionless units. Add axis labels, a grid, and a caption.

16. Adhesion of gas molecules on a solid surface at a constant temperature is described by the Langmuir adsorption equation $\theta = \frac{bP}{1+bP}$ in which θ is called surface coverage of an adsorbed substance, P, and b is pressure and a constant of the given substance at a given temperature (Langmuir isotherm). Plot two graphs in two separate Figure Windows:

a) The graph of $\theta(P,b)$ when P is given in the range 0...1 with step 0.01, and 50 values of the b coefficient is given in the range 0.1 ... 100; and

b) The graph $\theta(P)$ with four lines corresponding to the four values of the b constant: 5, 10, 20, and 100.

Add the graph axis labels, grid, and captions to each plot, and add a legend to the second plot.

17. A bio-film lense used in ophthalmology and some other medical applications has nano-size surface roughness that can be modeled by the equation $h = \text{asin}(\sin 2\pi kx) + \text{asin}(\sin 2\pi ky))$ in which x and y are dimensionless surface coordinates changed in the range 0 ... 1 each with the step 0.01; k is the wave number and is equal to 5. Plot a rough surface graph $h(x,y)$ with the azimuth and elevation angles: -24 and 82 respectively, add a caption to the graph and remove the plot axis.

3.6. ANSWERS TO SELECTED QUESTIONS AND EXERCISES

3) (c) subplot

6)

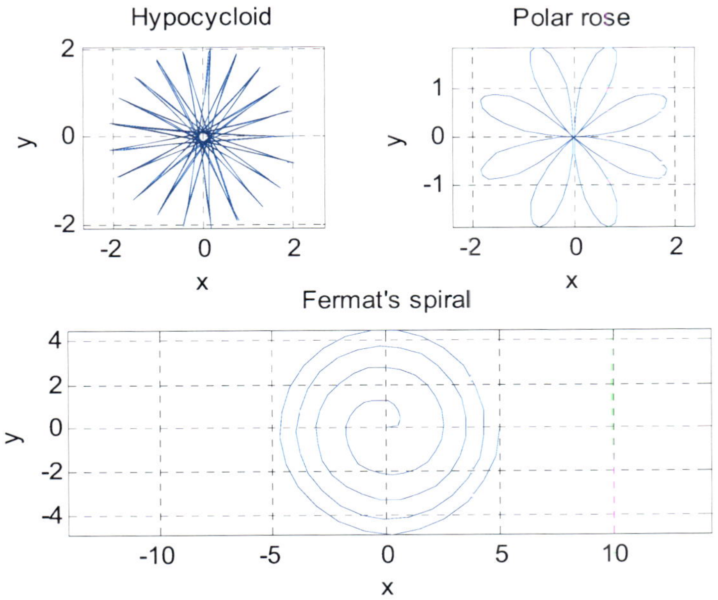

Hypocycloid
Polar rose
Fermat's spiral
x
y

9)

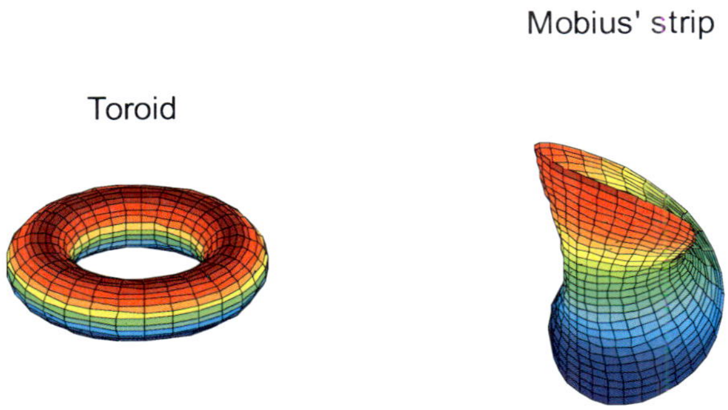

Mobius' strip
Toroid

13)

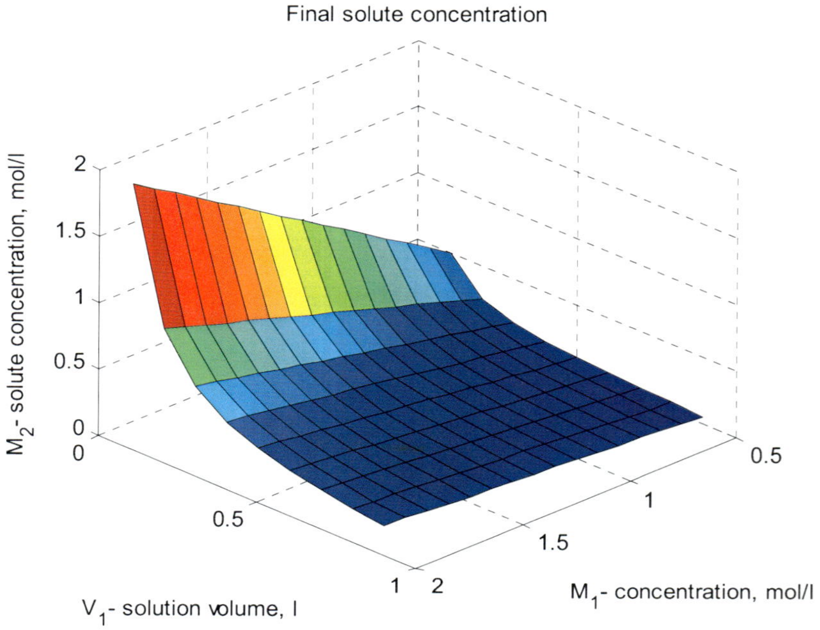
Final solute concentration
M2- solute concentration, mol/l
2
1.5
1
0.5
0
0
0.5
1
2
1.5
1
0.5
V1- solution volume, l
M1- concentration, mol/l

16)

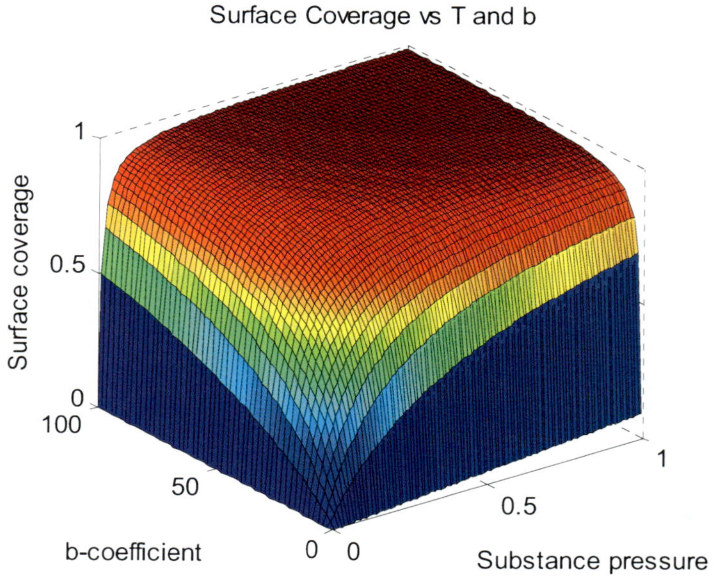
Surface Coverage vs T and b
Surface coverage
1
0.5
0
100
50
0
0
0.5
1
b-coefficient
Substance pressure

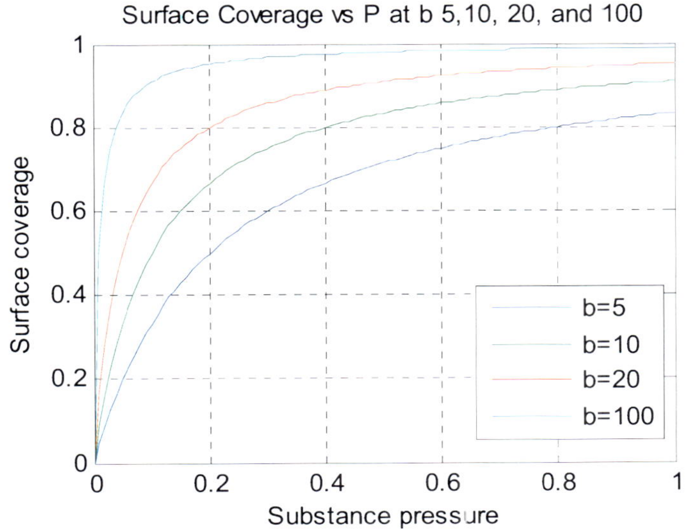
Surface Coverage vs P at b 5,10, 20, and 100
Surface coverage
Substance pressure
0
0.2
0.4
0.6
0.8
1
b=5
b=10
b=20
b=100

Primary MATLAB® for Life Sciences: Guide for Beginners, 2013, 130-172

CHAPTER 4

Writing Scripts and Functions: Some Functions Used in Bio-Computations

Abstract: Editor Window, script- and function files are accurately described. The commands for solving algebraic equation, for integration, differentiation, interpolation and extrapolation are introduced with applications to numerical problems of bioengineering, particularly such as heat sterilization time, population dynamics, bacterial population amount, *etc.* The questions and life-science problems together with answers to some of them are given in conclusion.

Keywords: Editor; script, functions; integration; differentiation; interpolation and extrapolation; life science applications; bacterial population amount; heat sterilization.

INTRODUCTION

In the previous chapters all the commands described were typed and entered interactively in the Command Window and were not saved. Therefore, they cannot be used again. Using commands in this way has additional disadvantage: to correct a command, the command must be called to the command line; after correction, all previous commands including the corrected and subsequent commands should be sequentially executed sequentially in order to obtain the correct result. If it becomes necessary to repeat the calculations, all commands have to be reentered. Readers of the preceding chapters have obviously experienced this inconvenience. In order to avoid these situations, all command sequences should be written and saved in separate files; in this case, the files can be run when necessary. MATLAB® provides two options for this purpose: writing script files or function files, which are described in this chapter. In addition, this chapter introduces useful MATLAB® functions for numerical analysis[1] and presents examples related to life science and biotechnology calculations.

4.1. WRITING, SAVING AND RUNNING SCRIPT FILES

A sequence of commands that is executed without user interaction is called a program. In MATLAB®, these written commands is called a script; the file, in

[1]Detailed mathematical background of numerical analysis, interpolation and approximation can be defined for example here [10, 11].

Leonid Burstein

which these commands are saved, is called a script file. MATLAB® executes these commands in the order in which they are written. Each correction, new command or any other extension may be entered directly into the script. The file is saved with name that you provide to him and with extension '.m'; therefor such generated files are called m-files. The MATLAB® Editor should be used to type and save m-files. The Editor can be opened in different ways; the two most suitable are: Entering the edit command in the Command Window (a) or selecting the 'Script' item in the 'New' line of the 'File' menu option (b). Immediately after executing one of these operations, the Editor Window appears (see Fig. **4.1**).

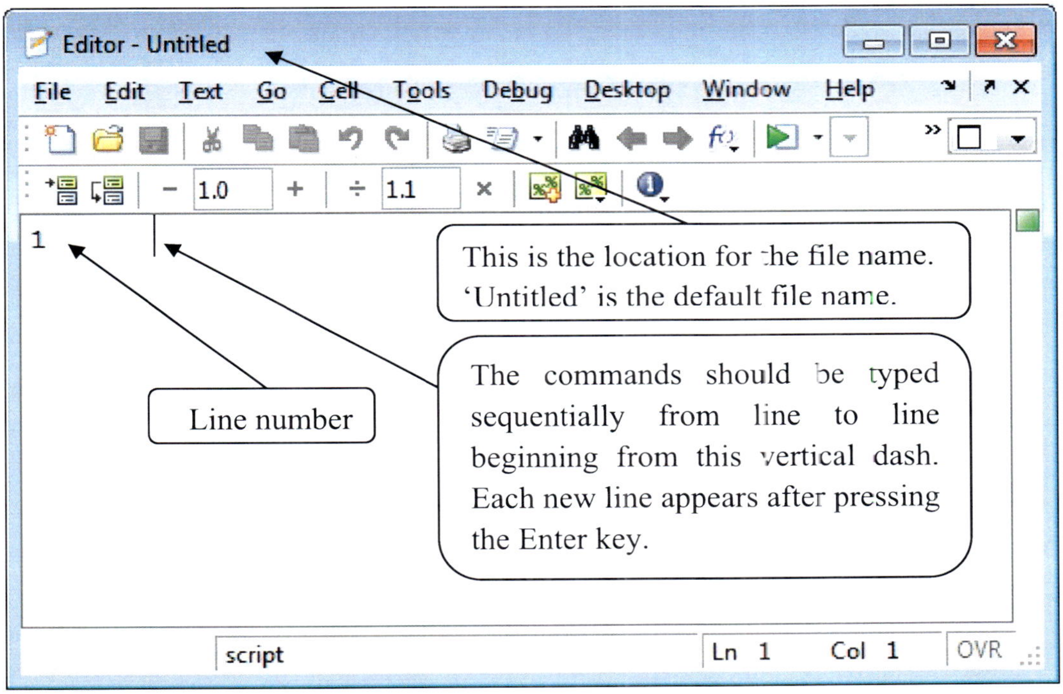

Figure 4.1: The MATLAB® Editor.

The commands are typed line by line in the Editor; herewith, two or more commands can be typed on the same line with commas or semicolons between them. To access a new line, press the Enter key; a new line automatically appears with a serial number on the left vertical strip. It is possible to use any other non-MATLAB® editor to write commands; these can then be copied into the MATLAB® Editor window.

An elementary script file typed in the Editor window is presented in Fig. **4.2**. The file, named EditorExample1, contains:

- Three lines with explanatory comments that are usually typed on the first lines using the comments sign %; comments are printed in green and are not executed when the program is running.

- Two lines with commands intend for calculations of the ribosomal RNA volume (see interactive calculations of the rRNA volume in Subsection 2.1.8.1); the commands appear in black for better readability.

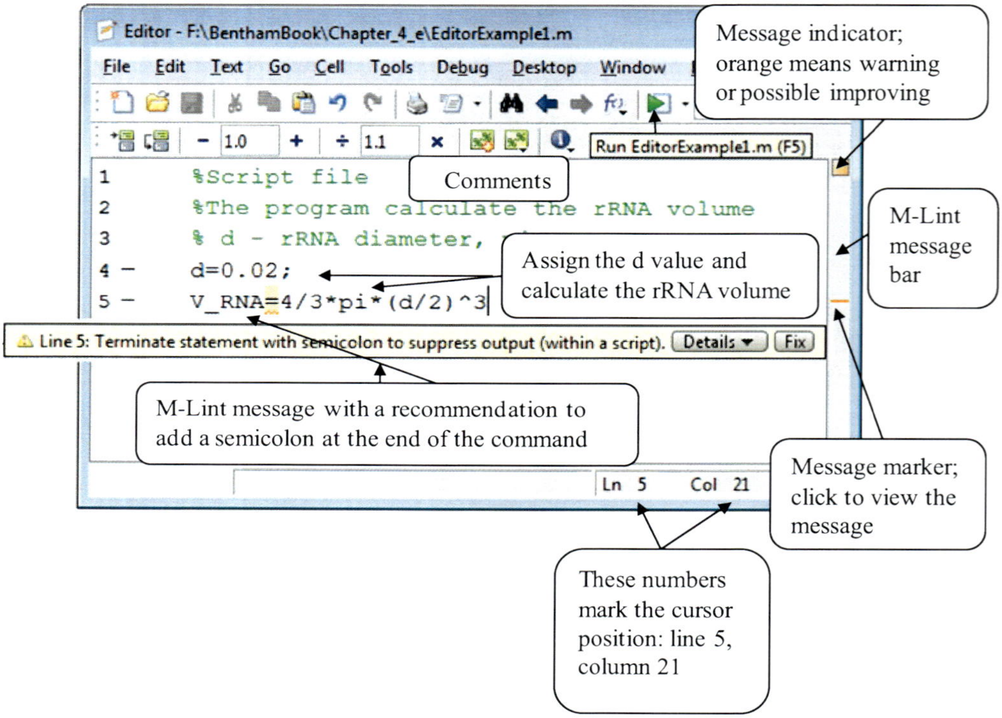

Figure 4.2: The Editor Window with the script file and the M-Lint message bar.

On the right vertical bar of the Editor Window, the so-called M-Lint analyzer is located; it checks written commands and places the message markers which designate detected errors and/or present comments and recommendations for better program performance. On the top of the message bar is located the message indicator ■, its color changes according to the analysis executed by the M-Lint analyzer program. A green indicator shows that everything is correct; a red indicates that syntax errors were detected; an orange signs that there are no errors but the analyzer warns or recommends possibly improvements. In the two latter cases, the appropriate program text appears underlined/highlighted and a horizontal line appears on the message bar. To see the comment message, the cursor should be placed on this line. The comment that appears is shown in the Fig. **4.2**.

Note:

- Warnings and recommendations that do not require corrections are shown in the fig. **4.2**; the comment message requires the addition of a semicolon, but this should not be executed, because we want to display the resulting ribosomal RNA volume value, V_RNA.

- The Editor Window includes the M-Lint analyzer by default. To disable the analyzer uncheck the 'Enable integrated M-Lint warning and error messages' check box, which can be found in the Code Analyzer Preferences dialog-box, accessed by selecting the Code Analyzer option of the Preferences window; the latter can be opened from the File option of the Editor Window or from the Desktop menu.

After writing the script into the Editor Window, it should be saved. To do this, follow these steps:

- Chose the 'Save As …' option from the 'File' menu;

- Type the desired file location into the 'Save in' field of the 'Save file as …' window; the default folder named MATLAB (frequently located in the 'My Documents' directory) is selected for saving your script file. If another directory/folder is preferred, click on the arrow to the right of the 'Save in:' field of the window.

- Type a file name into the 'File name:' field of the 'Save file as …' window; the file name is automatically terminated with the '.m' extension.

Note:

- The script file name should begin with a letter and cannot be longer than 63 characters;

- The name should not contain signs of mathematical operations (*e.g.* +, -, /, *) or repeat the user-defined and predefined variables, MATLAB commands and functions (*e.g.* sin, cos, sqrt, linspace, format, *etc.*). It is also not recommended to include spaces in the name.

To save the file, first check if the file is in the current MATLAB folder; if the folder does not contain your file, the folder with your file should be selected; then type and enter the file name, without the '.m' extension, from the Command Window.

Current Folder

The folder currently used by MATLAB® and the files in it is shown into the 'Current Folder' field and in the 'Current Folder' field on the MATLAB Desktop (see Fig. **4.3**). If the desired file is not in the current folder, you need to set the folder with the file; the simplest way is:

- Open the 'Browse for Folder' window by clicking on the icon with three dots [...] to the right of the Current Folder field;

- Select the desired folder, which appears in the 'Select a new folder' field and click the OK button.

In the Fig. **4.3** the location of the script file EditorExample1.m is shown; the file was saved in the 'MATLAB' folder of the 'My Documents' directory located in the 'Users' folder in Disk C. To run this file, type the file name (without the m-extension) in the Command Window, and press the Enter key:

```
>> EditorExample1    % runs the script written into the EditorExample1 file
V_RNA =
4.1888e-006
```

The RNA volume is displayed in the Command Window and calculated by running the script EditorExample1file

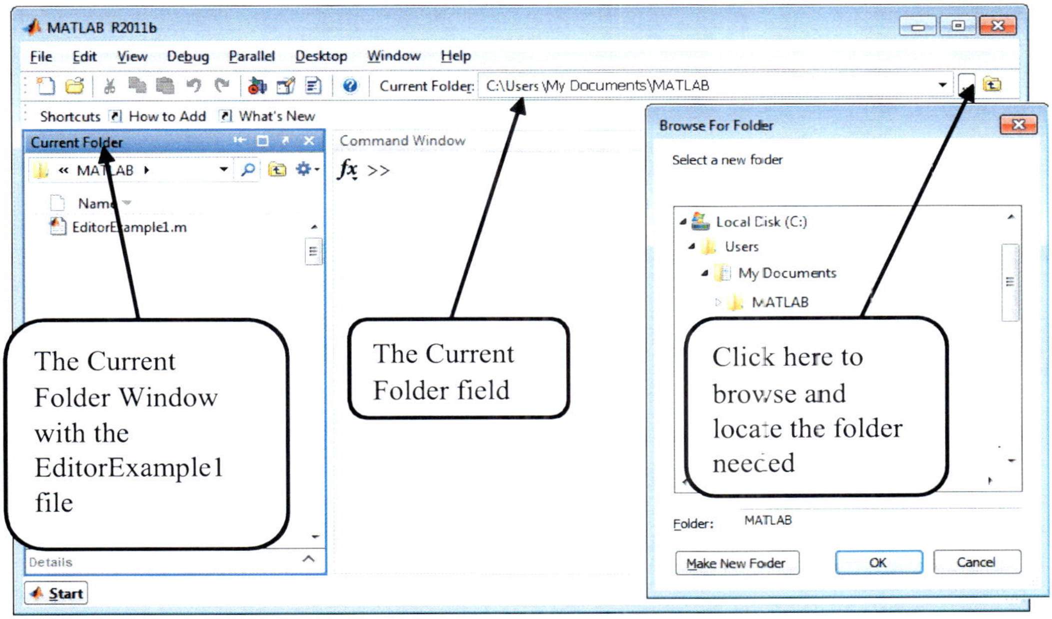

Figure 4.3: The 'Current Folder' field, 'Current Folder' and 'Browse for Folder' windows.

When a file is located in another folder, for example, if the EditorExample1 is located in disk D in the folder named Chapter 4, the current directory should be changed to D:\Chapter4 using the three dots button. The script file should then be run by typing and entering the file name from the Command Window.

4.1.1. Inputting Values into a Script File

The values for variables can be assigned directly in the script file. However, in this case, the file should be changed and saved every time new values are used. This is not suitable when the file is used frequently for calculations with different variable values. A better method is to assign the desired value to the variable that appears in the file using the input command, which can be written in two forms:

```
Numeric_Variable = input('String to display')

Character_Variable =input('String to display','s')
```

where the 'String to display' prompt is displayed in the Command Window after running the script file, the Numeric_Variable and Character_Variable are names of variables to which a numeric or character value should be inputted, and 's' notes that the inputted value is a string.

When the string written in the input command is displayed in the Command Window, the user should type and enter a number or string depending on the applied command form; the entered number or string values are assigned to the Numeric_Variable and Character_Variable respectively.

For example, the input command is used in the following script that converts a liquid volume, v_gal, given in US gallons to liters, v_L by the relationship v_L=3.78541v_gal:

```
%Gallon to liter convertor
v_gal=input('Enter liquid volume in gallons, V = ');
v_L=3.78541178*v_gal;
fprintf('\n The volume is%5.1f liters\n',v_L)
```

These commands are saved in the script file under the name Gallon2Liter. To run the file, type and enter this name in the Command Window, following which the 'Enter liquid volume in gallons, V=' prompt displays on the screen; now type a volume value (in gallons) directly after the '=' sign and press enter; values converted to liters appear on the screen.

```
>> Gallon2Liter
Enter liquid volume in gallons, V = 9
The volume is 34.1 liters
```

Note:

- Vectors and matrices can be inputted with the input command entered in the same way as for a variable, using numbers or characters in brackets.

- When the second form of the input command is used, inputting characters should be typed without quotes.

4.2. COMMANDS PRESENTED AS A FUNCTION AND SAVED AS A FUCTION FILE

In algebra, mathematical functions are presented in the form $y=f(x)$, where the right member contains one (x) or more arguments (parameters): x_1, x_2, x_3, ... After assigning values to the arguments, the y values are obtained. Many of previously studied MATLAB® commands were written in this form, *e.g.*, exp(x), log(x), tan(x), cot(x), plot(y), surf(z), *etc.* and, therefore, can be used for different calculations by typing their name with the argument presented as a number, numerical vector, or matrix. Analogously to these functions, MATLAB® presents the possibility to create new functions that are generated and can be used with the desired values of arguments in different programs; a function produced by the user is called 'user-defined'. Such functions can represent not only a specific expression, but also a complete program. The user can save a program defined as a function as a function file.

An example of such file is shown below in Fig. **4.4**. The function presented in the figure is named solute and calculates the molar concentration of a solute after dilution. The function and the function file have the name solute, three input arguments (the solute % concentration C1 and the solution volume V1, both before dilution, and solution volume V2 after dilution), and one output argument (the solute % concentration C2 after dilution).

Each user-created function consists of three parts: function definition, help lines and function body. The requirements and recommendations regarding these function parts are given below.

The Function Definition Line

The command for the definition of a function is:

```
function [output _arguments]=function_name(input_ arguments)
```

This function definition is written as the first program line with the word function typed as the first word of the file; the word appears in blue in the Editor Window. function_name is the name of the function; it is located to the right of the ' = '

sign, and is given by the user. The function name should follow the same rules as those for variable names (see Subsection 2.1.4). The input_ arguments, written between the parentheses, and output _arguments, written between square brackets, present lists of arguments that are transferred into and derive from the function. Commas divide the arguments; in cases of a single output argument, the brackets can be omitted.

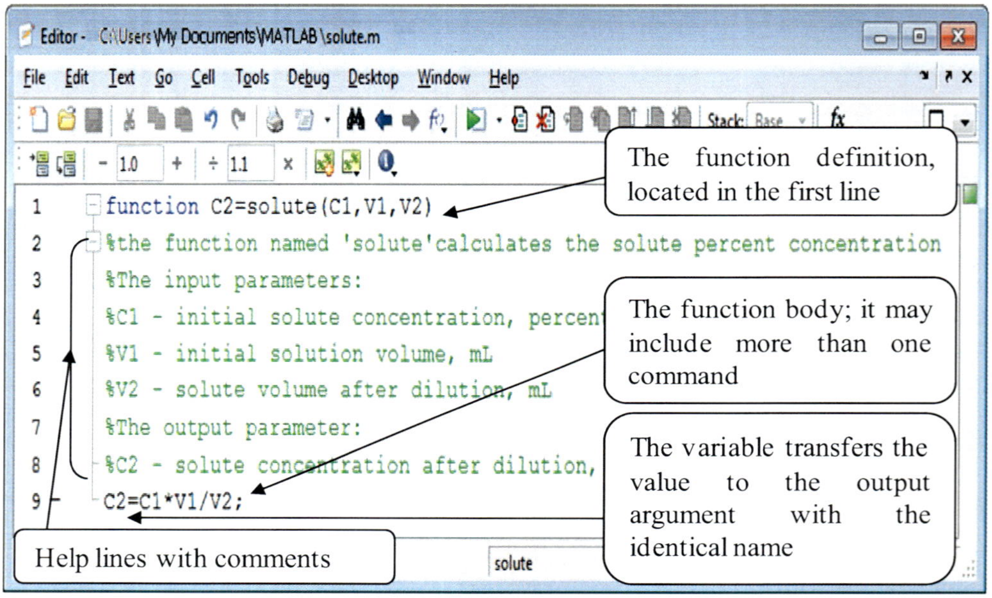

Figure 4.4: Editor Window with typical function file.

The function definition can be also written by omitting the arguments completely or partially. Examples of possible function definition lines are:

function [A,B]=ex1(a,b,c) – Function name 'ex1', three input and two output arguments;

function [A,B,C]=ex2 – Function name 'ex2', without input arguments and with three output arguments;

function ex3(a,b,c) – Function name 'ex3', without output arguments and with three input arguments;

function ex4 – Function name 'ex4,' without input and output arguments

Note: the word function should be written in lower-case letters.

Help Lines with Comments

Help lines contain comments concerning function and its arguments. They are placed just after the function definition line and before the first command of the function body. The first line of this part of the function should succinctly specify the function. This line is displayed by the lookfor command when this command outputs defined information, *e.g.*, typing and entering ookfor solute in the Command Window yields:

```
>> lookfor solute
solute - the function named 'solute' calculates the solute percent concentration
...
```

Note that the lookfor command in this example searches not only your function, but any MATLAB® function with the word 'solute' in its first help line; thus, list of defined functions may contain more than a single solute function.

The help command displays all written lines with the help comments when the the function name is typed after it; for example, typing and entering help solute in the Command Window yields:

```
>> help solute
the function named 'solute' calculates the solute percent concentration
The input parameters:
C1 - initial solute concentration, percent
V1 - initial solution volume, mL
V2 - solute volume after dilution, mL
The output parameter:
C2 - solute concentration after dilution, percent
```

Function Body, Local and Global Variables

One or more commands that perform actual calculations represent the body of the function; between or at the end of these commands, the command should be written that assigns a calculated value to the output argument. For example, in Fig. **4.4**, the last function command calculates solute concentration after dilution and assigns a computed value to the variable C2, which is defined as an output parameter in the function definition line.

The values of the input parameters should be assigned before running the function.

The variables in the function file are local and relevant only within the file. This means that after running the function, the variables are not saved and no longer appear in the workspace. In order share some or all of them with other function/s they have to be made them accessible; this is done using the global command:

global variable_name1 variable_name2 ...

A space (not a comma) is placed between the word global and the first variable name (variable_name1) and between other variable names, *e.g.*, variable_name1 variable_name2.

The command should be placed in the function before the variable is firstly used and should be repeated in every other functions wherever the variable is to be used.

4.2.1. Saving a Function as a Function File

Similarly to a script, a function should be saved in a file before it is used. To save a function as a function file, select 'Save As' from the 'File' menu and enter both the desired file folder and file's name. It is recommended to give the file the name of the function; for example the solute function should be saved in a file named solute.m.

Below are examples of function names that appear in the function definition lines and the names that should be given to the function files:

function M2=dilute(M1,V1,V2) – The function file name: dilute.m;

function [v, m]=r_RNA(d,h) – The function file name: r_RNA;

function heights2(age) – The function file name: heights2.m.

When a program contains more than one function, the function file should be named for the function that starts the program (the main function).

4.2.2. Running a Function File

The function saved in the function file can be run using the Command Window or by using another file. For this the function definition line should be typed without the word 'function' and with assigned values of the input arguments. For example, the solute.m function file (shown in the Fig. **4.4**) runs as follows:

```
>>C2=solute(2,0.5,0.6)
C2 =
     1.6667
```

Or, in the other way, by pre-assigning the input variables:

```
>> a=2;b=0.5;c=0.6;
>> C2= solute(a,b,c)
C2 =
     1.6667
```

The function created by the user can be used for calculations by another mathematical expression or by any other program. For example, the solute function calculates the C2 solute concentration in percentages that should be presented in mg/mL. In biochemistry, 1% of the solute is usually 10 mg of solute in 100 mL of the solution; thus C2_mg_per_mL =10*C2 mg per ml. The following commands should be typed in the Command Window:

```
>>a=2;b=0.5;c=0.6;   % defines values for the input parameters in solute
>>k=10;         % percentage to mg/mL coefficient
```

```
>> C2_mg_per_mL=k*solute(a,b,c)  % solute amount in mg/mL
C2_mg_per_mL =
16.6667
```

<u>Script and Function Files: Similarities and Differences</u>

As it is possible to solve most life sciences problems using the script file only or, interactively, by inputting commands directly from the Command Window, it is difficult to the beginners to understand the differences between script and function files. Similarities and differences between the two file types appear below:

- Both file types are produced using the Editor and saved as m-files (files with the extension m);
- The function definition line is the first line of the function file; this is not the case with a script file;
- The function file should have the same name as the function it contains;
- The data is inputted and outputted from the function files through the input and output arguments of the function definition line, respectively; when using script files, the data is assigned into the file, either by inputting using the `input` commands or by defining them directly in the workspace;
- The variables of a function file of are local; in contrast, all variables of the script file are global;
- The user-defined function files can be used in the same way as other MATLAB® functions in other files or simply by typing and entering them in the Command Window.

4.3. USEFUL FUNCTIONS FOR BIO-COMPUTING

In life science- or biotechnological- labs, various calculations [8, 9] are performed using mathematical operations such as interpolation, extrapolation, the solution of algebraic equations, integration, differentiation and fitting. MATLAB® has special functions for these purposes; the most frequent appearing below.

4.3.1. Data Interpolation and Extrapolation

In tables with measured, sampled, or calculated data, it is often necessary to estimate values between or out of the table points. In these cases interpolation or extrapolation methods are used for, respectively, the points lying inside or outside the data range. For example, the numbers of a rare breed among the tiger population were 21, 120, 340, 430, and 500 in the years 1940, 1971, 1985, 1996 and 2009 respectively. These data points are presented in Fig. **4.5**. Calculating the number of tigers in the years 1960 and 2000 (values between data points) is an interpolation problem while evaluating the number of tigers in the years 1935 and 2012 (values outside data points), an extrapolation problem.

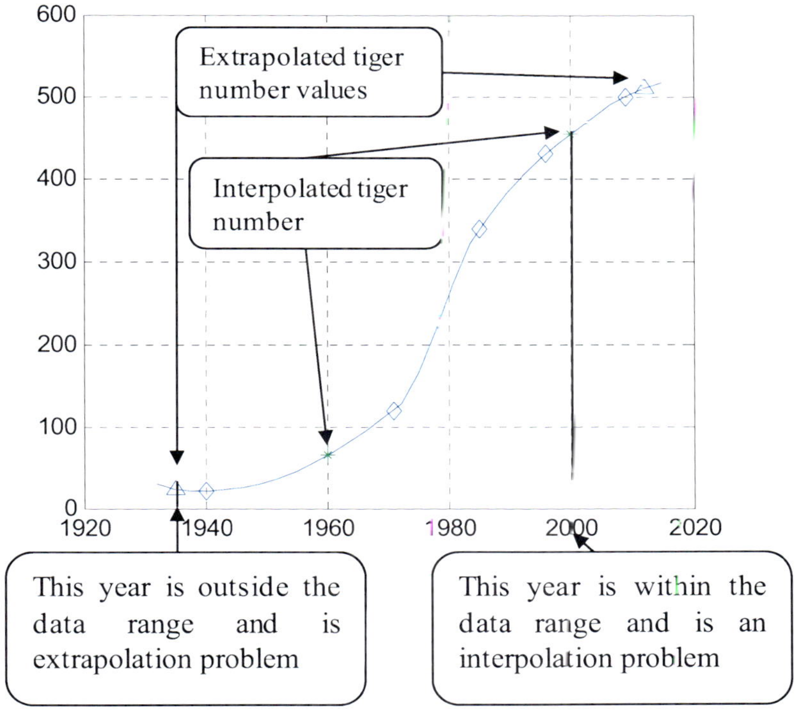

Figure 4.5: Interpolation and extrapolation: ◊ - Original data points; * - interpolation points; Δ - extrapolation points.

Both interpolation and extrapolation operations can be carried through the interp1 function which has the following forms

y_i=interp1(x,y,x_i,'method') or y_i=interp1(x,y,x_i,'method','extrap')

where the y_i is a single or vector of values obtained by inter- or extrapolation at the desired x_i point/s; x and y are the vectors of data values; the 'method' string specifies the name of the mathematical algorithm that is used for the y_i calculation. Some of names of available methods is – 'linear', 'cubic', and 'spline'; a default name is 'linear'; when the first command form is used this word can be omitted; for extrapolation or for simultaneous inter- and extrapolation, use the 'extrap' string.

The first form of the interp1 command performs interpolation only in default mode ('linear'); however, extrapolation but can also be carried out using the 'cubic' or 'spline' method.

The commands for the calculation of interpolated and extrapolated values represented in Fig. **4.5** are:

```
>>tiger=[21, 120, 340, 430, 500];                % the x-data
>>t=[1940, 1971, 1985, 1996, 2009]               % the y-data
>>ti=[1960 2000];                                % x-points to interpolation
>>te=[1935 2012];                                % x-points to extrapolation
>>y_interpolated=interp1(t,tiger,ti,'cubic');    % defines interpolated y-values
>>y_extrapolated=interp1(t,tiger,te,'cubic','extrap'); % defines extrapolated y-
values
>>y_interpolated,y_extrapolated                  % displays defined values
y_interpolated =
64.9353 455.0297
y_extrapolated =
24.1335 510.2463
```

In this example, the 'cubic' algorithm is used for extrapolation with the second form of the interp1 command. However, the first command form can also be used. The amount of tigers should be represented by an integer and the resulting values should be truncated using the floor command (Table **2.4**):

```
>> floor(y_interpolated),floor(y_extrapolated)
ans =
64 455
ans =
24 510
```

4.3.2. Solution of the Nonlinear Algebraic Equation

Solution of sets of linear algebraic equations presented in matrix form has been presented in Chapter 2 (Subsections 2.2.2, 2.3.4.1). If it is necessary to solve a single nonlinear equation $f(x) = 0$ the computer uses a special algorithm that finds such x where this equation is equal to zero. The function to be used for this process and for a nonlinear equation solution is fzero; whose general form is

```
x=fzero('function', x0)
```

This function searches for solutions near the point x0 (called the guess point) that graphically presents the x-value where the function is zero; 'function' is the string representing an actual equation or the name of the user-defined function with an equation to be solved.

Define, for example, activation energy E_a from the modified Arrhenius equation

$$\frac{k}{A} = \left(\frac{T}{T_0}\right) e^{-\frac{E_a}{RT}}$$

where $k/A = 8.7 \cdot 10^{-14}$ was defined at T=310 K and the reaction-to-reference temperature ratio was T/T_0=1.3, R=8.314 J/(K·mol).

To define E_a with the fzero function, the equation should be presented in the form

$f(x) = \frac{k}{A} - \left(\frac{T}{T_0}\right) e^{-\frac{x}{RT}}$ where x denotes E_a. For physical reasons, the value of x0 must be positive and can be selected as $1 \cdot 10^4$ J/mol (one of the known E_a for many chemical reactions).

The command for realizing this solution is:

```
>> Ea=fzero('8.7e-14-1.3*exp(-x/(8.314*310))',1e4)          % Ea in J/mol
Ea =
7.8184e+004
```

As can be seen, all the values of the variables are written into the fzero function because the string with the solved equation can include only the name of a variable to be selected. It cannot include pre-assigned variables, *e.g.*, it is not possible to define k_A=8.7271e-14, R=8.314, T=300 and then write 'k_A-exp(-x/(R*T))' into fzero.

To include pre-assigned variables into the equation written in the fzero function, another form of fzero can be used:

x=fzero(@ (x) fun(x, variables1, variables2,...), x0)

@ (x) fun[2] is a user-defined function containing the equation with the additional arguments variables1, variables2,... that should be assigned first.

Now, we can write the example above as a function with, for instance, the name activation_energy

```
function Ea=activation_energy(k_A,R,T,T_T0,x0)
% activation energy calculation
% k_A is ratio of reaction constant to frequency factor
% R - gas constant, J/mol/K
% T_T0 - real-to-reference temperature ratio
% T – temperature, K
% x0 – initial Ea
Ea=fzero(@(x) myf(x,k_A,R,T,T_T0),x0);
function f=myf(x,k_A,R,T,T_T0)
f=k_A-T_T0*exp(-x/(R*T));
```

This function has the input parameters k_A, R, T, T_T0, and x0, and the output parameter Ea, and includes the myf sub-function that is used by the command x=fzero(@ (x) myf(x,k_A,R,T,T_T0), x0). The function definition line of the

[2]The symbol @ is used to denote the so-called anonymous functions, which fall outside the scope of this book.

myf function should appear as function f=myf(x.k_A,R,T,T_T0). The activation_energy function should be written in the Editor Window and saved into the function file with the name activation_energy.m. Following these steps, the function can be run from the Command Window with the assigned arguments k_A, R, T, T_T0 and x0:

```
>> Ea=activation_energy (8.7e-14, 8.314, 310,1.3,1e4)
Ea =
7.8184e+004
```

4.3.3. Integration

An integral is the area between the curve of the function and the *x* axis and integration is a process used to calculate the size of this area. For this purpose, the area is divided into a number of small geometrical elements of identical form, *e.g.*, rectangles, trapezoids, *etc.*

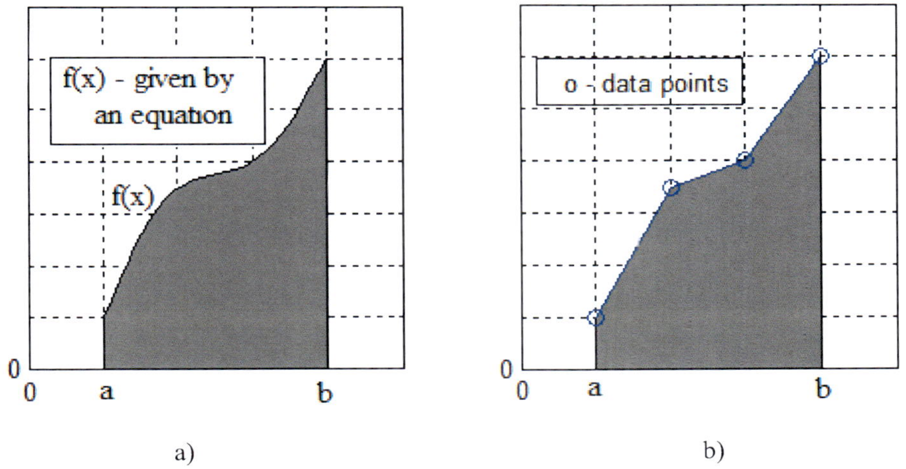

Figure 4.6: Integral (the shaded area) of the function given analytically (a) and by the data points (b). (Produced with a MATLAB script file that includes the fill command)

The area of each of these elements can be easily calculated and the integral can be defined as the sum of the squares of these elements.

The function f(x) for which the integral is defined can be given in the form of equation or data points, such as those shown on the Fig. **4.6 a,b**. MATLAB®

functions for the integration of each of these cases are the quad and trapz functions, respectively.

Integration with the quad Function

The function takes the form:

q=quad('function',a,b,tolerance)

where 'function' is a string representing an expression f(x) to be integrated, or the name of a function file containing the expression (this file should be created by the same way as that for the fzero command); a and b present the interval of integration (or the integration limits) and tolerance denotes the desired value of absolute error who default value is no more than $1 \cdot 10^{-6}$ (the tolerance arguments is optional and can be omitted); the obtained value of the integral is assigned to the q variable.

The quad function realizes the adaptive Simpson's sum method, in which the area beneath the integrated function is divided by elements, each two of which contains a cubic parabola as a line that fits the function piece; the number of elements increases by using special subdivision method for those parts of the integrated area where the function is behaving 'badly'. A detailed explanation of this integration method is available in classic courses of numerical analysis.

The f(x) integrated expression should be written with element-wise operators '.*', '.^', and './'.

For example, to calculate the integral $q = \int_1^4 x^{-3} dx$ (the x^n function appears, for example, in equations for reaction rates, in population dynamics, *etc.*) typy and enter the following command from the Command Window:

```
>>q=quad('1./x.^3',1,4) %Note: the element-wise operations are used for 1/x^3
q =
0.4688
```

Another option for use of the quad command is to write the function in the Editor Window as follows:

```
function y=Ch4_ Ex(x)
y=1./x.^3;
```

This user-defined function should be saved in a file with the name Ch4_ Ex.m. Next, to integrate, the quad command should contain the name Ch4_ Ex instead of the '1./x.^3' expression. To calculate the integral, type and enter from the Command Window:

```
>> q=quad('Ch4_ Ex',1,4)
q =
0.4688
```

To use other variables/arguments (and not only x) in the 'function' string, they should be previously assigned in the same way as for the fzero command in Subsection 4.3.2.

Integration with the trapz Function

The trapz function uses when a function for integration is presented as set of data points. The simplest form of this function is

q=trapz(x,y)

where x and y are coordinate vectors representing a set of points.

For example, the microorganism mass growth rates were measured in a laboratory and are given in the following table:

t, hour	1	2	3	4	5	6
v, pg/hour	4.1	10.2	22.1	44.3	88.6	356.9

Problem: Calculate the microorganism mass increment during the time of the measurements, that is between 1 and 6 hours

$$m = \int_{1}^{6} v(t)dt$$

where $v(t)$ under the integral is the data given numerically in the table.

To solve this problem, the following commands should be inputted from the Command Window:

```
>>t=1:6;
>>v=[4.1 10.2 22.1 44.3 88.6 356.9];
>>m= trapz(t,v)
m =
345.7000
```

4.3.4. Derivatives of Function

In numerical calculations the derivative $y'(t)$ of the $y(t)$ function is the function change Δy between the two neighboring t points, or when the distance between the t points is very small:

$$y'(t) = \lim_{\Delta t \to \infty} \frac{\Delta y}{\Delta t} \approx \frac{y_{i+1} - y_i}{t_{i+1} - t_i}$$

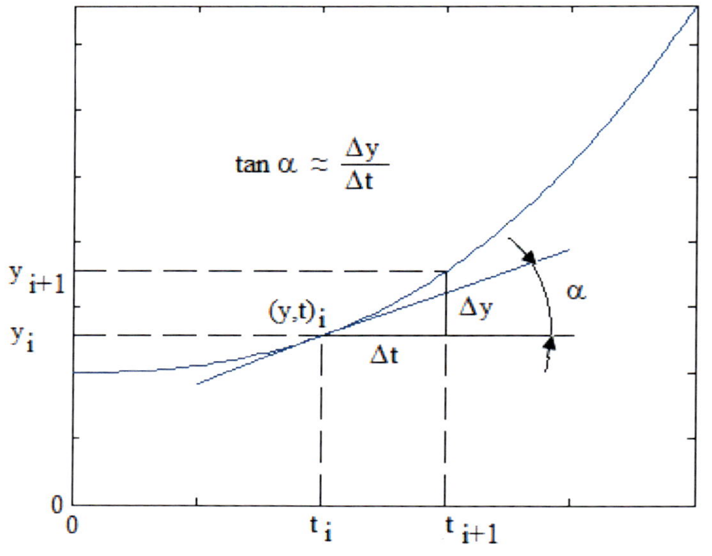

Figure 4.7: A graphic interpretation of a derivative.

Geometrical interpretation of this definition is the slope of the tangent to the curve at the y_i,t_i – point, as shown in Fig. **4.7**.

According to this premise, the derivative at each i-point can be calculated as the ratio of y- and x-differences that are computed between the i+1 and i-th points. The MATLAB® command that calculates these differences is named diff and has the forms:

dy=diff(y) or dy_n=diff(y,n)

where y is the vector of the y- or any other variable, *e.g.*, t, at points $i = 1, 2, \ldots$; the n denotes the order of the difference or shows that the command should be applied n times, for example, if n=2 the diff should be applied twice and it is the same as diff(diff(y)); the dy and dy_n are returned vectors containing determined values of the differences of the 1st and n-th order respectively.

The length of the dy vector is one element shorter than length of the y vector; the length of the dy_n vector is n elements shorter than y, *e.g.*, if vector y has 10 elements then vector dy has 9 elements, and the fourth order difference vector dy_4 has 6 elements only.

See, for example, the insect population size p, in individuals, that growths over time t, day, as shown in the table below.

t, day	1	2	3	4	5	6	7
p, unit	5500	7000	7750	8200	8500	8714	8875

<u>Problem</u>: calculate the insect population growth rate $r = \frac{dp}{dt}$, unit/day, and acceleration $a = \frac{dr}{dt} = \frac{d^2p}{dt^2} = \frac{\Delta p_i - \Delta p_{i+1}}{\Delta t^2}$.

The commands for calculating population growth rate are:

```
>> t=1:7;
>> p=[5500 7000 7750 8200 8500 8714 8875];
>> dt=diff(t);dp=diff(p);       % t and p differences
>> r=dp./dt;    % element-wise operations
```

```
>>disp('  t  r'),disp([t(1:end-1)' r'])
     t     r
     1   1500
     2    750
     3    450
     4    300
     5    214
     6    161
```

The command that calculates the population growth acceleration is

```
>>a=diff(r)./diff(t(1:end-1))   % t(1:end-1) is used as r is one element shorter
a =
-750 -300 -150 -86 -53
```

The values of a are negative and indicate deceleration in the insect population growth. The same results for the acceleration can be reached applying the second-order dp differences:

```
>>a=diff(p,2)./diff(t(1:end-1)).^2
a =
-750 -300 -150 -86 -53
```

Note, that if the values in the vector t are changed with a constant step h, then it can be used to change diff(t); for example, the latter command can be written as a=diff(p,2)./h^2.

In the example above, the p function was defined as a table. If the function is given by an equation, the derivatives can be determined in the same way as tabulated data, but the step in t in this case may be smaller, that leading to more precise values of the calculated derivatives.

For an example, we will assume that the equation p=10000-9000/(1+t) very accurately describes the insect population data in the above table.

Problem: Calculate the population growth rate r of each half-day with the p given by the equation above; use the fprintf function for displaying t and r values

The solution is:

```
>> h=0.5;
>> t=1:h:7;p=10000-9000./(1+t);
>> r=diff(p)./h;
>>fprintf(' t r\n')
>>fprintf('%7.1f %7.0f\n',[t(1:end-1);r])
      t      r
    1.0   1800
    1.5   1200
    2.0    857
    2.5    643
    3.0    500
    3.5    400
    4.0    327
    4.5    273
    5.0    231
    5.5    198
    6.0    171
    6.5    150
```

When these results and the results of previous examples are compered, we see significant deviations of the *r* values for the corresponding *t* points meaning that there are not enough points in the table for an exact numeric determination of derivatives. Apparently, more points are necessary to achieve a more accurate result that can be easily realized for analytically given function.

In certain cases, the derivative should be determined at a specific point, *e.g.*, population size at a specific date, reaction rate at a desired moment, *etc.* In this case, the argument *t* (or any other argument of a solved problem) should be assigned at one additional point after that point. Thus, if, as in the example above, the required rate value is $t=7$, the points for numerical differentiation are $t=7$ and $t+h = 7.5$, when h is 0.5.

4.4. APPLICATION EXAMPLES

4.4.1. Celsius to Fahrenheit Convertor

The expression

$$F = \frac{9}{5}C + 32$$

is used for converting degrees of Celsius °C into degrees of Fahrenheit °F.

Problem: Write a script that can be used as a C-to-F converter; display the degrees Celsius with one decimal place and the resulting degrees Fahrenheit with two decimal places.

The script that solved the problem is:

```
% Centigrade to Fahrenheit convertor
C=input('Enter temperature in Celsius = ' );
F=9/5*C+32;
fprintf('\nTemperature %5.1f degrees Celsius is %5.2f degrees Fahrenheit \n',F,C)
```

After writing these commands in the Editor Window, they are saved in the script file under the name C2F. The user types and enters this name in the Command Window; after the string ''Enter temperature in Celsius = ' appears, the user types and enters a temperature value in degrees Celsius. The script commands convert the inputted Centigrade value into degrees Fahrenheit and display both inputted and calculated temperatures with the required decimal places.

Below is an example of this script, run in the Command Window:

```
>> C2F
Enter temperature in Celsius = 25.5
Temperature 25.5 degrees Celsius is 77.90 degrees Fahrenheit
```

4.4.2. Heat Sterilization Time

Heat sterilization process (HSP) is used for the elimination of all forms of microbial life under height temperatures. The time *t* required for sterilization is different for various media and as an example can be described by the exponential equation

$$t = 7.13e^{-0.021(T-170)}$$

where T is temperature in °C, t – time in sec.

Problem: write the script that calculates and displays the sterilization time at temperatures of 110, 120, …, 200 C; present the results in graph with time as a function of temperature T; add axis labels, a grid, and a caption to the graph.

The script solving this problem saved as the SterilTime script file is:

```
% Sterilization time
T=110:10:200;
t=7.13*exp(-0.021*(T-170));
disp([' Temperature',' St.time'])
disp([T',t'])
plot(T,t)
xlabel('Temperature, C'),ylabel('Time,min')
title('Sterilization time vs. Ttemperature')
grid
```

After typing and entering the script file name SterilTime into the Command Window, the program displays the following numeric and graphic results:

```
>> SterilTime
  Temperature   St.time
   110.0000     25.1363
   120.0000     20.3751
   130.0000     16.5157
   140.0000     13.3874
   150.0000     10.8516
   160.0000      8.7961
   170.0000      7.1300
   180.0000      5.7795
```

```
190.0000        4.6847
200.0000        3.7974
```

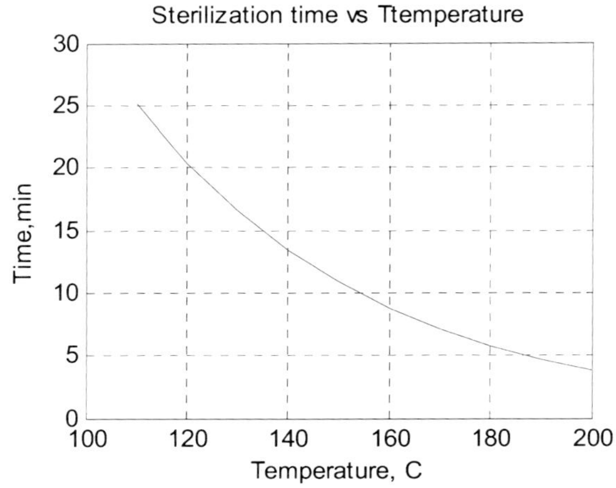

4.4.3. Gas Volume at a Given Pressure and Temperature

A relation between volume, pressure and temperature of gas may be described with the Redlich-Kwong equation:

$$P = \frac{RT}{V - b} - \frac{a}{\sqrt{T}V(V + b)}$$

where P is pressure in atm, V – is volume in L/mol, T is temperature in K, R is ideal gas constant in atm/(mol K), and a and b are gas-specific constants that can be defined from the expressions:

$$a = \frac{0.4275R^2T_c^{5/2}}{P_c}$$

$$b = \frac{0.08664RT_c}{P_c}$$

where T_c and P_c are temperature and pressure at a critical point of a substance.

Problem: Write the function file that calculates the gas volume at the following given values of the P, T, P_c, and T_c parameters: P=6 atm, T=30 C (303.15 K), P_c=49.8 atm, and T_c=154.6 K (oxygen); universal gas constant R=0.08206

L·atm/(mol·K). Use the fzero function for obtaining volume V with the initial volume value V_0=22 L/mol.

When using fzero, the variable V in the expressions above should be named x and the Redlich-Kwong equation should be rewritten as $f(x)=0$:

$$P - \frac{RT}{x-b} - \frac{a}{\sqrt{T}x(x+b)} = 0$$

The function for solving this problem is:

```
function V=RedlichKwong(P,T,Pc,Tc)
% defining V, L/mol, from the Redlich-Kwong equation
% P - pressure, atm
% T - temperature, K
% Pc – critical point pressure, atm
% Tc - critical point temperature, K
V=fzero(@(x) myf(x,P,T,Pc,Tc),22);
function y=myf(x,P,T,Pc,Tc)
R=0.08206;
a=0.4275*R^2*Tc^(5/2)/Pc;
b=0.08664*R*Tc/Pc;
y=P-R*T/(x-b)-a/(sqrt(T)*x*(x+b));
```

This function should be written in the Editor Window and saved as function file RedlichKwong.m. The function definition line (the first line of the function file) contents the P, T, Pc, and Tc variables as input arguments, and V variable as output.

The fzero function in written file is used in form with the P, T, Pc, and Tc pre-assigned variables (see Subsection 4.3.2) and with the myf sub-function, that includes these variables as input arguments.

The command for running the file and the result of the calculations are displayed in the Command Window:

```
>>V=RedlichKwong(6,303.15,49.8,154.6)
V =
4.2068
```

4.4.4. Population Dynamics

The population of New York City between 1920 and 2010 is qiven in the following table:

Year	1920	1940	1960	1980	2000	2010
People, million	5.620	7.455	7.781	7.072	8.008	8.175

Problem: Write a function file with the name NY that predicts and displays the expected population of New York in 2015. Use for prediction the interp1 function for the prediction with these three extrapolation alternatives: 1 – linear; 2- cubic; 3 - spline.

The function definition line should include the function name NY and the input and output arguments. The specified input arguments are: yi – the target year; and meth_num, the number representing the chosen alternative: 1- for the linear; 2 – for the cubic; and 3 or any other number (except 1 and 2) – for the spline. The argument specified for output is NYi (the predicted population).

To solve this problem the function file should be written as follows:

```
function NYi=NY(yi,num)
% Ney York population prediction
% yi - year for prediction
% num - mehod number: 1-linear,2 - cubic, 3 - spline
y=[1920:20:2000 2010];
p=[5.620 7.455 7.781 7.072 8.008 8.175];
if num==1
method='linear';
elseif num==2
method='cubic';
else
```

```
method='spline';
end
NYi=interp1(y,p,yi,method,'extrap');
```

The if … elseif … else … end statement is used for assigning appropriate string ('linear', 'cubic', or 'spline') to the method variable for further inputting into the interp1 function. For example, the NY population prediction by the 'cubic' method should be made the following command entered in the Command Window:

```
>>NYi=NY(2015,2)
NYi =
8.1707
```

4.4.5. Parallel Reactions

In these two first-order parallel reactions A→B and A→C, the concentration of the main product, C, can be expressed as:

$$[C]=[A]_0\frac{k_2}{k_2-k_1}\left(1-e^{-(k_1+k_2)t}\right)$$

where $[A]_0$ is the initial reactant concentration, k_1 and k_2 are the reaction rate constants in the first and the second parallel reactions respectively, and t is time.

Problem: Write a function file with name paralrtime that evaluates and displays time t when the product C reaches the desired concentration. The initial reactant concentration $[A]_0$=2.5 mol/L, the product concentration $[C]$=1 mol/L, the reaction rate constants $k_1=5\cdot10^{-3}$ sec^{-1} and $k_2=9\cdot10^{-3}$ sec^{-1} and initial (guess) time value that is necessary for a solution using the fzero function is x_0=2 seconds.

For solution, this equation should be rewritten in the form $f(x)=0$:

$$-[C]+[A]_0\frac{k_2}{k_2+k_1}\left(1-e^{-(k_1+k_2)x}\right)=0$$

where x denotes searching time t.

To solve this problem, write the following in the Editor Window and save the function file:

```
function t=paralrtime(A0,C,k1,k2,x0)
% time of the current main product concentration in parallel reactions, t
% Ao is initial concentration of the initial reactant A, mol/L
% C - the main product concentration, mol/L
% k1 - rate constant of the A-to-B reaction
% k2 - rate constant of the A-to-C reaction
% x0 - initial time for the fzero function
t=fzero(@(x) kinetics(x,A0,C,k1,k2),x0);
function f=kinetics(x,A0,C,k1,k2)
f=-C+A0*k2/(k2+k1)*(1-exp(-(k1+k2)*x));
```

The input arguments included in the function definition line are: the concentrations $[C]$ and $[A]_0$, the reaction rate constants k_1 and k_2, and the initial value x0; the output argument is the reaction time t.

The Command Window displays following run command together with the result:

```
>> t=paralrtime(2.5,1,5e-3,9e-3,2)
t =
69.5321
```

4.4.6. Bacterial Population Amount

The proliferation rate of a bacterial population is given as $v(t) = 0.6931 \cdot N_0 \cdot 2^t$, cell/h; N_0 is the initial bacterial amount in the cells, and t is the time in hours. The amount of the bacterial population N during a specific time t can be calculated with the expression

$$N = \int_a^t v(t)dt$$

where a is the low integration limits; the upper integration limit t can be changed in the time range from a to b (the final upper limits).

Problem: write a script that calculates the amount of bacteria during each hour, from 0 to 7, using the quad function and plot the graph $N(t)$. The initial bacterial amount N_0 was equal to 10 cells. Include in the script the calculation of the bacterial amount after 7 hours using the left Riemann sum expression:

$$N=\Delta t(v_1+v_2+\ldots+v_{n-1})$$

where n is the number of points in the integration interval $[a,b]$, a and b are the lower and upper integration limits respectively, $\Delta t=(b-a)/(n-1)$ is the spacing of the time points, f_i is the function value at point i=1, 2, ..., n-1; take n=1000.

For natural reasons, the amount of the bacterial cells should be integer; thus the floor command should be used.

To solve the problem, use the following steps:

- Define the t vector of value from 0 to 7 with step 1;
- Organize a loop with the for...end command for the bacterial amount N, calculated at different upper time limits; use the quad function for integration, in which the upper integration limit repeatedly changes from 0 to 7 with the one hour step;
- Display the results with the fprinntf command;
- Plot the graph with the plot command;
- Define the No, dx and t values to calculate the integral with the left Rieman sum;
- Calculate N with the left Riemann sum;
- Display the results at t=7 are with the fprinntf command for Riemann and Simpson's sums;

The script file for solving the problem is:

```
% Amount of bacteria
clear, close all% clear the memory and close all preceding graphs
t=0:7; % times for integration
for i=1:length(t) % the loop for integration by the quard command
q(i)=quad('0.6931*10*2.^t',0,t(i));
end
fprintf('\n Bacterial amount\n Hour Cell\n') %title for resulting table
fprintf(' %5.0f %8.0f\n',[floor(t);q]) %displays resulting table
plot(t,q,'-o') %plot the graph
title('Bacteria amount')
xlabel('Time, h'),ylabel('Amount,cell')
grid
n =1000;a=0;b=7;dt=(b-a)/(n-1);
t=a:dt:b;
f=0.6931*10*2.^t;
N7=floor(dt*sum(f(1:end-1)));
fprintf('\nBacterial amount after 7 hours by the\n')
fprintf(' Left Riemann N=%5.0f Simpson N=%5.0f\n',N7,q(end))
```

Name this script BactAmount and save it as a script file. When the file is run, the following will display in the Command Window:

```
>> BactAmount
 Bacterial  Amount
    Hour      Cell
      0          0
      1         10
      2         30
      3         70
      4        150
      5        310
      6        630
      7       1270
Bacterial amount after 7 hours by the
Left Riemann N= 1266 Simpson N= 1270
```

The resulting graph is:

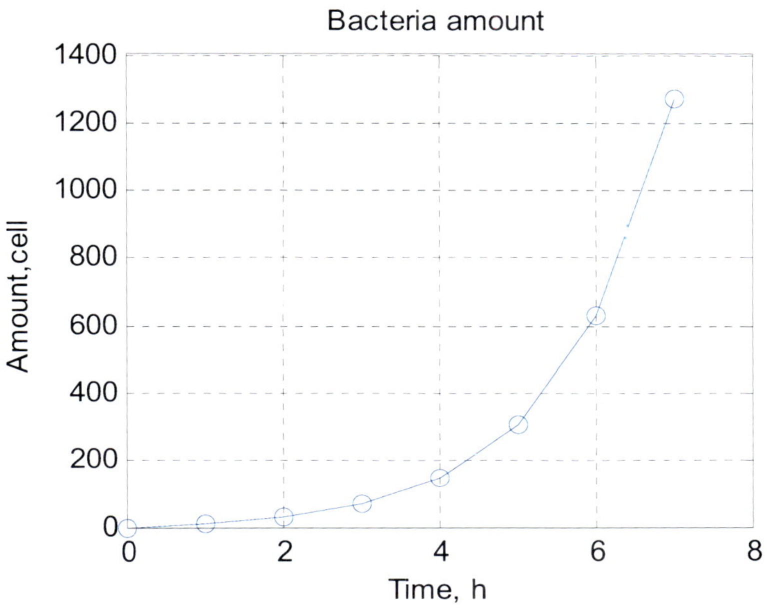

The left Riemann sum method of numerical integration is not as accurate as Simpson's method and is very sensible to number of points for integration. When the number of points increase the difference in the *N* values defined by the left Riemann and Simpson's sums decreases; nevertheless, it is accompanied by a significant increase in the volume of the calculations.

4.4.7. Growth Rate

A microorganism population-time data are described by the polynomial

$$p = 10^6 + 10^4 t - 10^3 t^2$$

where *p* is population amount and *t* is time in hours.

Problem: write a function file that determines numerically the growth rate $v = \frac{dp}{dt}$ at *t*=4 hour; take the p vector with values defined at one step (Δt) longer time than required, *e.g.* *t*= 0, Δt, 2 Δt, …,4, 4+ Δt. Plots the *p*(*t*) and *v*(*t*) curves in two graphs in the same Figure Window and calculate for the *p* and *v* values at *t*= 0, 0.01, …, 4 hour.

The program solving the problem is realized in the form of a function and saved in the GrowthRate.m file. The function has the following input arguments: tstart the starting time, h the Δt time step, and t_required the time point for defining the growth rate; the output argument v_required is the variable to which defined growth rate is assigned.

To solve this problem the following steps should be taken:

- Calculate the population vector p at t points for the entire time interval (from tsatrt to tend with step h);

- Calculate the population growth rates as the diff(p) to h ratio and assign results to the vector v;

- Plot the population and growth rate values with the subplot and plot commands; then add the commands for the axis and plot captions; to represent p and t vectors together with the one element shorter v vector, the p and t vectors should be shortened by the one last element.

The function file attained is:

```
function v_required=GrowthRate(tstart,h,t_required)
% microorganism population growth rate at the required time
% tstart - starting time
% t_required - time point for the growth rate calculation
% h - time step
tend=t_required+h;
t=tstart:h:tend;
p=1e6+1e4*t-1e3*t.^2;
v=diff(p)./h;
v_required=v(end);
subplot(2,1,1)
plot(t(1:end-1),p(1:end-1))
xlabel('Time, hour'),ylabel('p, unit')
title('Population growth'),grid
subplot(2,1,2)
```

```
plot(t(1:end-1),v)
xlabel('Time, hour'),ylabel('dp/dt, unit/hour')
title('Growth rate'),grid
```

After running this function file the Command and Figure windows appears as displayed below:

```
>>v_required=GrowthRate(0,0.01,4)
v_required =
1.9900e+003
```

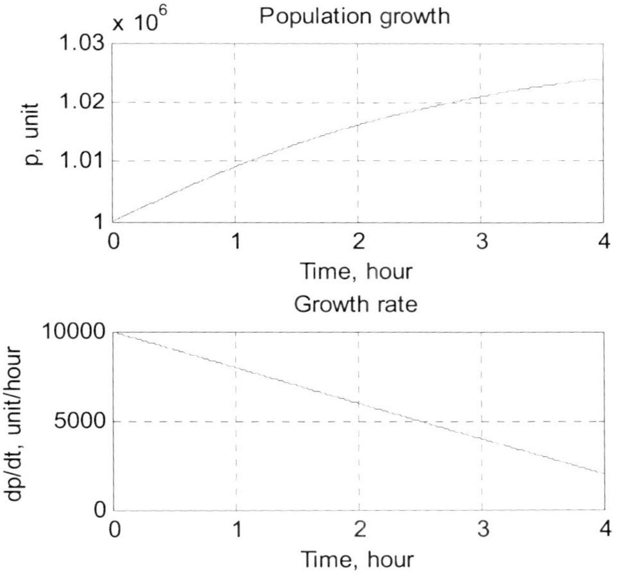

4.5. QUESTIONS AND EXERCISES

1. The first line of the help comments of the user-defined MATLAB function should be: (a) Define of variables to input/output; (b) The function definition; (c) Defines the function in short; Choose the correct answer.

2. Global variables are: (a) All variables used within the function file only; (b) Input/output arguments, written in the function definition line; (c) The variables that are available for any function, script or interactive work. Choose the correct answer.

3. Which of the following written unterp1 functions should be used for the extrapolation: (a) unterp1(x,y,xi); (b) unterp1(x,y, 'method'); (c) interp1(x,y,x_i,'method','extrap'). Note: The variables in these commands correspond to those indicated in Subsection 4.3.1.

4. To define t with the fzero function, the equation $C=A_0e^{-k/t}$ should be written: (a) $-C+A_0e^{-k/t} = 0$; (b) $\ln(C/A_0) = -k/t$; (c) No change, as it is written: $C=A_0e^{-k/t}$.

5. Which of the following written commands can be used to define derivatives of the $y=\sin(x)$ function at the $x = 0, \pi/10, \ldots, \pi$: (a) dydx=diff(x); (b) x=linspace(0,pi,11);y=sin(x);dydx=diff(y)./diff(x); (c) x=0:pi/10:pi;diff(x); (d) answers (b) and (c) are correct; (e) None of the above.

6. The body mass index

$$\text{BMI} = \frac{G}{h^2}$$

relates the body weight G in kg and the height h in m; a BMI of between 20 and 25 kg/m^2 is normal for humans; below 20 is considered underweight (too thin), between 25 and 30 overweight (large); and above 30, obese (too large).

Write and save a script that asks the recipient to enter their weight and height and then calculates and displays the BMI together with one of the next conclusions: 'too thin', 'normal', 'large', or 'too large'. To display use the fprintf command

7. The basal metabolic rate:

$$\text{BMR} = \begin{cases} 655 + 9.6w + 1.8h - 4.7a, & \text{for women} \\ 66 + 13.7w + 5h - 6.8a, & \text{for men} \end{cases}$$

is the minimal human daily energy requirement in cal/day; here w is weight in kg; h is height in cm and a is age in years. Write and save a script in the file with the name Ch4_7 that calculates and displays BMR using the fprintf command.

8. The component concentrations in solutions are measured in various units, such as molarity M in mol/L, molality m in mol/kg, and molar fraction χ

(dimensionless, as it is the mole solute to mole solution ratio). The following expressions are used to convert M to m and to χ:

$$m = \frac{1000M}{1000d - MM_1}$$

$$X = \frac{m}{m + 1000M_2}$$

where d is the solution density, g/L; M_1 the molecular weight of the solute, g/mol; and M_2=18 g/mol is the molecular weight of water. Write and save a function file that calculates and outputs solute molality and molar fraction by the inputted solute molarity M, its molar mass M_1, and the solution density d. Calculate the molality and the molar fraction for M=3 mol/l, d=1.5·10^3 g/l, and M_1=40g/mol (sodium hydroxide).

9. The population of Asia is presented in the table below:

Year	1750	1800	1850	1900	1950	1999	2010
Population, millions	502	635	809	947	1402	3634	3879

Write and save a function with the name Ch4_9 that predicts and outputs the value estimated for 2013. For this prediction use the interp1 function, which can be used with any of three possible extrapolation methods: linear (to enter the number 1); cubic (for the number 2); and spline (for the number 3). Generate a plot with a curve for the table with the data signed by the point marker, and with the predicted value signed with the red circle marker.

10. In the A→B→C consecutive reaction, the concentration of reactant B can be calculated using the expression:

$$[B] = [A]_0 \frac{k_1}{k_2 - k_1}\left(e^{-k_1 t} - e^{-k_2 t}\right)$$

where t is time; $[A]_0$ is the initial concentration of the reactant A; k_1 and k_2 are the rate constants of the $A \rightarrow B$ and $B \rightarrow C$ reactions respectively. Write and save a function file that uses the fzero command to evaluate and display the time t during which the intermediate reactant B breaks down to the current concentration. Use the following data as input arguments: $[B]$=0.012 mol/l, $[A]_0$=2.3 mol/l, $k_1 = 2.6\cdot10^{-3}$ sec^{-1}, k_2=9.5·10^{-3} sec^{-1}, and initial (guess) time value is 3 sec.

11. The decay rate of a compound is expressed as

$$v = -0.69e^{-2.3t}$$

where t is time in h, and v - in mol/h. The amount m of the compound after time t is:

$$m = m_0 + \int_0^t v(t)dt$$

where m_0=0.3 mol is the initial amount of the compound. Write a script that calculates the amount of the compound each quarter of an hour over 2.5 hours. Use the quad function to calculate the integral. Using the fprinntf command, display a table comprising two columns, with inputted times and calculated compound amounts. Plot a $m(t)$ graph.

12. Solve the integral (see Subsection 3.4.6)

$$N = \int_a^t 0.6931\cdot N_0\cdot 2^t dt$$

with the Simpson sum using the quad command and with the right Riemann sum with the equation:

$$N = \Delta t(f_2+f_3+\ldots+f_n)$$

where t is time in hours, N_0 is the initial bacterial amount in cells, Δt is the spacing of the time points and f_i is the integrand value at point i=2, 3, …, n, n= 3000. Write and save a function with a, b, n, and N_0 as input arguments and with bacterial amounts calculated by Simpson's and Riemann rules as output arguments.

Note: The outputted bacterial amount values should be integers.

13. Calculate the reaction rate $r=-\frac{dm}{dt}$ for species that dissociates according to the equation

$$m = m_0 e^{-kt}$$

where m_0 and m are the species amounts at starting and at time t respectively, and k is the dissociation constant. Write and save a function that displays the r at t= 0, 0.25, …, 2 min, k=1.8 min^{-1}, m_0 = 5 mg, and plots the $m(t)$ and $r(t)$ curves in the same graph. Write the function without output arguments and with the following input arguments: m0- the species amount at starting time; k – the reaction constant; tstart – the starting time; tend – the end time; and h – the time step. Using the fprintf command, display the t and r values with 2 and 5 decimal digits respectively.

4.6. ANSWERS TO SELECTED QUESTIONS AND EXCERCISES.

2. (c) the variables that are available for any function, script or interactive work.

4. (a) $-C+A_0e^{-k/t} = 0$.

7.

```
>> Ch4_7
Enter the sex: 1 - male, 2 - female 2
Enter your weight in kg 78
Enter your height in m 1.71
Enter your age in years 50
Your BMP is 1171.9 cal/day
```

9.

```
>>Asia_Population=Ch4_9(2013,1)
Asia_Population =
3.9458e+03
```

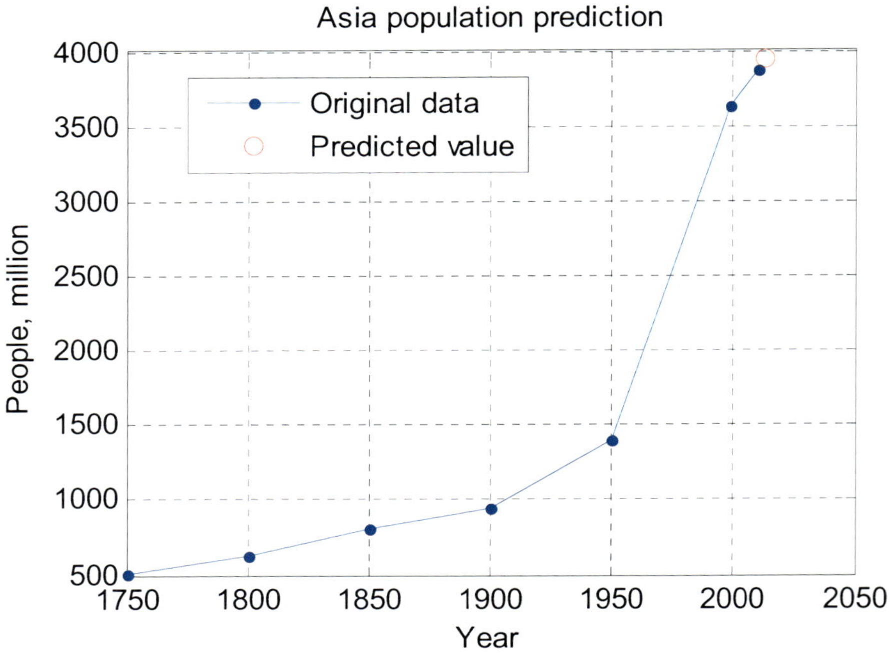

11.

```
>> Ch4_11
    Compound  amount
    Hour      Mole
    0.50      0.09499
    0.75      0.05345
    1.00      0.03008
    1.25      0.01692
    1.50      0.00952
    1.75      0.00536
    2.00      0.00302
    2.25      0.00170
    2.50      0.00095
```

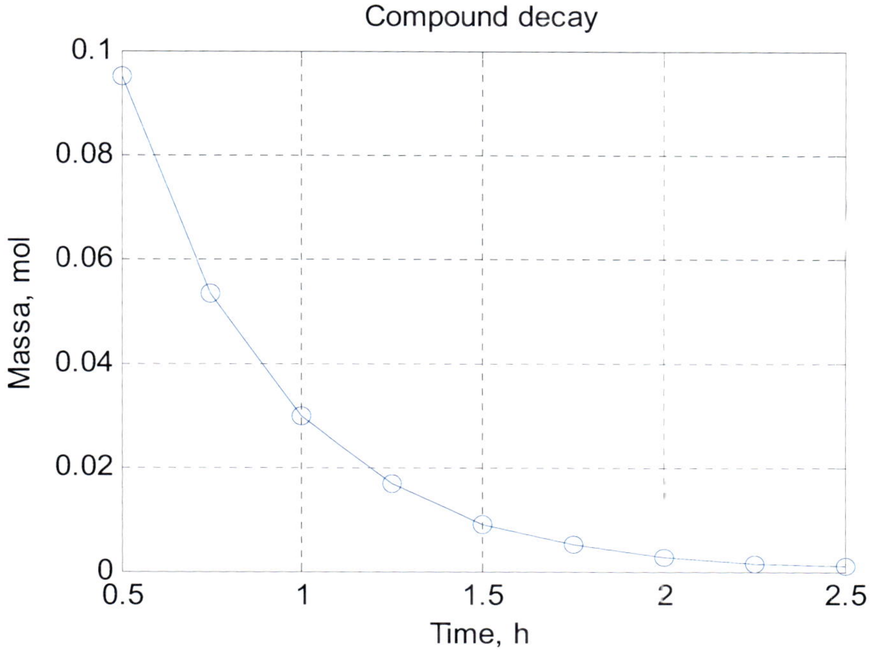

13.

```
>> Ch4_13(5,1.8,0,2,.2)
      t          r
          0    7.5581
     0.2000    5.2731
     0.4000    3.6789
     0.6000    2.5667
     0.8000    1.7907
     1.0000    1.2493
     1.2000    0.8716
     1.4000    0.6081
     1.6000    0.4243
     1.8000    0.2960
```

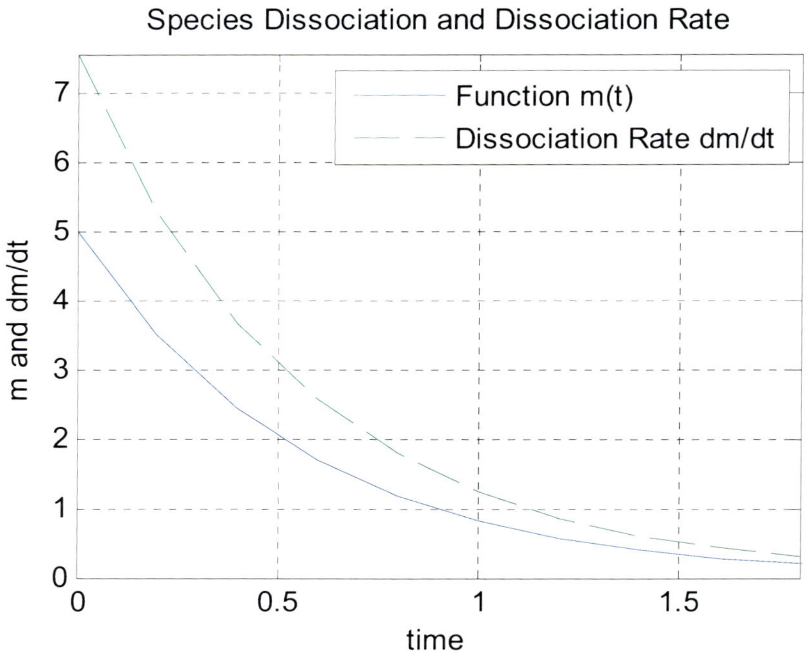
Species Dissociation and Dissociation Rate
Function m(t)
Dissociation Rate dm/dt
m and dm/dt
time
0
1
2
3
4
5
6
7
0
0.5
1
1.5

Send Orders for Reprints to reprints@benthamscience.net
Primary MATLAB® for Life Sciences: Guide for Beginners, 2013, 173-204

CHAPTER 5

Ordinary Differential Equations and Tools for Their Solution

Abstract: Specific ordinary differential equations and the ODE solver are briefly presented together with examples for bio-systems that can be represented by differential equations, one or a set. The solutions are demonstrated for the bio-molecular reaction, the predator-prey model, the drug dissolution, the batch reactor, *etc*. The questions and life-science problems together with answers to some of them are given in conclusion.

Keywords: Ordinary differential equations, ODE solvers, solution steps, bio-molecular reaction, predator-prey, drug dissolution, batch reactor.

INTRODUCTION

Differential equations with one independent variable are one of the main mathematical tools used in technology and the sciences, particularly in the life sciences. These equations, called ordinary differential equations (ODE), are applied to simulate and analyze a variety of processes and phenomena in the environmental sciences, earth and atmospheric sciences, ecology, biology, bio-kinetics, medicine, epidemiology, pharmacology, genetics, and other biosciences. In many cases, these equations have no exact analytical solution and are solved by a number of computerized numerical methods [7, 12]. There are a number of such methods and MATLAB® provides a number of special functions, called as ODE solvers, which implement these methods, permitting a solution for ordinal differential equations. This chapter provides descriptions of these solvers together with examples from the biosciences; herewith, a basic familiarity with ODE is assumed.

5.1. SOLVING ORDINARY DIFFERENTIAL EQUATIONS WITH ODE SOLVERS

A single set or sets of ordinary differential equations can be solved if the equations are presented in the form of first-order ODEs:

Leonid Burstein

$$\frac{dy_1}{dt} = f_1(t, y_1, y_2, ..., y_n)$$

$$...$$

$$\frac{dy_n}{dt} = f_n(t, y_1, y_2, ..., y_n)$$

where t is the independent variable and $y_1, y_2, \ldots, y_n$ are the dependent variables; n is the number of ODEs; any other variable can be used instead of t, for example, the variable x.

To solve high-order ODEs, they should be reduced to the first order equations, for example:

- The equation $a\frac{d^2y}{dt_2} + b\left(\frac{dy}{dt}\right) + cy = \cos(\omega t)$ can be rewritten as two first-order equations $\frac{dy_1}{\partial t} = y_2, \frac{\partial y_2}{\partial t} = -\frac{b}{a}y_2 - \frac{c}{a}y_1 + \cos(\omega t)$

- The equation $\frac{d^3y}{dx_3} + \varepsilon\left[\left(\frac{d^2y}{dx_2}\right)^2 + y\right] = \sin(x)$ can be rewritten as three first-order ODEs: $\frac{dy_1}{dx} = y_2,\ \frac{dy_2}{dx} = y_3,\ \frac{dy_3}{dx} = -\varepsilon\left(y_3^2 + y_1\right) + \sin(x)$.

However, as first order ODEs are the most common problems in the practical life sciences, solutions for these equations are discussed in depth.

Unfortunately, there is no universal method for numerical solutions of ODEs; to solve an actual ODE, a number of solvers realizing different methods are used. The available solvers, the numerical method they utilize, and sort of differential equation that can be solved with each solver, are presented in Table **5.1**.

Table 5.1: ODE solvers, Their Assignments, and Their Associated Numerical Methods[1].

Solver Name	Numerical Method	Sort of Problem	Assignment
ode45	Explicit Runge-Kutta method	Nonstiff differential equations	Use first when the solver is unknown; suitable for nonstiff equations
ode23	Explicit Runge-Kutta method	Nonstiff differential equations	For nonstiff and moderately stiff problems. While often quicker, but less precise than ode45
ode113	Adams' method	Nonstiff differential equations	For problems with stringent error tolerances or for solving computationally intensive problems
ode15s	Numerical differentiation formulas, NDFs (backward differentiation formulas, BDFs)	Stiff differential equations and differential algebraic equations, DAEs	For stiff problems when ode45 is slow. Try first when you do not know which solver is suitable to your stiff equation.
ode23s	Rosenbrock's method	Stiff differential equations	For stiff problem when ode15s is slow
ode23t	Trapezoidal rule	Moderately stiff differential- and differential algebraic equations, DAEs	For moderately stiff problems
ode23tb	Trapezoidal rule/second order backward differentiation formula,TR/BDF2	Stiff differential equations	For stiff problems, sometimes more effective than ode15s
ode15i	Backward differentiation formulas, BDFs	Fully implicit differential equations	For any ODEs given in implicit form $f(t, y, \frac{dy}{dt})=0$

All the solvers presented are solved ODEs with the given initial value of the function; for example, function value y=0 at time t=0 for an actual $\frac{dy}{dt} = f(t, y)$ equation. The ODE solution with the initial value belongs to what is called the initial-value problem (IVP), with the initial value is called the initial condition. An ODE solution with two boundary values specified at opposite ends of the range is called a two-point boundary value problem (BVP). Only IVP equations will be studied, as the BVP equations are beyond the scope of this book.

[1]The table is from the author's book [2]; with the permission of Biohealthcare Publishing (Oxford) Limited.

5.2. NUMERICAL METHODS AND TYPES OF PROBLEMS THAT CAN BE SOLVED WITH THE ODE SOLVER

The primary method for solving ODE equations is in replacing the derivatives by finite differences according to the equation: $\frac{dy}{dt} \to \lim_{\Delta t \to 0} \frac{\Delta y}{\Delta t} = \frac{y_{i+1} - y_i}{t_{i+1} - t_i}$. In this equation, the argument and function differences, Δt and Δy, are very small, but finite (non-zero); *i* is the point in the argument range [*a*,*b*]. By knowing the initial y_0 value at t_0 and calculating the derivative at this point by the solving equation $\left.\frac{dy}{dt}\right|_0 = f(t_0, y_0)$, we can determine the y_1 value at the second *t*-point as $y_1 = y_0 + \left.\frac{dy}{dt}\right|_0 (t_1 - t_0)$. Now, by calculating $\left.\frac{dy}{dt}\right|_1 = f(t_1, y_1)$ by the defined t_1, y_1 values, we can determine $y_2 = y_1 + \left.\frac{dy}{dt}\right|_1 (t_2 - t_1)$ and repeat this process to the end of the *t*- range, so that each function value in the range is defined. This solution method, originally realized by Euler, is called the method of finite differences. It was, and is still used today with improvements and complications, for example, in more advanced methods such as Runge-Kutta, Adams, Rosenbrock, *etc.*

ODE solvers can solve three kinds of problems – non-stiff, stiff, and fully explicit. There is no one rigorous criterion for defining stiffness in the two first categories of the ODEs. When we solve an equation that contains terms that lead to jumps in the function, or holes, ruptures, or other singularities resulting in a divergence of the numerical solution, even when size steps are very small, then this ODE type is known as stiff. In contrast, non-stiff ODEs are characterized by a stable convergence solution. Unfortunately, it is impossible to define the stiff category of equations and to determine in advance what ODE solver is suitable. In cases when solving the ODE that simulates a real phenomenon, it can be helpful to use the needed ODE solver. For example, fast chemical reactions, explosions, volatile processes, *etc.* should be described with stiff ODEs and the appropriate ODE solvers are used (see Table **5.1**). Sometimes, as a criterion of the stiffness, the ratio of the maximal and minimal coefficients of the ODE is used; when this ratio is larger than 1000 the problem is categorized as stiff. This criterion is not always correct, however, and it is therefore hard to determine in advance what ODE solver to use.

Note: If the category of the solving ODE is unknown, it is recommended to use the ode45 solver first followed by the ode15s solver.

For the third sort of ODEs, for equations represented in the implicit form, $f(\frac{dy}{dt},t,y)=0$, that cannot be transformed to the explicit form, $\frac{dy}{dt}=f(t,y)$, the ode15i solver should be used. The implicit form is rarely found in the bio-sciences and there is no need to discuss it further.

5.3. THE SIMPLEST FORM OF ODE SOLVER COMMANDS AND STEPS FOR SOLUTION

All ODE commands, except the ode15i, have an identical form that in the simplest case is:

```
[t,y]=odeNN(@ode_fun,t_range,y0)
```

where:

- Argument t is the output vector of *t*-points at which the y-values were calculated;
- y is the output vector with calculated function values that were calculated by the solver for the ODE; when more than one ODEs y is a matrix in which the first column is y_1 values, the second column is y_2, *etc.*;
- The odeNN is one of the solver names, *e.g.*, ode45 or ode15s and the @ode_fun is the function or function file name where the differential equations are written. The line with the function definition should be:

```
function dy=function_name(t,y)
```

In the lines added below this function definition, the first-order differential equation/s must be presented in the form

```
dy=[right side of the first ODE; right side of the second ODE; ...];
```

- t_range specifies the integration interval, *e.g.*, [1 14] defines a *t*-interval from 1 to 14; this vector can be written with more than two values. This is for cases when we want to display a solution at point values written in this vector, *e.g.*, [1:3:10 14] means that the results of a solution lie in the *t*-range of 1…14 and will be displayed at t-values of 1, 4, 7, 10, and 14. The values given within the t_range affect the output, but not the step that ensures the tolerance, so that the resulting y- values are computed with a default absolute tolerance of 0.000001.

- y0 is a vector with values of y-functions at the initial t-point; in other words, when this vector contains the initial conditions, for the set of two first-order differential equations with the initial function values $y_1=0$ and $y_2=4$, this vector is y0=[0 4]; vector y0 can also be given also as a column, *e.g.*, y0=[0;4].

Note: The odeNN commands can be used without the output parameters t and y; in this case, a plot automatically appears with the obtained $y(t)$ solution.

The Sequence of Steps for Solving an ODE

First present the equation in the form:

$$\frac{dy}{dt} = f(t,y), \qquad a \le t \le b,$$

with the initial condition

$$y = y_0 \ \text{ at } t = t_0$$

This and the next steps are demonstrated by an example of the rate equation solution of a bimolecular reaction A+B → C:

$$\frac{dx}{dt} = k(a-x)(b-x)$$

x is the amount of the product C at time t and k is the reaction rate constant; a and b are the initial amounts of the A and B reactants. For an example, k=0.007 sec^{-1}, a= 2 and b=3 mol, the reaction time range is 0 … 10 min, and the initial amount of the product at the beginning of the reaction is 0 mol.

For a numerical solution using one of the ODE solvers, this equation should be rewritten as:

$$\frac{dy}{dt} = k(a-y)(b-y)$$

where x, amount of C, is signed now by y.

Second, create the function files containing the used-defined function with the solving equation. The definition line of this function must include input arguments t and y and the output argument dy denoting $\frac{dy}{dt}$, the left side of the ODE. In the next lines, write the ODE/s as a vector of right-hand parts of equation/s with the ; (semicolon) sign between them. Type the commands in the Editor Window and then save with a name given in the definition line.

In our example, such a function is

```
function dy=myfirstODE(t,y)
dy=[0.007*(2-y).*(3-y)];
```

This function should be saved in the m-file with the name myfirstODE.

Note:

- In cases when the t- argument is absent in the right part of the differential equation, the character ~ (tilde) can be written instead and the function definition line may appear as: function dy=myfirstODE(~,y).
- In cases when there is a set of ODEs, the right parts of these equations can be written on separate lines of the dy vector, *e.g.*, two ODEs

$$\frac{dy_1}{dt} = y_2$$

$$\frac{dy_2}{dt} = -0.2y_2 + 0.03y_1 + \cos(\omega t)$$

can be written as

```
dy=[y(2) -0.2*y(2)+0.03y(1)+cos(omega*t)]
```

instead of

```
dy=[y(2); -0.2*y(2)+0.03y(1)+cos(omega*t)]
```

In the final step, the stiffness of the ODE should be assumed together with the necessery numerical method of the solution; then, the corresponding ODE solver should be chosen from Table **5.1**. For our example, when specific recommendations about appropriate methods are absent, the ode45 solver should be selected. Type and enter the following comman in the Command Window:

```
>> [t,y]=ode15s(@myfirstODE,[0:100:600],0) % t=0…600 sec, step 100; y0=0
t =
     0
   100
   200
   300
   400
   500
   600
y =
         0
    1.5046
    1.8030
    1.9110
    1.9589
    1.9803
    1.9906
```

The process starts with initial value of y=0 mol at t=0; the final time of the process is assumed as t=10·60=600 sec; the step of time for displaying results was chosen as 100 sec; thus, the vector of the time span, t_range, was inputted as 0:100:600.

Given commands yield the resulting numbers but do not generate the plot. To plot, use the plot command; however achieved seven t,y-points are insufficient to generate a smoothed curve. To produce both results - the numbers t,y and their plot – input t_range with the start and final t-values. In this case, the default t-steps values will be chosen automatically and the point number will be sufficient to generate a smoothed $y(t)$ plot; the commands that should be entered for this target are:

```
>> [t,y]=ode45(@myfirstODE,[0 600], 0); % t=0 ...600 s with default step
>> plot(t,y)
>> xlabel('Time, sec'),ylabel('Amount of C, mol')
>> title('Solution of the second order reaction rate equation')
>> grid
```

The generated plot is:

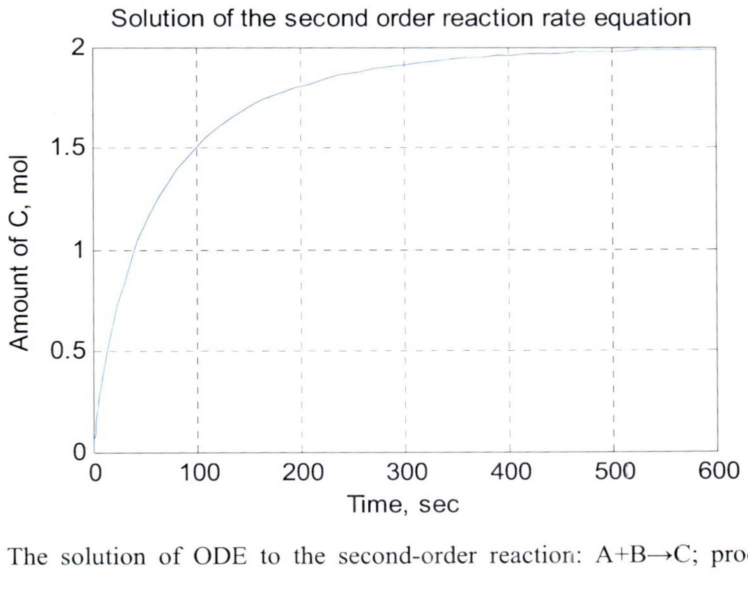

Figure 5.1: The solution of ODE to the second-order reaction: A+B→C; product C, amount change.

In the described solution, parts of commands were written and saved in the myfirstODE function file, and parts of commands, the ODE45 and the plot and plot formatting, were written in the Command Window. In order to create a single program that includes all these commands a function file should be written. For the example, this file, named SecOrdReaction, reads as follows:

```
function t_A=SecOrdReaction(ts,tf,y0)
% Solution of the ODE for second order reaction rate
% t – time, sec; y – amount of the C-product, mol
% t_range=[ts tf], sec;y0=0, mol;
% To run:>> t_A=SecOrdReaction(0,600,0)
close all % closes all previously plotted figures
t_range=[ts,tf];
[t,y]=ode45(@myfirstODE,t_range,y0);
plot(t,y)
xlabel('Time, sec'),ylabel('Amount of C, mol')
title('Solution of the second order reaction rate equation')
grid
t_A=[t y];
function dy=myfirstODE(~,y)
dy=[0.007*(2-y)*(3-y)];
```

To run this file, input following command in the Command Window:

```
>>t_A=SecOrdReaction(0,600,0)
```

After entering the command, the t and y values are displayed in two columns, each having 69 rows (not listed here for reasons of space), and the graph (see Fig. **5.1**) with the C product amount as a function of time, is also plotted.

5.4. SOME ADDITIONAL FORMS OF THE ODE SOLVER COMMANDS

When the ODE includes parameters such as the reaction rate constant and the reagent amounts, discussed in the previously example, and it is necessary to pass them to the function containing the differential equation, a more complicated odeNN form is necessary:

[t,y]=odeNN(@ode_fun,t_range,y0,[ ],arg_name1,arg_name2,…)

where [ ] denotes an empty vector. In general, this is the location for various integration and display control options[2]; when this vector is empty, the default values are used. In most cases, a satisfactory solution is obtained, and it is unnecessary to use these options. arg_name1, arg_name2, … are the names of the arguments that it is our intention to transmit to the ode_fun function.

The parameters named in the odeNN solver command should be written into the function containing the ODE with these parameters.

In the previous example, the k, a, and b coefficients in the SecOrdReaction function can be introduced as arguments:

```
function t_A=SecOrdReaction(k,a,b,ts,tf,y0)
% Solution of the ODE for second order reaction rate
% t – time, sec; y – amount of the C-reactant, mol
% % tspan=[ts tf], ts=0, sec tf=600, sec; y0=0, mole;
% To run: >> t_A=SecOrdReaction(0.007,2,3,0,600,0)
close all % closes all previously plotted figures
t_range =[ts,tf];
[t,y]=ode45(@myfirstODE, t_range, y0,[],k,a,b);
plot(t,y)
xlabel('Time, sec'),ylabel('Amount of A, mol')
title('Solution of the second order reaction rate equation')
grid
t_A=[t y];
function dy=myfirstODE (~,y,k,a,b)
dy=[k*(a-y).*(b-y)];
```

Type and enter the following command in the Command Window:

```
>> t_A=SecOrdReaction2(0.007,2,3,0,600,0)
```

The results are identical to those discussed in Subsection 5.3.

---

[2]For more details, type and enter help odeset in the Command Window.

This form, with additional arguments, is more advanced and has more versatility, *e.g.*, the SecOrdReaction function with the k, a, and b arguments can be used for second-order reaction with varies reactant amounts and different reaction-rate constants.

In forms discussed above, the ODE solver was used with the function written in a separate file or in a sub-function of the general function file. There is an option to include the ODE directly in the odeNN solver command; the general command form is:

```
[t,y]=odeNN(@(t,y) ode_fun(t,y, arg_name1,arg_name2,…),t_range,y0)
```

where @ (t,y) ode_fun(t,y, arg_name1,arg_name2,…) is a function containing the right part of the ODE with the additional arguments arg_name1,arg_name2,…that should be assigned beforehand (see Chapter 4, Section 4.3.2); in this case, the ode_fun function can be written directly into the odeNN solver command.

This form permits the creation of a program with less restrictions than the previous cases. This command, with the included ODE, can be written and saved in a function or script file or printed directly in the Command Window. To realize the latter possibility, write the following commands in the Command Window.

```
>>t_range =[0,10,50,100,600];k=0.007;a=2;b=3;
>>[t,y]=ode45(@(t,y) k*(a-y).*(b-y), t_range, 0)
t =
    0
   10
   50
  100
  600
y =
        0
   0.3573
   1.1139
   1.5051
   1.9899
```

The results are displayed here at five arbitrary time points t=0, 10, 50, 100, and 600 sec.

5.5. APPLICATION EXAMPLES

In the examples below all the programs are written for the most part in the form of a function. In general, the first help line of the function should describe in brief the purpose of the function and the subsequent lines should explain the input and output parameters of the function as described in the preceding chapter. In order to reduce their numbers, the help line is written as a single line containing a command that should be inputted into the Command Window to run the function.

5.5.1. Predator-Prey Model

In many life-science areas where one organism (plant, animal, individual) eats another organism the predator-prey model is widely used. Mathematical equations describing these phenomena were originally developed by V. Volterra and A. J. Lotka at the beginning of the previous century. The model includes two differential equations for the velocities of the predator and prey population changes. Prey survival, death, and proliferation decline due to crowding, and predator survival and death rates are described in this model by the following set of equations:

$$\frac{dx}{dt} = k_1 x - k_2 xy - k_5 x^2$$

$$\frac{dy}{dt} = k_3 y + k_4 xy$$

where x and y are the populations of the prey and the predators, k_1 and k_3 are the survival factors of the prey and predator populations, k_2 and k_4 are the death factors for each of the populations and k_5 is the prey crowding factor.

Problem: Solve these equations and plot $x(t)$ and $y(t)$ curves. Use k_1=1.011 1/year, k_2=1.002 1/year, k_3=-0.999 1/year, k_4=1.006 1/year, k_5=0.101 1/year, the time interval 0 … 20 years, and initial prey and predator populations x_0=3 and y_0=3 in thousands. In addition generate the phase plane grapg, x *versus* y.

First represent the sets of these ODEs in the form suitable for the ODE solvers:

$$\frac{dy_1}{dt} = k_1 y_1 - k_2 y_1 y_2 - k_5 y_1^2$$
$$\frac{dy_2}{dt} = k_3 y_1 + k_4 y_1 y_2$$

Then select the suitable ODE solver. Since there is no specific information about the stiffness of the solving equations, the ode45 solver should be selected.

The final step is to create a function file with the ODE solver and the sub-function containing the set of ODEs. The PredatorPrey function that solves the problem is:

```
function PredatorPrey(k1,k2,k3,k4,k5,ts,tf,x0,y0)
% >> PredatorPrey(1.011,1.002,-.999,1.006,.101,0,20,3,3)
close all
tspan=[ts,tf];
[t,y]=ode45(@PPM,tspan,[x0;y0],[],k1,k2,k3,k4,k5);
subplot(1,2,1)
plot(t,y)
axis square
xlabel('Time, year'),ylabel('Amount of x and y species, thousand')
title('Prey and predator amounts')
legend('Prey','Predator')
grid
subplot(1,2,2)
plot(y(:,1),y(:,2))
axis square
xlabel('Prey'),ylabel('Predator')
title('Phase plane')
grid
function dy=PPM(t,y,k1,k2,k3,k4,k5)
```

```
dy=[k1*y(1)-k2*y(1)*y(2)-k5*y(1)^2
-k3*y(2)+k4*y(1)*y(2)];
```

This function is written as a function without output arguments. The input arguments k1, k2, k3, k4, k5 are the same as the k_1, k_2, k_3, k_4, and k_5 in the original set; ts, and tf are the start and the end times used by the ode45 in the t_range vector; x0 and y0 are the initial populations of the prey and predator respectively. The solving-equations set is contained in the PredatorPrey-function within the sub-function called PPM. For a more aesthetic plot, the axis square command is used.

To run this function, type and enter the following command in the Command Window:

```
>>PredatorPrey(1.011,1.002,-0.999,1.006,0.101,0,20,3,3)
```

After this the following graphs will be generated:

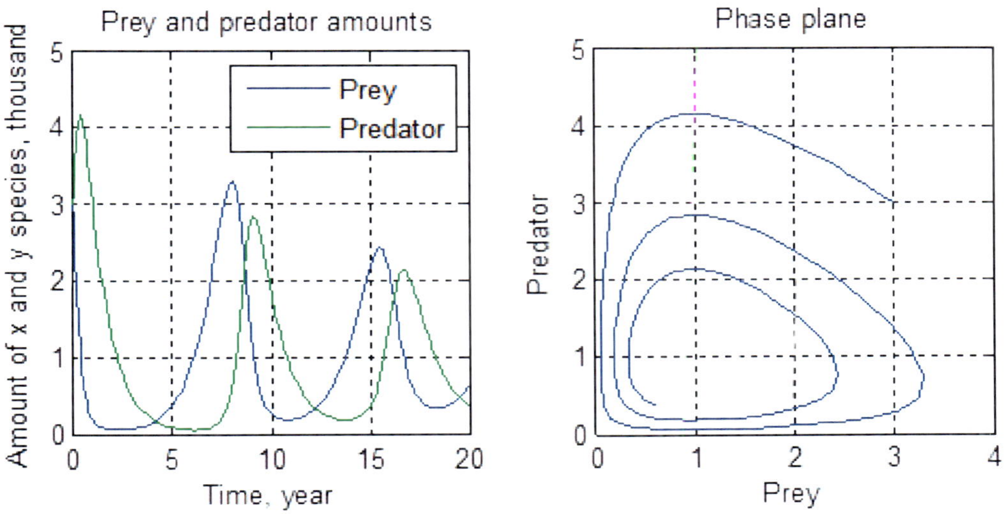

5.5.2. Subsequent Reaction

The rate equation set for the subsequent A→B→C reaction is

$$\frac{d[A]}{dt} = -k_1[A]$$
$$\frac{d[B]}{dt} = k_1[A] - k_2[B]$$
$$\frac{d[C]}{dt} = k_2[B]$$

where [*A*], [*B*], and [*C*] are concentrations of the *A* and *B* reactants and the *C* product respectively and k_1 and k_2 is the rate constants of the *A*→*B* and *B*→*C* reactions respectively.

Problem: Solve the set of ODEs in the time range 0 …4 min with the initial [*A*]=2.5, [*B*]=0, and [*P*]=0, in mol/L and the reaction rate constants: k_1=2, and k_2=6, in min^{-1}. Plot the component amounts as functions of time and display the obtained data.

First represent the set of equations in the form required by the ODE solver:

$$\frac{dy_1}{dt} = -k_1 y_1$$
$$\frac{dy_2}{dt} = k_1 y_1 - k_2 y_2$$
$$\frac{dy_3}{dt} = k_2 y_3$$

where [*A*], [*B*], and [*C*] are denoted as y_1, y_2, and y_3 respectively; the time range is $0 \le t \le 4$, the rate constants are k_1=2, k_2=6 and the initial y values are y_1=2.5, y_2=0, and y_3=0.

Then, select the appropriate solver. In the absence of considerations regarding the stiffness of the equations, the `ode45` solver should be used.

The final step is to write the commands that solved the problem. The `SubsequentReaction` function, which was created for this purpose is:

```
function t_A_B_C=SubsequentReaction(k1,k2,ts,tf,A0,B0,C0)
```

```
% To run >>t_A_B_C=SubsequentReaction(2,6,0,6,2.5,0,0)
t_range=[ts tf];
[t,y]=ode45(@SR,t_range,[A0,B0,C0],[],k1,k2);
plot(t,y);
title('Subsequent reaction A->B->C')
xlabel('Time, min'),ylabel('A, B, C amounts, mol')
legend('A','B','C')
grid
t_disp=[ts.5 1:tf];% times for displaying
y_disp=interp1(t,y,t_disp,'spline');% y for displaying
t_A_B_C=[t_disp' y_disp];
function dy=SR(~,y,k1,k2)
dy=[-k1*y(1);
k1*y(1)-k2*y(2);
k2*y(2)];
```

The k1, kr1, k2, A0, B0, C0 is the input arguments that correspond to k_1, k_2, $[A]_0$, $[B]_0$, and $[C]_0$ in the original set; the ts and tf arguments represent start and final time values intended for the t_range vector. The t_A_B_C output argument is a matrix with the time and the A, B and C component amounts. To reduce the number of displayed data, the y values are outputted at the ts, 0.5, 1, 2, …, and tf time values, the vector of these values called t_disp; for y-calculations at these t points, the interp1 command and their 'spline' option is used.

The following command should be typed and entered in the in the Command Window to run the function, display the results and generate a graph:

```
>> t_A_B_C=SubsequentReaction(2,6,0,6,2.5,0,0)
t_A_B_C =
         0    2.5000         0         0
    0.5000    0.9197    0.3977    1.1826
    1.0000    0.3383    0.1661    1.9956
    2.0000    0.0458    0.0229    2.4313
    3.0000    0.0062    0.0031    2.4907
    4.0000    0.0008    0.0004    2.4987
```

5.0000	0.0001	0.0001	2.4998
6.0000	0.0000	0.0000	2.5000

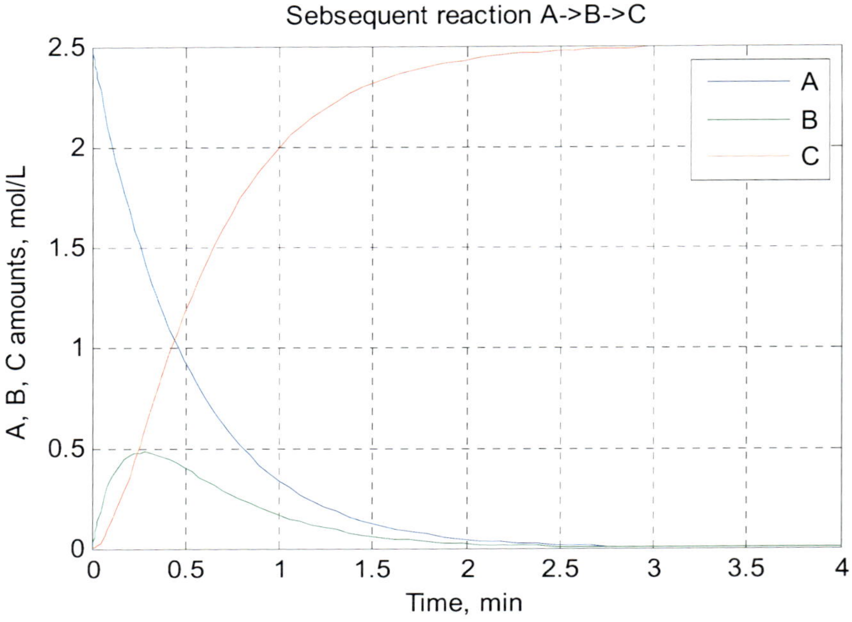

5.5.3. Drug Dissolution

In common pharmacology models, particularly in pharmacokinetics, the dissolution rates of a drug in the digestive system (DS) and in the blood are described correspondingly by the following set of two Noyes-Whitney type equations:

$$\frac{dx}{dt} = -ax + D(t)$$

$$\frac{dy}{dt} = ax - by$$

where x and y are the drug amounts in the DS and in the blood respectively; a and b are the half-life of the drug in the DS and in the blood respectively; $D(t)$ is the dosing function. It is assumed that:

- The problem is stiff;

- A drug dissolves within one half-hour and is taken every six hours, and the dosing function is:

$$D = \begin{cases} 4, & t - 6 \cdot \text{floor}(t/6) < 0.5 \\ 0, & \text{otherwise} \end{cases}$$

where D is in mg, the 'floor' is the math function name that denotes rounding towards minus infinity.

Problem: Solve the set of ODEs and plot the resulting $x(t)$ and $y(t)$ curves. The a and b coefficients are 1.38 h^{-1} and 0.138 h^{-1} respectively. The initial drug amounts in the DS and in the blood equal zero. Desired time values for the displaying of the results are 0, 0.15, 0.3, 0.6, 0.9, 1, 1.5, 2, 2.5, 3, 4, 5 and 6 hours.

First, represent the set of equations in the form required by the ODE solver:

$$\frac{dy_1}{dt} = -ay_1 + D$$
$$\frac{dy_2}{dt} = ay_1 - by_2$$

where D is described by the above equation, which does not require any changes in its form.

Then, select the `ode15s` solver as the problem under study is stiff.

To solve this problem use the following commands:

```
function t_DS_Blood=DrugDissolution(a,b,ts,tf,x0,y0)
% To run: >> t_DI_Blood=DrugDissolution(1.38,0.138,0,6,0,0)
close all
t_range=[ts:0.15:0.9,1:0.5:2.5,3:tf];
[t,y]=ode15s(@Drug,t_range,[x0;y0],[],a,b);
t_plot=linspace(ts,tf);
y_plot=interp1(t,y,t_plot,'spline');
plot(t_plot,y_plot)
```

```
xlabel('Time, hour'),ylabel('X and Y concentrations, mg')
title('Drug concentrations in the DS and Blood')
legend('DS','Blood')
grid
t_DS_Blood=[t,y];
function dy=Drug(t,y,a,b)
if t-6*floor(t/6)<0.5
D=4;
else
D=0;
end
dy=[-a*y(1)+D;a*y(1)-b*y(2)];
```

The a, b, x0, and y0 are the input arguments for the DrugDissolution function; they correspond respectively to the *a* and *b* coefficients and to the start drug amounts in DS, *x*, and in blood, *y*, in the original set; the ts and tf input arguments represent start and final time values intended for the t_range vector. The t_GS_Blood is an output matrix with the time and component amounts calculated at the desired time points that are given in the t_range vector. The generation of a plot with two smooth curves requires the greatest number of t,y_1 and t,y_2 points. To do this, the linespace and the interp1 command are used; the latter command includes the 'spline' argument.

To run this function and achieve the desired results, type and enter the following command in the Command Window:

```
>> t_GI_Blood=DrugDissolution(1.38,0.138,0,6,0,0)
```

After running this function in the Command Window, the following results are displayed and plotted:

```
t_GI_Blood =
         0         0         0
    0.1500    0.5420    0.0576
    0.3000    0.9826    0.2143
```

```
0.4500    1.3409    0.4493
0.6000    1.2538    0.7190
0.7500    1.0191    0.9365
0.9000    0.8285    1.1058
1.0000    0.7219    1.1966
1.5000    0.3630    1.4621
2.0000    0.1822    1.5386
2.5000    0.0915    1.5233
3.0000    0.0460    1.4656
4.0000    0.0116    1.3083
5.0000    0.0029    1.1476
6.0000    0.0007    1.0017
```

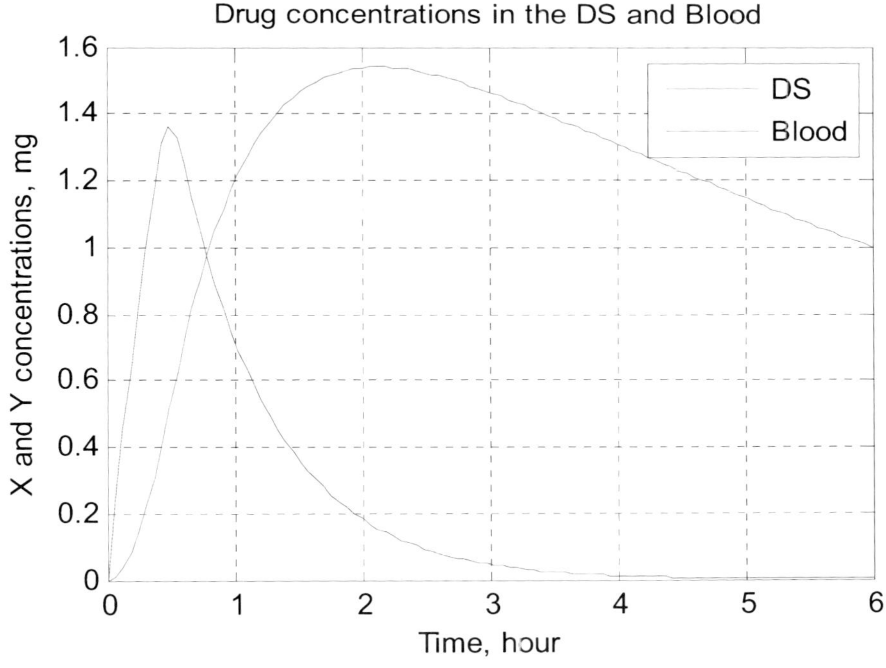

5.5.4. Batch Reactor

In industry, various batch reactors are used to produce new products as a result of reactions of the initial reactants and catalysts. Assume the processes in a batch reactor are described by the following set of ordinary differential equations:

$$\frac{d[A]}{dt} = -k_1[A] - k_2[A]^2$$
$$\frac{d[P]}{dt} = k_1[A]$$
$$\frac{d[U]}{dt} = k_2 A^2$$

where $[A]$. $[P]$, $[U]$ are the amounts of the species of the reactant A, the desired product P and the undesired product U respectively; the basic reactions that take place are $A \rightarrow P$ and $A+A \rightarrow U$ having the k_1 and k_2 reaction-rate constants respectively.

Problem: Solve these equations, display the results and plot the $[A](t)$, $[P](t)$ and $[U](t)$ curves in the time interval 0 … 2. Use time values equal to 0, 0.1, 0.2, 0.3, 0.4, 0.6, 0.8, 1, 1.5, 2; the rate constant k_1=2 is for the first reaction and k_2=1 is for the second. The initial amounts of the reagents are $[A]_0$=2 and $[P]_0$=$[U]_0$=0. All values are given here in arbitrary units; the time points are selected to display a small number of the t-points and to obtain and generate a plot having curves that are as smooth as possible.

First, transmit the set of differential equations to the form required by the ODE solvers:

$$\frac{dy_1}{dt} = -k_1 y_1 - k_2 y_1^2$$
$$\frac{dy_2}{dt} = k_1 y_1$$
$$\frac{dy_3}{dt} = k_2 y_1^2$$

Since there is no specific information concerning the stiffness of the ODE set, the `ode45` solver should be used.

To solve this problem create a function file:

```
function t_A_P_U=BatchReactor(k1,k2,ts,tf,A0,P0,U0)
```

```
% To run: >> t_A_P_U=BatchReactor(2,1,0,0.3,2,0,0)
close all
t_range=[ts:.1:.4 0.6 0.8 1 1.5 tf];
[t,y]=ode45(@BR, t_range,[A0,P0,U0],[],k1,k2);
plot(t,y)
xlabel('Time'),ylabel('A, P, U -species amount')
title('Isotermal Batch Reactor')
legend('A','P','U')
grid
t_A_P_U=[t,y];
function dy=BR(~,y,k1,k2)
dy=[-k1*y(1)-k2*y(1)^2;k1*y(1);k2*y(1)^2];
```

The input arguments: k1, k2, and A0,P0,U0 are respectively the same as the k_1, k_2, and y_1, y_2, and y_3 values at t=0 in the original set; the t_range is a two-element vector with starting, ts, and end, tf, time values. The t_A_P_U output argument is a three-column matrix with the time, reagent amount values, and the amounts of the desired and undesired products.

After running this function in the Command Window the following results are displayed and plotted:

```
>>t_A_P_U=BatchReactor(2,1,0,2,2,0,0)
t_A_P_U =
         0    2.0000         0         0
    0.1000    1.3862    0.3332    0.2806
    0.2000    1.0082    0.5699    0.4219
    0.3000    0.7565    0.7448    0.4987
    0.4000    0.5796    0.8774    0.5430
    0.6000    0.3547    1.0599    0.5854
    0.8000    0.2246    1.1736    0.6018
    1.0000    0.1452    1.2463    0.6085
    1.5000    0.0511    1.3360    0.6129
    2.0000    0.0185    1.3681    0.6134
```

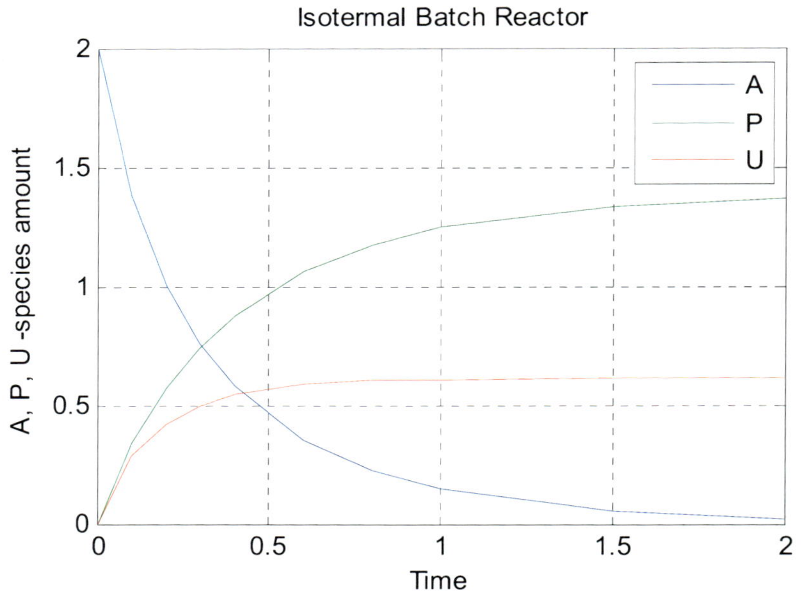

5.6. QUESTIONS AND EXCERCISES

1. When the stiffness of a differential equation is unknown, which ODE solvers are recommended to solve the problem? Choose the correct answer: a) ode23 first and then ode23t; b) ode45 first and then ode15s; c) ode15s first and then ode45; d) ode113 and ode15s.

   Which ODE solvers should be selected for a nonstiff differential equation? a) ode23tb, b) ode15i, c) ode45, d) ode113.

2. To specify the interval for a differential equation solution, the t_range vector of an ODE solver should contain: a) The single starting point value; b) Two values only, the starting and end points; c) The starting point, the desired values within the interval and the end points, d) the answers (a) and (c) are correct, e) the answers (b) and (c) are correct.

3. To solve a set of two ODEs, the *y*0 vector in the ODE solver should include: a) The *y* value for the first ODE only; b) The *y* values of each of the ODEs at the initial point; c) The *t* values at the starting points for each of the ODEs.

4. What occurs when the ODE solver command is written without output arguments: a) An error message appears in the Command Window; b) the Figure Window automatically appears with a plot of the obtained solution; c) The obtained solution values automatically appear in the Command Window.

5. The enzyme-catalyzed reactions $\mathrm{E+S} \rightleftharpoons \mathrm{ES} \rightarrow \mathrm{E+P}$ are described by L. Michaelis and M. Menten using the following set of ordinary differential equations:

$$\frac{d[S]}{dt} = k_{1r}[ES] - k_1[S][E]$$

$$\frac{d[E]}{dt} = \left(k_{1r} + k_2\right)[ES] - k_1[S][E]$$

$$\frac{d[ES]}{dt} = k_1[S][E] - \left(k_{1r} + k_2\right)[ES]$$

$$\frac{d[P]}{dt} = k_2[ES]$$

where the [ ] brackets denote the amounts of substrate *S*, the free enzyme *E*, the substrate-bound enzyme *ES*, and the product *P*; k_1 and k_{1r} are the direct and reverse rate constants in the $E+S \rightleftharpoons ES$ reaction and k_2 is the rate constant of the $ES \rightarrow P$ reaction. Create a user-defined function to solve the set of ODEs in the time range 0 … 6 sec with an initial [*S*]=8 mol, [*E*]=4 mol, [*ES*]=0, and [*P*]=0. The reaction rate constants are k_1=2 sec^{-1}, k_{1r}=1 mol^{-1}sec^{-1}, k_2=1.5 sec^{-1}. Solve using the function form with the input arguments for transferring the given numeric values; perform the defined times and component amounts in a five-column matrix and use it as the function output argument. Plot the component amounts as a function of time; output the obtained data at ten equidistant time points.

6. A chemostat-type bioreactor[3] has volume *V*. The differential equations that describe the concentrations of bacteria *N* and nutrients *S* are:

---

3 Sometimes referred to as a CSTB continuous stirred tank bioreactor.

$$\frac{d[N]}{dt} = [N]\left(\frac{r[S]}{a+[S]} - D\right)$$

$$\frac{d[S]}{dt} = D([R]-[S]) - \frac{1}{\gamma}[N]\frac{r[S]}{a+[S]}$$

where R is the fresh nutrient concentration, $D=F/V$ is the dilution rate, F is the continuously added fresh medium, r is the maximal growth rate, a is the half-saturation constant and □ is the growth yield; square brackets [ ] signify concentration.

7. Solve the set of ODEs in the time range 0 … 10 h with $r=1.35$ h^{-1}, $a=0.004$ g/L, $D=0.25$ h^{-1}, $[R]=6$ g/L, $\gamma=0.23$ 1/L, $[N]_0=0.1$ g/L and $[S]_0=6$ g/L. Use the `ode15s` solver. Write a function and save it in the function file. Assign the variables, with numeric values, as input arguments of the function; perform defined times and component amounts in a three-column matrix at ten equidistant t-points and use it as the function output argument to be displayed in the Command Window. Plot the nutrient and bacteria concentrations as a function of time.

8. One of the ODEs used to simulate a population growth is the Malthus-Verhulst equation

$$\frac{dN}{dt} = rN\left(1-\frac{N}{K}\right)$$

where N is the population size, r is the population growth/decline rate coefficient, and K is the maximum population the environment can support. Solve this equation with an initial $N_0=10$ million people and constants $K=387.7$ and $r=1.413$ 1/year. The time t is given here as a centered and scaled parameter $(t_1-1890)/62.05$ with $t_1=1790$, 1810, …, 2050 year. Solve the ODE, write and save the user-defined function which has no output arguments and has the following input parameters: K and r constants and t_1 vector containing given year values. Display the t_1 and N in two columns with the `fprintf` command.

Generate $N(t_1)$ a curve and use the axis tight command to set the plot axis limits to the actual t_1 and N ranges.

9. The simplest Lotka-Volterra model of predator-prey behavior can be represented by these two differential equations:

$$\frac{dx}{dt} = k_1 x - k_2 xy$$

$$\frac{dy}{dt} = -k_3 y + k_4 xy \qquad 10.$$

where k_1, k_3 are the growth rate of the x (preys, *e.g.* rabbits) and y (predators, *e.g.* foxes) species respectively and k_2, k_4 are coefficients characterizing the interactions between the species, the start *ts* and the end *tf* times are 0 and 15 (dimensionless) respectively and an initial x=5000 (rabbits), y=100 (foxes). The growth rate constants are k_1=2, k_2=0.01, k_3=0.8, k_4=0.0002. Solve this set of ODEs; write a user-defined function for this that has given rates, times, and initial population amounts as the input arguments and a matrix with the obtained values as the output argument. Display the obtained t, x, and y data in three columns at 15 equidistantly spaced time points; plot the species populations as a function of time.

10. According to the simple susceptible-infectious-recovered (SIR) model of epidemiology, the rates of S, I, and R are described by the following set of differential equations:

$$\frac{dS}{dt} = -\beta SI$$

$$\frac{dI}{dt} = \beta SI - vI$$

$$\frac{dR}{dt} = vI$$

where S is the day susceptible number, I is the number of infectious and R is the number of new cases per day (called the basis reproductive number). Solve this equation with an ODE solver in the time range 0 … 60 days, with β=0.001 day^{-1}people^{-1}, v=0.1 day^{-1}, and initial S_0=700, I_0=1 and R_0=0 people. Write a function with input and output arguments, and save the function in a function file. Display a matrix containing the obtained *t*, *S*, *I*, and *R* values at the eight equidistant time points and plot the *S*(*t*), *I*(*t*), and *R*(*t*) curves in the same graph.

11. In a metabolically based model, the mass growth of a cancer tumor is described by the following ordinary differential equation:

$$\frac{dm}{dt} = bm^{3/4} - am$$

where *m* is the tumor mass, kg. The coefficients *a* and *b* equal 0.03 day^{-1} and 0.026 kg$^{1/4}$day^{-1} respectively. Solve this equation using an ODE solver with the following start and end time values ts=0 and tf=600, in days; the initial m_0 value is 0.001 kg. Write a function with input and output arguments, and save it in a function file. Display the obtained *t* and *m* values at eight equidistant time points and plot the *m*(*t*)– graph.

12. A leaf-surface growth rate can be described by an ODE. For a circled leaf of the *Victoria regia* species, the equation is:

$$\frac{dS}{dt} = k_1 S^{3/2} \cos(k_2 t - \pi)$$

where *S* is the leaf surface, k_1 is the proportionality coefficient, and k_2 is the coefficient connected to the amount of sunlight obtained by the leaf. Solve this equation with an ODE solver; use the option including the solving equation directly to the selected solver command. The start and the end time is *ts*=6 and *tf*=18, in hours; k_1= 0.001309 cm$^{-3/2}$h^{-1} and k_2=0.2618 rad·h^{-1}; the initial leaf surface is S_0 is 1600 cm^2. Write a function with input and output arguments and save the function in a function file. Display the obtained *S* values at ten equidistant time points; plot the *S*(*t*)– graph.

5.7. ANSWERS TO SELECTED QUESTIONS AND EXCERCISES

2. e) the answers (b) and (c) are correct.

4. b) the Figure Window automatically appears with a plot of the obtained solution.

6.

```
>>t_S_E_ES_P=Ch5_6 (2,1,1.5,0,6,8,4,0,0)
t_S_E_ES_P =
        0    8.0000    4.0000         0         0
   0.6667    3.6555    0.4409    1.9883    2.3562
   1.3333    3.0181    0.3063    1.1175    3.8644
   2.0000    2.6334    0.2074    0.6446    4.7220
   2.6667    2.3965    0.1373    0.3811    5.2224
   3.3333    2.2492    0.0895    0.2298    5.5210
   4.0000    2.1570    0.0578    0.1406    5.7024
   4.6667    2.0990    0.0370    0.0870    5.8140
   5.3333    2.0625    0.0236    0.0542    5.8833
   6.0000    2.0395    0.0150    0.0340    5.9266
```

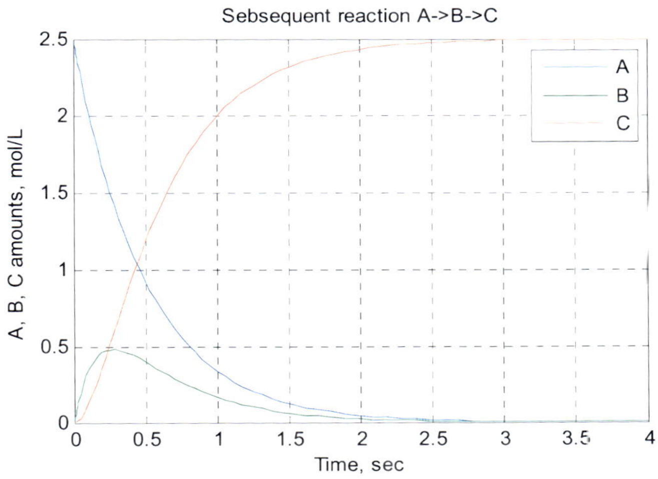

8.

```
>> Ch5_8(1.413,387.7,10,[1790:20:2050])
```

```
Year      People
1790       10.0
1810       15.5
1830       23.9
1850       36.4
1870       54.5
1890       79.4
1910      112.0
1930      151.3
1950      194.7
1970      238.0
1990      277.2
2010      309.4
2030      334.1
2050      351.9
```

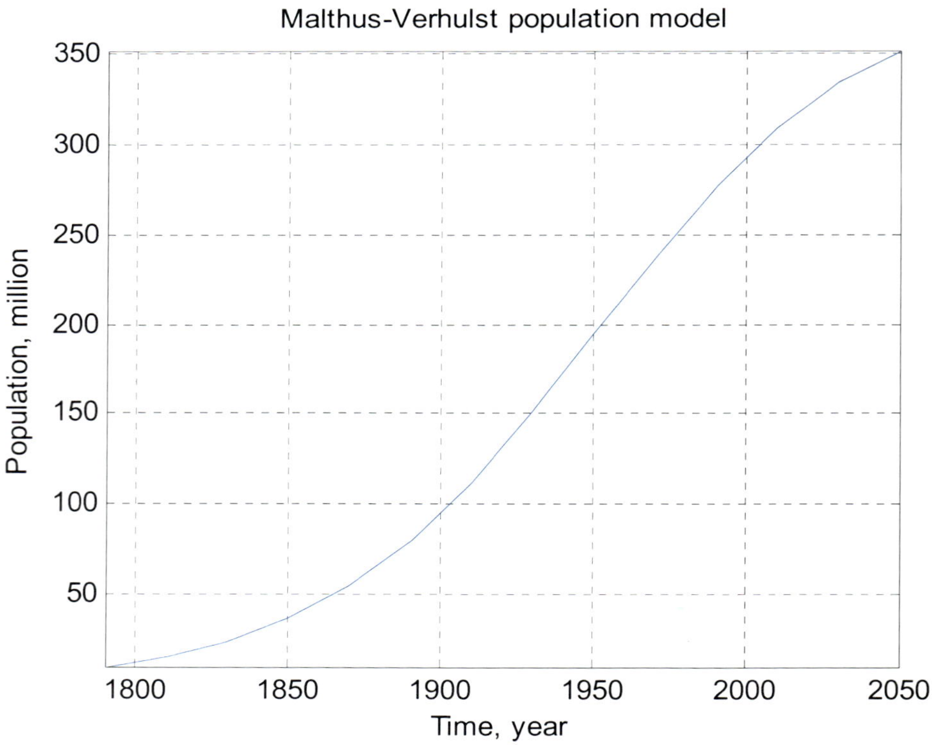

10.

```
>> t_Susceptible_Infected_Recovered=Ch5_10(0.001,0.1,[0 60],[500 1 0])
t_Susceptible_Infected_Recovered =
         0  500.0000    1.0000         0
    8.5714  465.3325   28.4828    7.1846
   17.1429  169.0849  223.4316  108.4836
   25.7143   25.3352  178.1435  297.5213
   34.2857    8.4629   85.5509  406.9862
   42.8571    5.1061   38.3583  457.5356
   51.4286    4.0793   16.9198  480.0009
   60.0000    3.6955    7.4221  489.8823
```

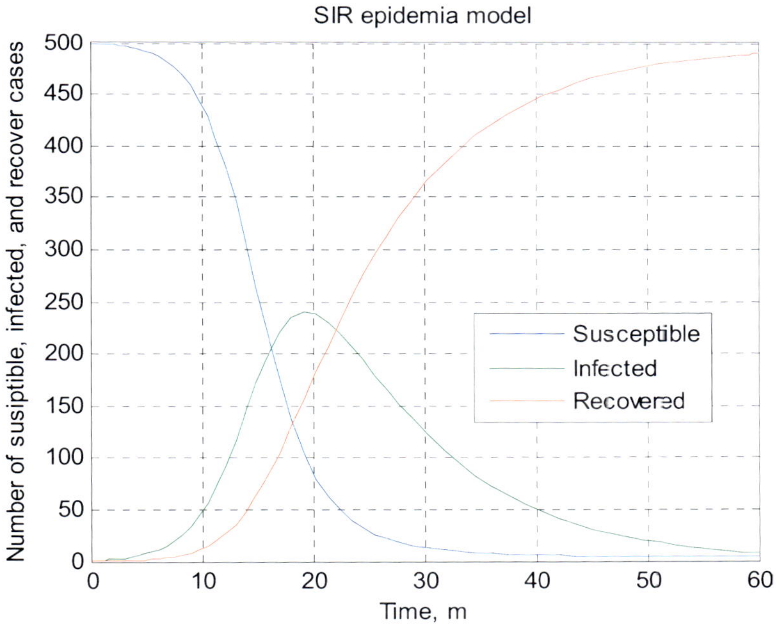

12.

```
>> t_LeafSurface=Ch5_12(0.001309,0.2618,[6,18],1600,10)
t_LeafSurface =
   1.0e+003 *
     0.0060    1.6000
     0.0073    1.6195
```

```
0.0087    1.6776
0.0100    1.7729
0.0113    1.9012
0.0127    2.0538
0.0140    2.2145
0.0153    2.3600
0.0167    2.4627
0.0180    2.5000
```

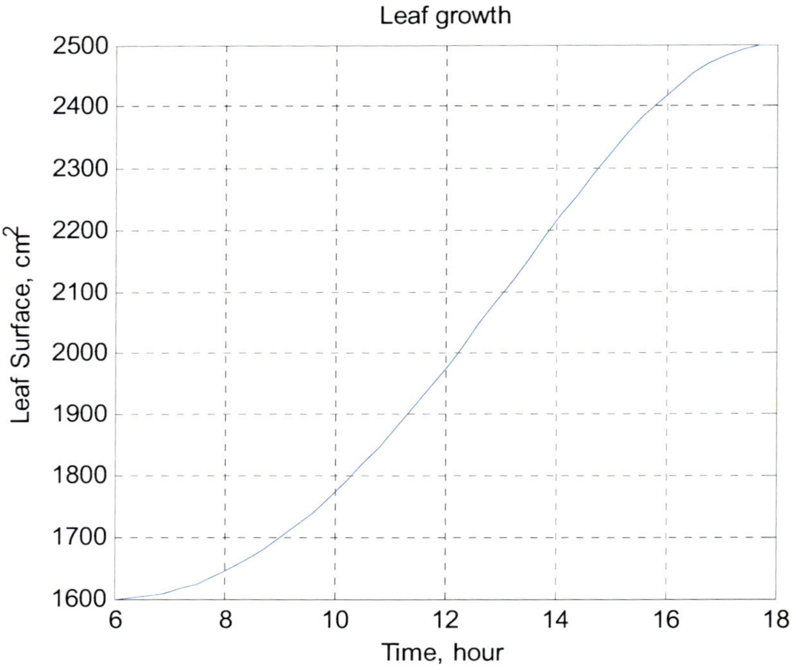

Send Orders for Reprints to reprints@benthamscience.net
Primary MATLAB® for Life Sciences: Guide for Beginners, 2013, 205-245

CHAPTER 6

Curve Fitting and Time Series

Abstract: The polynomial fitting commands and time series calculations are presented. The Basic Fitting and Time Series Tool interfaces are introduced through applications to the drug dose-blood pressure relation, the hazardous substances level in the air, the plankton concentration, time series forecasting, temperature monthly average predictions, and others. The questions and life-science problems together with answers to some of them are given in conclusion.

Keywords: Polynomial fitting; time series forecasting; trend and seasonality; Basic Fitting; Time Series Tool; life science applications.

INTRODUCTION

Variable data obtained in bio-laboratories or natural observations should be fitted with mathematical expressions that can be assigned empirically or theoretically. In most cases, these expressions connect two variables; for example, injected drug dose and blood pressure of animals, binding and component concentrations, and biomass changes and temperatures. Obtained data is used for defining coefficients relations of this kind. This process is called fitting and the required relation is called regression.

In many cases, life science data are received as a function of time, for example, bacterial growth rate, animal population change with time, radioactivity decay and reaction rate. Such time data is called time series and is used in order to extract meaningful statistics, or for prediction. Time series analysis and forecasting are used for these objectives.

In this chapter, we show some of the commands and basic tools that MATLAB provides, which biologists can use for data fitting and time series analysis.

6.1. FITTING DATA WITH POLYNOMIAL EXPRESSION

In cases where we search polynomial relations between two variables, one of which is dependent, x, and other independent, y, the polyfit and polyval commands are used. The simplest forms of these commands are:

Leonid Burstein

a=polyfit(x_data,y_data,n) and y_fit=polyval(a,x_polyval)

where x_data is a vector of dependent data points and y_data is a vector of independent data points; a is a row vector of coefficients, in descending powers, that fit the data; x_polyval is a vector of values for calculating the y_fit values with the coefficients defined in polynomial fit; and n is the degree of the polynomial relation $y = a_n x^n + a_{n-1}x^{n-1} + a_{n-2}x^{n-2} + ... + a_1 x + a_0$ marking the number of a coefficients. For example, in the first-degree polynomial, n=1, we have two-element vector a containing two fit coefficients: a_0 in a(2) and a_1 in a(1), and in the second degree polynomial, n=2, three-element vector a contains a_0 in a(3), a_1 in a(2), and a_2 in a(1).

The first of these commands defines polynomial coefficients by the (x, y)-data points and uses the least-squares method for a better fit. In this method, the a-coefficients are determined by minimizing the sum of the squares of the differences between the polynomial- and data values; these differences are called residuals and denoted R.

The second command uses fit coefficients defined by the first command for y-value calculations by the fit polynomial and at interesting x points.

Define, for example, the relation between injected drug doses, x= 75, 62, 54 43, 37 mg per kg of animal, and changes in the blood pressures, y= 3, 13, 17, 25, 28 mmHg. For polynomial fit of this data by the first-degree polynomial (n=1), and for generating the fit curve and data plot, the following script file, named Ch6_fit, can be created.

```
% Polynomial fitting
% x_data - dosage, mg/kg
% y_data – blood pressure, mmHg
x_data=[75, 62 54 43 37];              % vector with dose data
y_data=[3,13,17,25,28];                % vector with blood pressure data
a=polyfit(x_data, y_data,1)            % defines fitting coefficients
```

```
x_pol=linspace(min(x_data),max(x_data));  % vector with 100 (default)
                                           % x values for plotting
y_fit =polyval(a,x_pol);                   % vector of y values calculated at x_pol
plot(x_data, y_data,'o', x_pol, y_fit)     % plots polynomial and data points
xlabel('Dose, mg/kg'), ylabel('Blood Pressure, mmHg'),grid
legend(' original data',' first degree polynomial fit')
```

After typing and entering the file name in the Command Window, the following coefficients are displayed and the graph is generated:

```
>> Ch6_fit

a =

-0.6572 52.8199
```

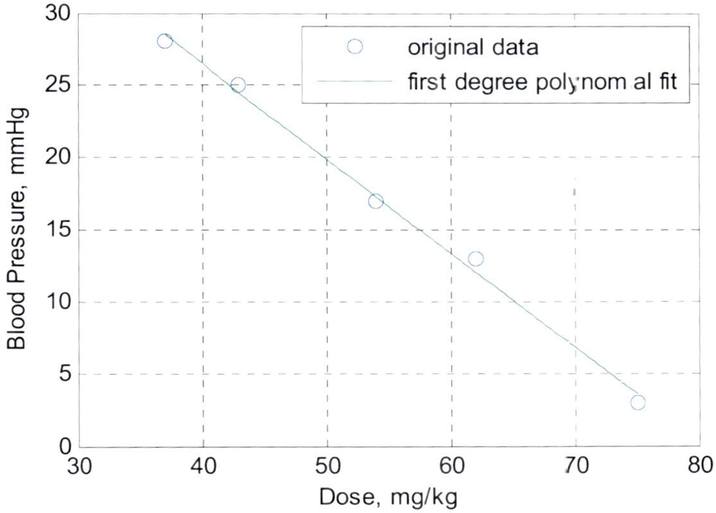

Various bio-applications frequently require an exponential or a logarithmic fitting function:

$$y = a_0 e^{a_1 x}$$

$$y = a_1 \ln x + a_0 \quad \text{or} \quad y = a_1 \log x + a_0$$

In these cases, the fitting function is rewritten as polynomial. For this purpose, the exponential function is transformed to $\ln y = a_1 x + \ln a_0$ and the polyfit function should be used in the following form—a=polyfit(x, log(y),1), where in the vector a the first element, a(1), is a_1 and the second, a(2), is $\ln a_0$, that is, a_0=exp(a(2)).

In cases of logarithmic functions, the polyfit is written as a=polyfit(log(x), y, 1) or a=polyfit(log10(x), y, 1), where in vector a the first element, a(1), is a_1 and the second, a(2), is a_0.

6.2. THE BASIC FITTING INTERFACE

In addition to polynomial fitting attained with the commands described above, MATLAB has a specific tool for interactive polynomial fit called Basic Fitting; the data in this tool can also be interpolated. The tool permits:

- Fitting data points by choosing linear, quadratic, cubic and up to 10th degree polynomials;
- Plotting one or more fit curves on the plot for better comparison and showing the polynomial equations with defined fit coefficients on this plot;
- Plotting the residuals for each polynomial fit with the norm of residual values;
- Computing the y-values by the fit polynomials at various points inputted by the user.

To start the interface, it is first necessary to plot the intended fit data. After the Figure Window with the plot appears, select the Basic Fitting line from the Tools option of the Figure Window menu as shown in the figure below, left. Following this action, the 'Plot fits' panel of the Basic Fitting window appears; see figure below, right.

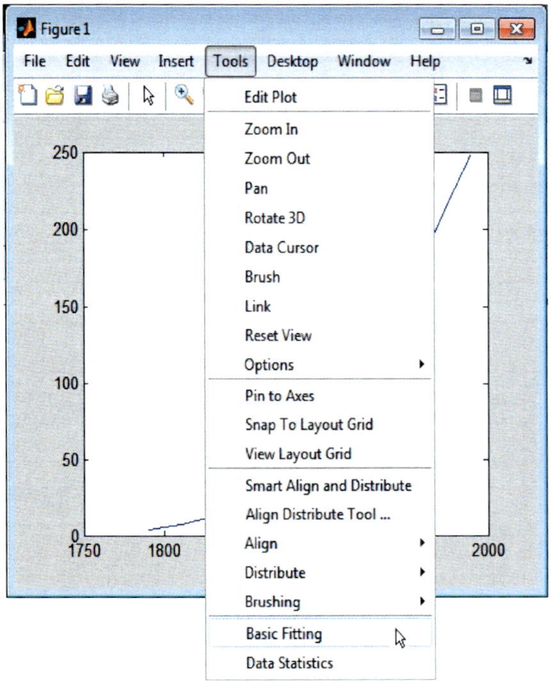

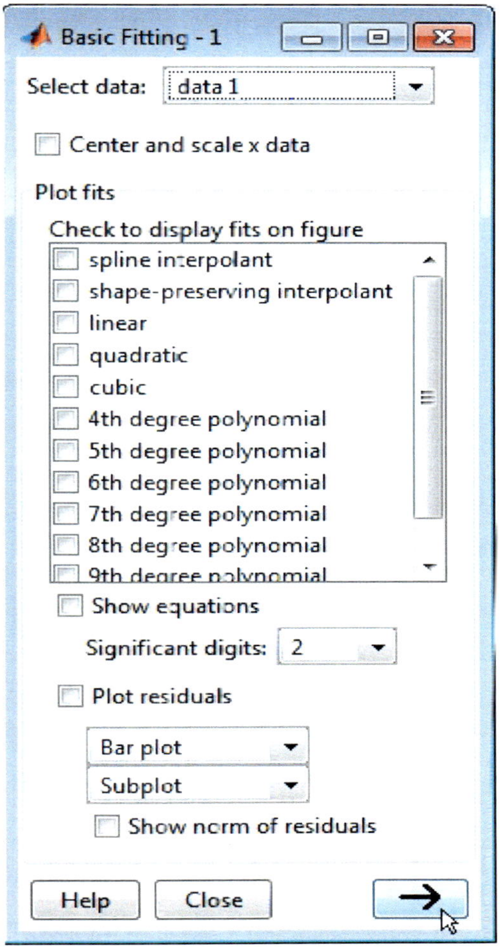

To receive the whole Basic Fitting window click the 'Show next panel' button →. The window extends and the 'Numerical Results' panel appears. The next click on this button extends the entire window form as shown in Fig. **6.1**. To minimize the last window and return to the previous panel, the 'Hide last button back' button ← should be clicked.

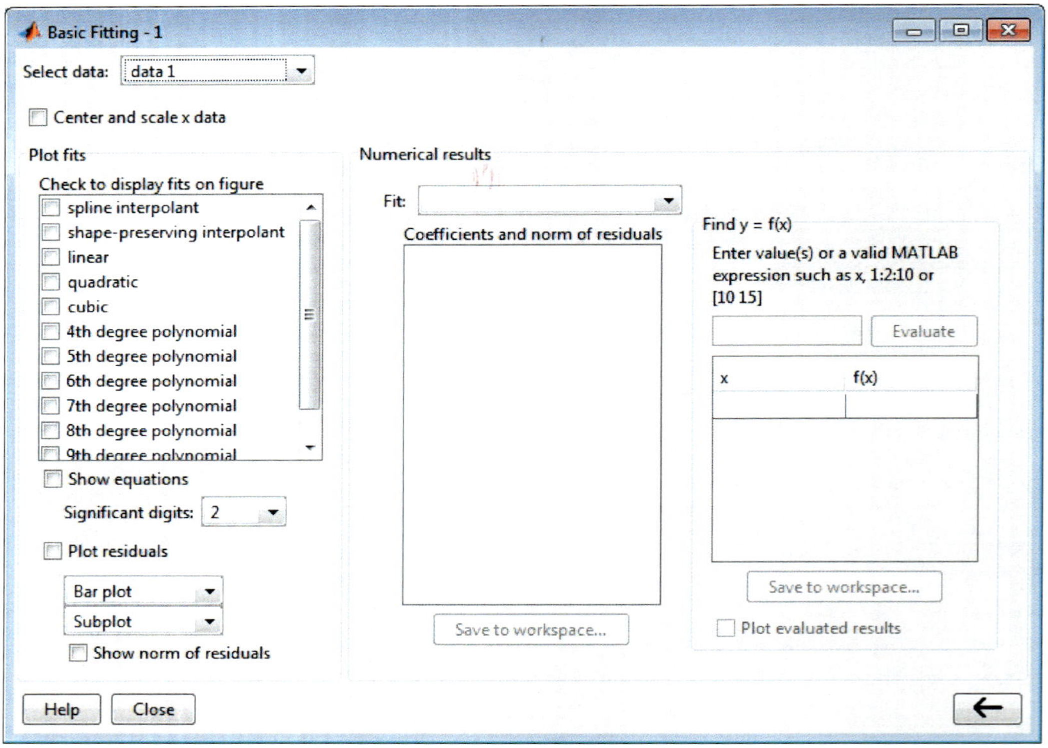

Figure 6.1: The Basic Fitting Window after two repeated extensions with the 'Show next panel' button.

The items located in each panel of the Basic fitting window are described below.

6.2.1. The 'Plot fits' Panel

Select data

In the Figure Window, more than one curve can be plotted for different data sets. However, only one data set should be chosen for the fit; only one set of points should be screened with this item.

Center and scale x data

For a better fitting of the x points of the *x, y*, data can be centered and scaled by marking this option. This is calculated for each data point, *i*, with the equation $z_i=(x_i-\mu)/\sigma$, in which μ is the average of *x*-values, σ is the standard deviation of *x*-values and *z* is *x* value after centering and scaling. In many cases, when the high-degree polynomial is selected to fit and this option is not marked, the special nameplate appears with the suggestion to center and scale the data.

Check to Display fits on Figure

This item includes fit by polynomials from the first (linear) degree to the tenth degree and interpolation by the spline or Hermite method. More than one fit option can be marked in this item box. When selecting the polynomials, the fit line appears immediately in the plot.

Show Equation and Significant Digits Fields

Mark the first of these items in order to display the fit equation on the plot. The number of significant digits in such an equation is chosen by marking the second item.

Plot Residuals with Two Adjustent Fields

Mark this item in order plot residuals that are calculated with the equation $R_i = y - y_i$, where the original y and the calculated y_i are polynomial data values at each i-point. For the first of the adjustent fields select the plot type bar, scatter or line. Select the second to figure in where the residuals should be displayed—separately or together with data set and fitted curve.

Show Norm of Residuals

For evaluation quality of the fit the norm of residuals can be displayed; mark this item to show the fit quality. This norm is calculatied as $\sqrt{\sum_{i=1}^{n} R_i^2}$ where n is the number of data points. The lower norm designates a better fit.

6.2.2. The 'Numerical Result' Panel

Fit

In order to explore a number of fits and to see fit equation, coefficients and residuel norm for one of them select the needed fit from the dropdown menu. Requested data are displayed in the 'Coeeficients and norm of residuals' box.

Coeeficients and Norm of Residuals

This item displays the selected polynomial, it coefficient values and norm of residuals.

Save to Workspace

The fit, residuals and norm of residuals can be saved in the MATLAB workspace by clicking the 'Save to workspace' button. After clicking this button, the window for indexes that were selected appears with the names for variables, as they should be saved

6.2.3. Find *y=f(x)* Panel

Enter Value(s) or a Valid MATLAB Expression... [1]

The values of x can be inputted in this field to calculate numerical y values for specified x. The resulting numbers will display in the box below after clicking the 'Evaluate' button to the right of this item field.

Save to Workspace...

In order to save evaluated values, click the 'Save to workspace...' button. Small windows appear in which the needed variables should be checked and the names for specified x values and for evaluated values should be inputted.

Plot Evaluated Results

When this item is checked, the evaluated values are displayed in the plot. An example of a problem using the Basic Fitting tool is given in the next subsection.

6.2.4. Fitting the Injection Dosage - Blood Pressure Data

The injection dosage—animal blood-pressure data were fitted in Subsection 6.1. using the polyfit command. Here, this data are used for the same target with the Basic Fitting interface.

Problem: Define linear and square polynomial equations that describe a drug dose-blood pressure set of data; show fitted coefficients and norm of residuals in

---

[1] The caption of this item contains long explanations and is shortened here and below

the Fit panel and on the plot, evaluate blood pressure under doses equal to 60 mg/kg by the fit equation with lesser norm of residuals; save defined equations, norm of residuals and evaluated dose value in the workspace.

First, the entire data set should to be inputted and plotted. Enter the following commands in the Command Window:

```
>> x_data=[75, 62 54 43 37]; % vector of dosages
>> y_data=[3,13,17,25,28];   % vector of pressures
>> plot(x_data, y_data,'o')  % plots data-points as circles
```

Then select the Basic Fitting line from the Tools menu in the Figure Window. This opens the Basic Fitting Window. It should extend in full with the 'Show next panel' button as described above. After marking the linear option in the 'Plot fits panel', the defined linear equation *y=p1*x+p2*, coefficients p1=-0.65719 and p2=52.82, and norm of residuals=1.3022 into the 'Coefficients and norm of residuals' box of the 'Numerical results' panel appears.

Check the 'Show equations', 'Plot Residuals' and 'Show norm of residuals'; two plots—the fit curve with the linear equation and original data and the residual bar graph with residual norm value appear in the Figure Window. Now select the 'quadratic' option in the 'Plot fits panel'. The defined quadratic equation y=p1*x^2+p2*x+p3, coefficients p1=-0.0022812, p2=-0.40247, p3=46.133 and norm of residuals=1.0424 appear in the 'Coefficients and norm of residuals' box in the 'Numerical results' panel. Both the linear and cubic polynomial curves together with the fit equations (default is coefficients with two significant digits) appear simultaneously on the upper subplot of the Figure Window; the residual bars with their norms appear in the next figure and on the lower subplot. The norm of residuals of the quadratic polynomial is slightly lower than the norm of residuals for the linear polynomial. Thus, this polynomial better describes the data and is therefore used for evaluation of the expected blood pressure at a 60 mg/kg drug-dose injection. Enter the number 60 in the 'Enter value(s) ...' field and press the 'Evaluate' button.

Check the 'Plot evaluate results' option to mark the evaluated point in the upper plot of the Figure Window.

The next two figures show the Basic Fitting tool window for quadratic fit and evaluation and the Figure window with both linear and quadratic fits.

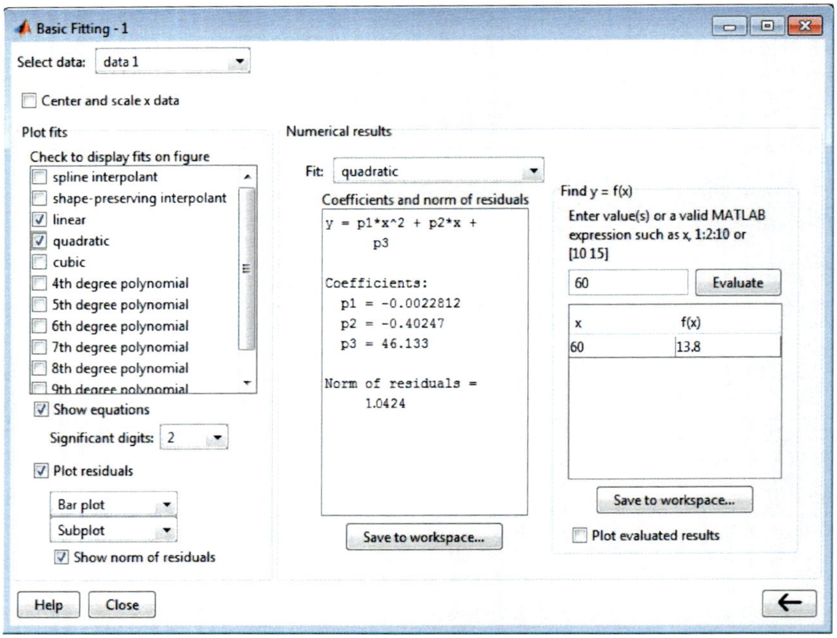

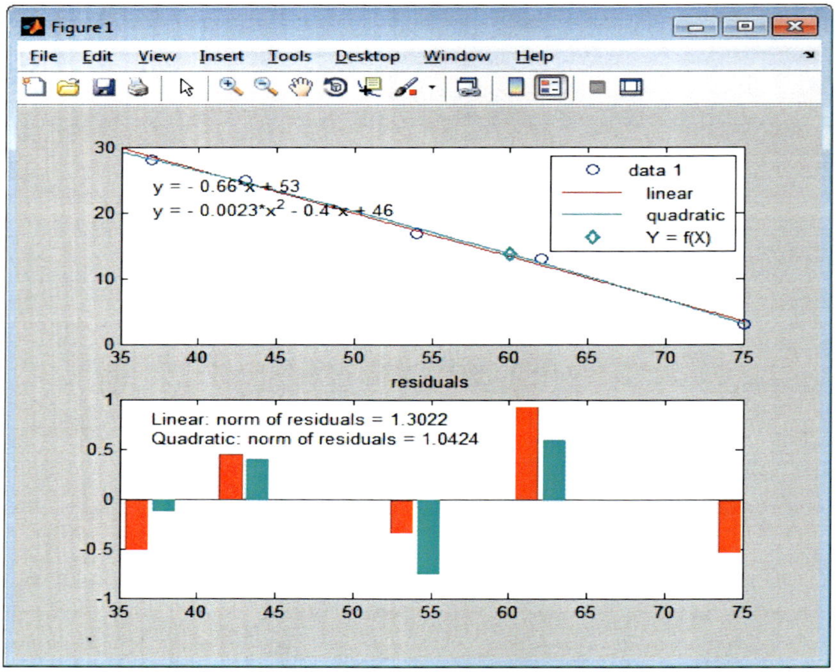

Press the 'Save to Workspace' button to export fits into the Workspace. The dialog box appears.

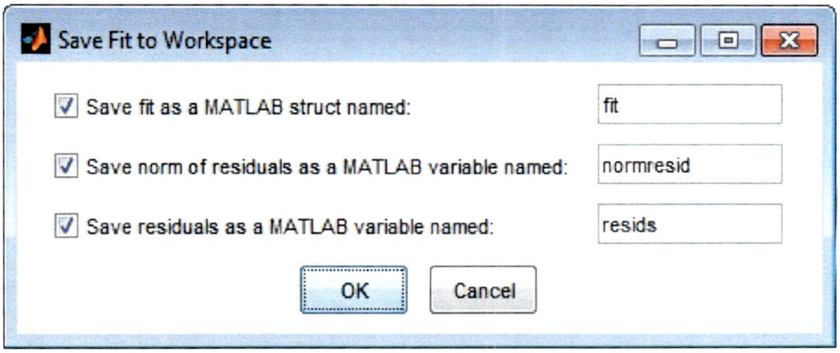

After clicking 'OK' the fit, normresid and resid variables are exported and appear in the Workspace Window. One of these variables, named fit, has a type called structure; this concept lies out of the scope of this book.

Enter the fit.coeff variable name into the Command Window to receive the fit coefficients from the fit structure. Do the same operation for evaluated value and press the 'Save to Workspace' button. Click OK in the dialog box that appears. This exports the x (the drug dose) and $f(x)$ (blood pressure) variables and they appear in the Workspace Window.

6.3. APPLICATION EXAMPLE

High levels of hazardous substances in the air at a manufacturing plant caused disease incidents. The 2, 2, 6, 7, 11, and 24 cancer incidents were fixed at the 1, 4.1, 10.2, 20.3, 30.4, and 41 mg/m^3 concentrations of a substance.

Problem: Fit the pollutant concentrations—disease incidents data—with the three-degree polynomial by the Basic Fitting tool and evaluate possible numbers of cancer incidents of 45.0 dangerous components in the air. Present resulting plots with original data, fitting curve, fit equations, residuals and residual norms.

The following steps should be executed:

- Enter the concentration-cancer data and plot them with the commands

```
>> concen=[1,4.1,10.2,20.3,30.4,41];          % concentrations
>> incend=[2,2,6,7,7,24];                     % diseases
>> plot(concen,incend,'o')                    %plotting the data points
```

- Select the Basic Fitting line in the Tools option of the Figure Window to open the Basic Fitting tool and extend fully the Basic Fitting window.

- Check 'Cubic', 'Show equations', 'Plot residuals' and 'Show norm of residuals' options in the 'Plot fits' panel. The following results will appear in the 'Coefficients and norm of residuals' box of the 'Numerical results' panel:

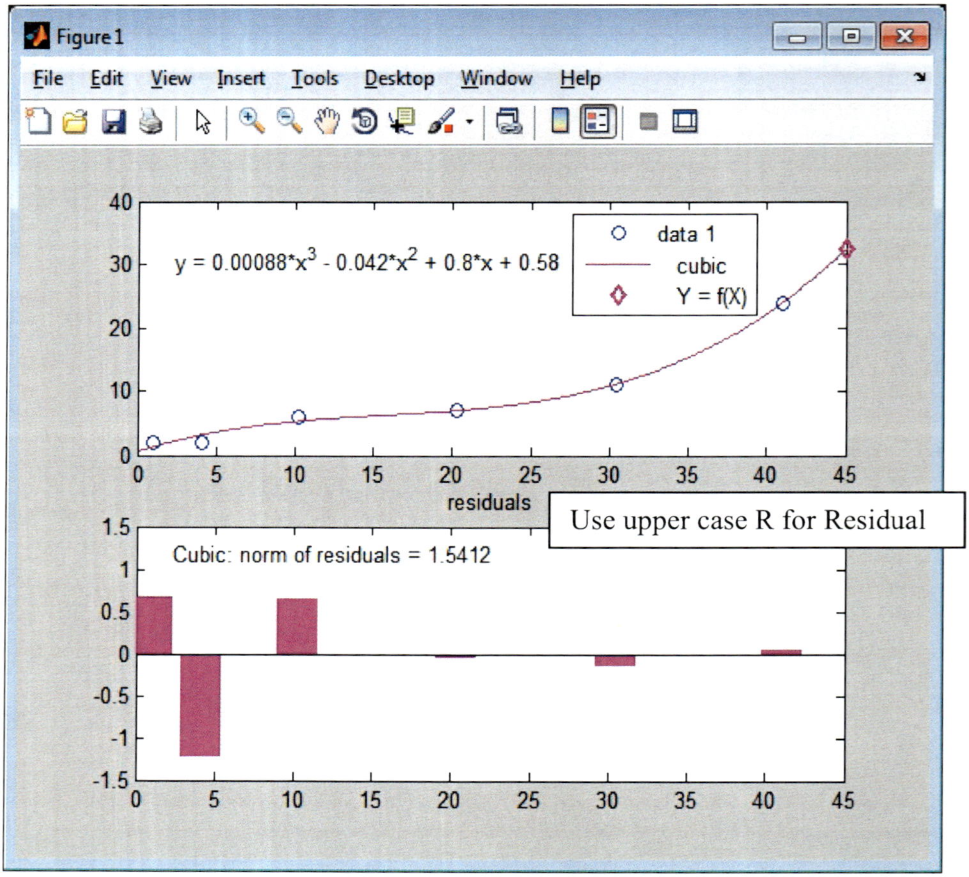

y = p1*x^3 + p2*x^2 + p3*x + p4
Coefficients:
p1 = 0.00087782
p2 = -0.0416
p3 = 0.80022
p4 = 0.57752
Norm of residuals =
1.5412

- Enter the number 45 in the 'Enter value(s)' field of the 'Find *y=f(x)*' panel. Click the 'Evaluate' button. The result, 32.3 (mg/m^3), appears in the column f(x) of the panel box. The resulting plots is:

6.4. ABOUT TIME SERIES

Data that change dynamically over time, *e.g.*, animal or human population evolution, electrocardiogram signals records, periodical disease data and various other data can be analyzed using time-series analysis. Such data are met frequently in various areas of the biosciences; thus, it is desirable to have a tool to process them. Solving such problems by special commands requires more knowledge than beginning students of the life sciences have. This knowledge is required to study objects, structures, constructors, methods and other specific programming concepts. Nevertheless, novices can use the simple commands studied in the previous chapters or the special interface—the Time Series tool—to override these problems and execute frequently used operations of time-series analysis. This analysis concentrates on three main problems: identifying, modeling, and predicting, the latter used most frequently. Under this analysis, the following operations are most frequently used: refilling missing data at certain time points by an interpolation procedure; cleaning data from outlying points; smoothing data by a filtering procedure; defining time trend and removing it from the data (this operation is called detrend); and building plots for these procedures.

The following subsections describe the time series prediction with commands presented in the previous sections and with the special tool for some time series operations, called Time Series Tools. The material presented here assumes a minimal acquaintance with time-series basics.

6.4.1. Prediction with Time Series

The datum Y observed in various biological observations often has a tendency to grow or a tendency T (trend) to decline. Additionally, the data often demonstrate periodical changes over time, or, such changes can be assumed; for example, annual plankton biomass fluctuations, monthly environmental temperature changes, animal population dynamics and seasonal growth rates of plants. Such periodicity is named seasonality S. In general, the data values can be presented in each time point, i, as the superposition of trend, seasonable, and random, R, components:

$$Y_i=T_i+S_i+R_i$$

where all variables vary over time.

Prediction, frequently called forecasting, is concluded by defining the trends and seasonal components and extrapolating their sum to times lying out of the original data period. For example, the average air temperature for a current month can be defined as the sum of temperatures obtained from trend relations and the monthly average temperature obtained for this month from the data of previous years; or, plankton seasonal biomass changes plus the derived tendency of biomass changes can be extrapolated to the current season.

For achieving this target by applying commands that were studied previously, the next steps should be executed:

- Input observed values—time points and their graphical representation;

- Define the data trend with the first- or two-degree polynomial fit and then detrend data by calculation of the differences Y_i-T_i;

- Define mean values of *S* at each identical time point, *e.g.*, the monthly mean: for the month of May over a period of several years, for the month of April, and so forth;

- Calculate and graphically present the random component as $R_i=Y_i-T_i-S_i$ to validate that data are really distributed randomly;

- Predict the value of *Y* as the sum of the *T* and *S* taken for the desired time, *e.g.*, the May (month) of the next to last year of the used data.

Show this by example on chlorophyll Chl-a concentration in the phytoplankton abundance. Say we have sequence of Chl-a bimonthly data along three years as it presented in the Table **6.1**.

Show this by example of chlorophyll, Chl-a, concentration in the abundance of phytoplankton, a sequence of Chl-a bimonthly data along three years as presented in Table **6.1**.

Table 6.1: The plankton Chl-a concentration data, $\mu g \cdot L^{-1}$

Year \ Bi-month*	1	2	3	4	5	6
1	0.04	0.073	0.1	0.12	0.12	0.11
2	0.08	0.12	0.14	0.13	0.13	0.13
3	0.13	0.09	0.12	0.14	0.17	0.15

* Bi-month number 1 refers to January–February, 2 to March–April. *etc.*

Problem: Write, save and run the function file that have the data of the Tab.6.1, detrend data with the first-degree polynomial fit, define seasonal component, and predict the Chl-a concentrations on the fourth year for March-April period.

The program realized solution of this problem is named ts_forecast and is presented below:

```
function Chl_a=ts_forecast(month2predict)
% To run: >>Chl_a=ts_forecast(6*3+2)
close all
```

```
Y=[0.0400 0.0733 0.1000 0.1200 0.1160 0.1060,...
0.1140 0.0880 0.1200 0.1380 0.1340 0.1260,...
0.1360 0.0920 0.1240 0.1440 0.1733 0.1500];
year=1:3;
bimonth=1:length(Y);                          % bi-month number
T_coeff=polyfit(bimonth,Y,1); % linear fit
T=polyval(T_coeff,bimonth);                            % trend
SR=Y-T;                                % detrend - seasonality
S=mean(reshape(SR, 6,length(year))'); % 6 months, each of 3 year
R=Y-T-repmat(S,1,length(year));             % random component
Chl_a=polyval(T_coeff,month2predict)+S(2); % prediction
%===============plot==================
subplot(3,1,1)
plot(bimonth,Y,'o',bimonth,T,'-'),grid
ylabel('Concentration'),title('Fit')
subplot(3,1,2)
plot(bimonth,SR),grid
ylabel('Y-T'),title('Detrend')
subplot(3,1,3)
plot(bimonth,R),grid
xlabel('bi-months'),title ('Random')
```

After running the program, the predicted concentration value, Chl_a, appears in the Command Window.

The running command with the bi-month number for prediction, 6*3+2 is March–April for the fourth year; displayed results with the Chl_a concentration value, mg L^{-1}, and the graph with three subplots containing the data points with linear fit, the detrend line and the line of the random deviations are presented below.

```
>> >> Chl_a=ts_forecast(6*3+2)
Chl_a =
0.1364
```

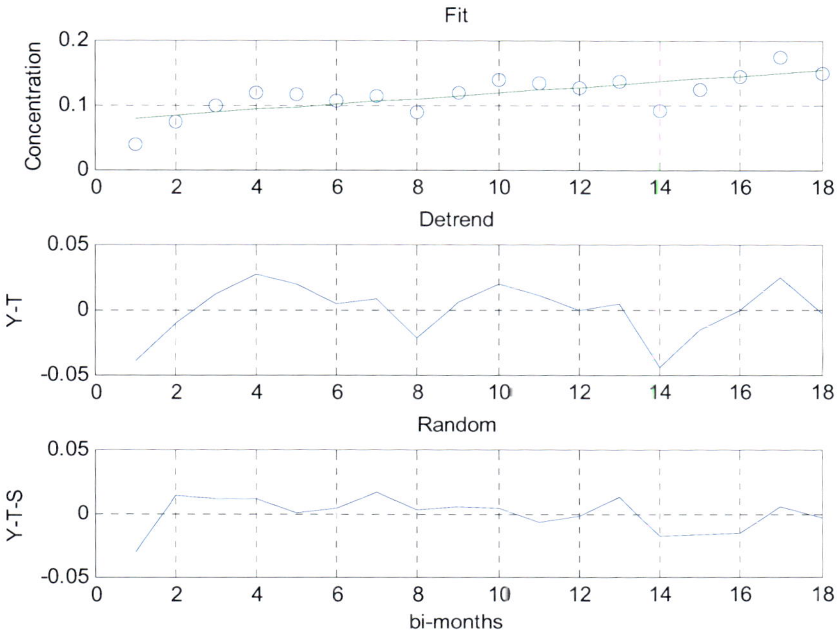

In the ts_forecast program, the Chl-a of plankton concentrations for three years are given in Y-vector and the year numbers, in the year vector; linear fit is executed with the polyfit command. After detrend, the *SR* vector of the *Y-T* difference is calculated; the *SR* vector is transformed in the 3x6 matrix with the reshape and transpose (') commands so that every column has the values of the same bi-month; then, the 1x6 S-vector with average seasonable values are calculated for each bi-month number with the mean command; the random value *R* is calculated as *Y-T-S* for which the vector *S* is repeated three times for each year; predicted concentrations are calculated for the 6*3+2 bi-month (three years in bi-months plus two months for March–April in the fourth year) as the sum of the extrapolated *T* value (with the polyfit command) and the seasonable value *S* for this bi-month (the second element of the *S* vector).

6.4.2. The Time Series Interface

This interface permits to execute some procedures with sequential data spaced at uniform time intervals without writing special commands. To activate this interface, load the data into the workspace and enter the tstool command in the

Command Window. This opens the Time Series Tools window presented in Fig. **6.2**. The window has a menu, a toolbar with the operations used most frequently and three main areas: the 'Time Series Session' tree, the 'Time Series' pane, and the 'Help' pane.

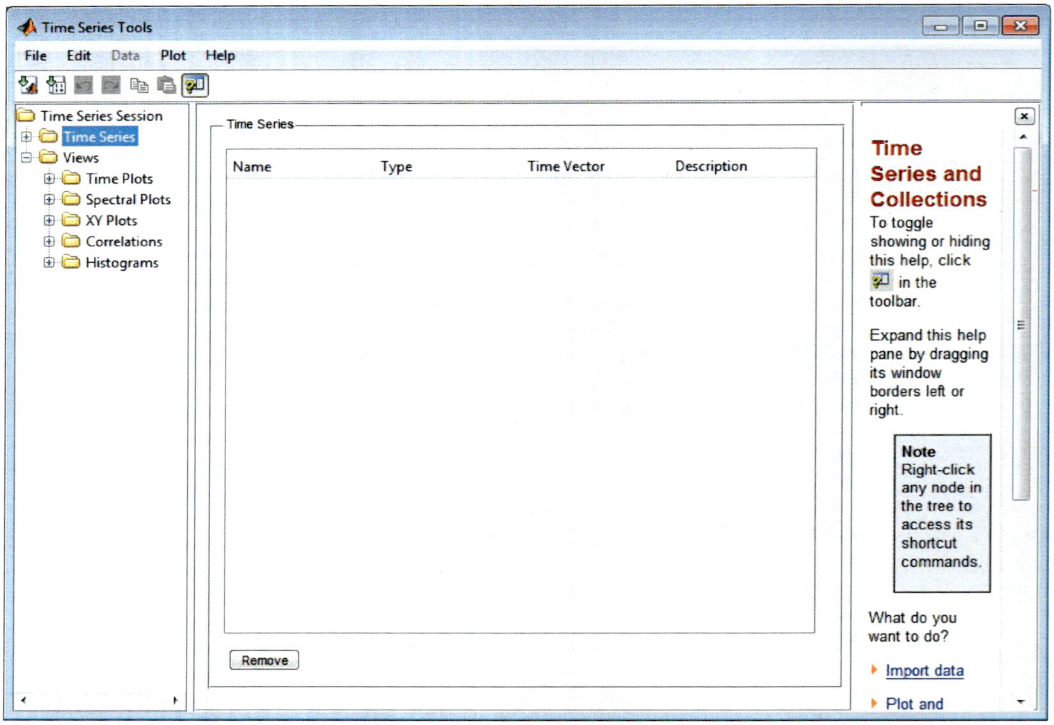

Figure 6.2: The Time Series Tools window.

6.4.2.1. Menu and Toolbar

The items in the tool menu and toolbar are summarized below.

Menu Options:

- **File**

Permits the import of data from the array or other sources located in the MATLAB Workspace, Excell Workbook, Text or in M-file. This item allows the export results and saves the code produced by the Time Series Tools. This option opens the Time Series Import Wizard that in three steps imports data to the tool for further processing (called 'choose the source…', 'specify the data and time', 'create time-series object and import').

- **Edit**

Gives a number of simplest editing options – undo, redo, copy, paste, or remove.

- **Data**

After the data import, this item permits most spread operations with time-series data: select needed data in the plot, remove time rows where data is missing, detrends, filters, interpolates, resamples, or transforms data with an algebraic expression.

- **Plot**

This option permits the selection of the needed plot: time series, spectral (the data after squared fast Fourier transform), XY (one-time series *versus* another time series), correlation (after or cross-correlation for matching the degree of the relationship between the data) or histogram (the view of data distribution with the rectangular bins). Line properties, such as style, color, marker and other properties are set by this option. When the data set is imported to 'Tools', a data plot can be created by dragging a 'Time Series' data node from the 'Time Series Session' tree and dropping it onto a 'Views' folder node.

- **Help**

Time series tool description from and case-sensitive help about currently executed options can be accessed with this item.

Toolbar Options

The toolbar is located just below the menu line of the tool and includes buttons for frequently used operations, namely, import or creation of time series, copy or paste, undo or redo and hide/show help.

6.4.2.2. The Time Series Tools Areas

The tool window has three main areas from left to right, briefly described below, with the items located in each of these areas. The items are explained in more detail in the next subsection by an example of use.

Time Series Session Area

The 'Time Series Session' tree is located here. It contains the 'Time Series' node icon and data icons that appear after entering them by means of the File menu option, and the 'Views' node with the plot icons. Data from the 'Time Series' folder can be presented in plot with this option. The forms of plot that can be selected are time-data, XY, spectral, correlation or histogram.

Time Series Area

This area appears empty, as shown in Fig. **6.2** until data are imported to the tool. After importing data, manifold options and settings appear here pertaining to the time-series node that is selected in the tree; two columns with time and data values appear in the 'Edit Data' and 'Plot time series' panels.

The first panel is for editing data and contains the 'Show event table' box; 'Attributes ...', 'Add row', 'Delete row(s)' and 'Uniform Time Vector ...' buttons; and 'Current time' information line.

The second panel is for plot generating and contains the 'Create new' and 'Add to existing plot' boxes, the 'Type' and 'Name' fields, and the 'Display' button.

When you edit the data you can:

- Check the 'Show event table' box to mark the data at a specific time. The marked event is displayed on a plot;

- Click the 'Attribute' button to open the 'Define Data Attribute' dialog box to enter: a quality value for each number in a data table; data units for plot axes; or the method of interpolation for missing data calculations;

- Add or delete rows in a data table with the 'Add row' and the 'Delete row(s)' buttons;

- Modify the data in uniform time intervals by clicking the 'Uniform time vector ...' button. This leads to the appearance of the 'Define

Uniform Time Vector'; enter here time display format, time units and start and end times.

The 'Plot time series' subarea allows you to generate plots: select the type of plot, *e.g.* 'Time Plots'; enter the plot name in the 'Name' field; and click the 'Display' button. The required plot appears in the separate 'Time Series Plot' window.

Note:

- Present the data uniformly distributed in time; use inputted units for plot and table presentations only. Time interval for analysis accounts for the number of time steps between data values, but not the actual time elapse. For example, say that you want to import a monthly data for 36 months, from January 31, 2009 until January 31, 2011. The 'Units' field of the Wizard (Step 2), only allows a selection of uniform time intervals, *e.g.*, days or weeks, and not months or years (both have varies day number).

- To access 'Data' operations right-click inside the plot after the plot with the data opens.

- Obtain data by interpolation in cases when one or more dates are missing between the data.

- Use the 'Remove' button located in the lower middle area of this tool to remove one or more time series from the 'Time Series' tree when data is still not imported.

Content-Sensitive Help Area

This help area is called context-sensitive as it provides information about options and settings currently shown in the tool.

6.4.3. Elephant Population Dynamics with the Time Series Tools

We used the Time Series Tools as an example for processing the elephant population in an African park monitored between the years 1987 and 1999, cn

December 31 of each year, with two interruptions—in 1989 and 1998. The number of elephants obtained was 6898, 7344, 7278, 7470, 7632, 7834, 7806, 8064, 8320, 8371 and 9152.

Problem: Input data into the Time Series Tools; interpolate loaded values for obtaining missing elephant numbers in the years 1989 and 1999 and detrend the data; plot the resulted time series and export the data into the MATLAB workspace.

Write the data as a column vector in the workspace using NaN (not a number) where there are data absences and then activate the Time Series Tools; enter the following commands for these operations:

```
>> elephant=
[6898;7344;NaN;7278;7470;7632;7834;7806;8064;8320;8371;NaN;9152];
>> tstool
```

The Time Series Tools window opens. Now import the elephant vector into the Time Series Tools by selecting from the File menu the option 'Import from Workspace'. Then select 'Array Data ...'.

The 'Time Series Import Wizard' window opens with the highlighted caption: 'Step 1: Choose the source that contains time series data' into the 'Current step' area. Select the 'MATLAB Workspace' option in the 'Data Source' area in the 'Import from:' field; clicking the 'Next' button opens the 'Import Time Series from MATLAB Workspace' window with the highlighted caption: 'Step 2: Specify the data and time'. In the 'Specify Data' box, mark the elephant vector and select 'columns' in the 'Data is arranged by' field. Input the 12/31/1987 data in the 'Start time' field of the 'Specify time vector' area. Select the 'Date Strings' and 'dd/mm/yy' options in the 'Use' and 'Format options' fields, respectively.

The figure below shows this window with inputted items.

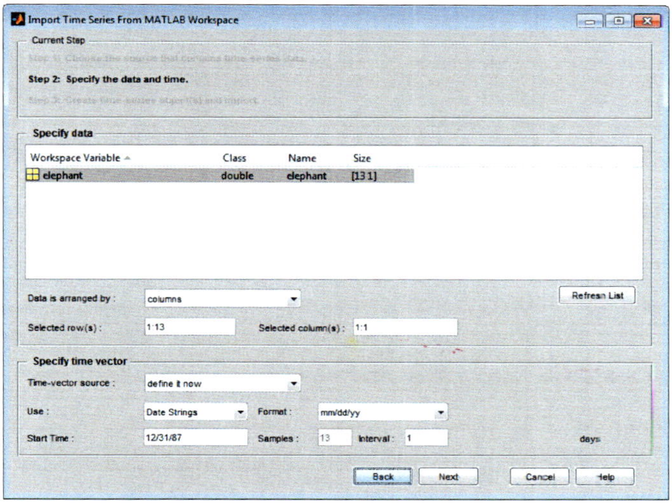

Click the 'Next' button in the Wizard window to open 'Step 3: Create time-series object(s) and import' in the 'Current Step' area. Check the 'Create a new time series with the name:' box and write 'elephant_1' for further processing and saving of obtained data. Then click the 'Finish' button. Fig. **6.3**. presents the Time Series Tools window modified by the above-mentioned operations.

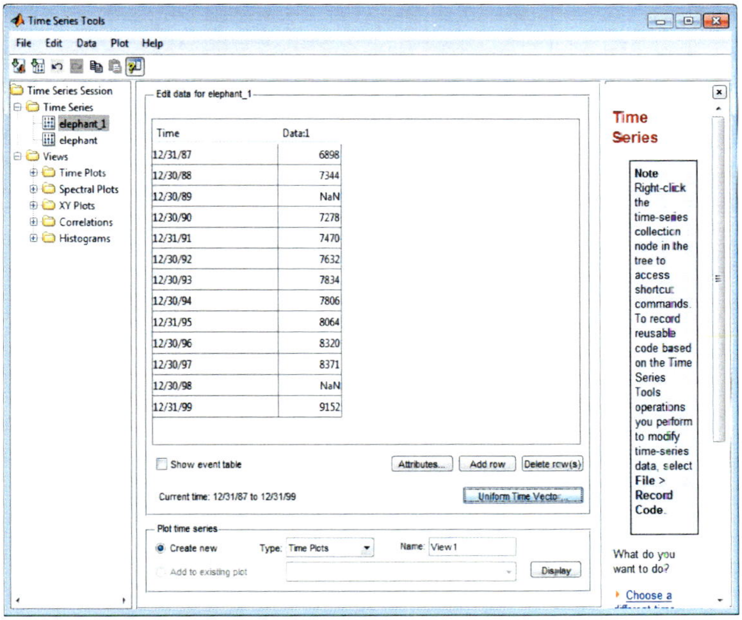

Figure 6.3: The Time Series Tools window with the elephant dynamic population data.

In this window, the years are inputted by the 'Uniform Time Vector …'. Click this button to access the 'Define Uniform Time Vector' box (see below).

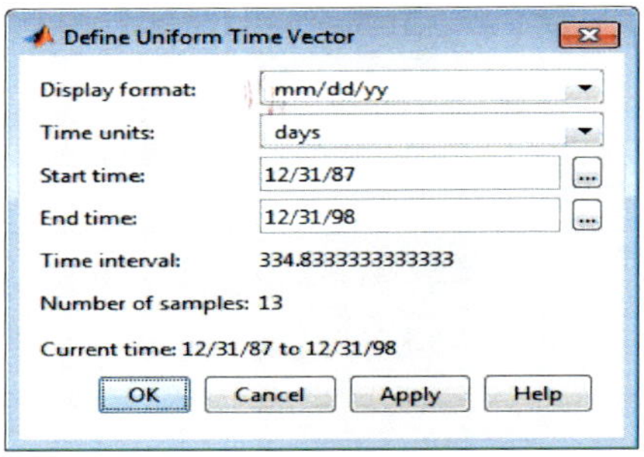

This box shows the selection of the 'mm/dd/yy' option in the 'Display format' item. Input the dates '01/31/98', and '12/31/98' respectively into the 'Start Time' and 'End Time' fields and click the 'Apply' button. The 'Time interval', 'Number of samples' and 'Current time' values are calculated and appear automatically in relation to the inputted dates and length of the date vector.

To interpolate data for defining the missing number of elephants in 1989 and 1998 years select the 'Interpolate…' line in the 'Data' option of the 'Time Series Tools' menu. Click the 'Apply' button when the 'Process Data' box appears. The interpolated values will appear in the 'Data:1' column of the 'Edit data for elephant_1' area. As the resulting values for the numbers of elephants should be integers, use the 'Transform Data Algebraically…' option in the 'Data' item of the tool menu. Select the 'elephant time series' in the box that appears and input the floor(aa) expression as per figure below:

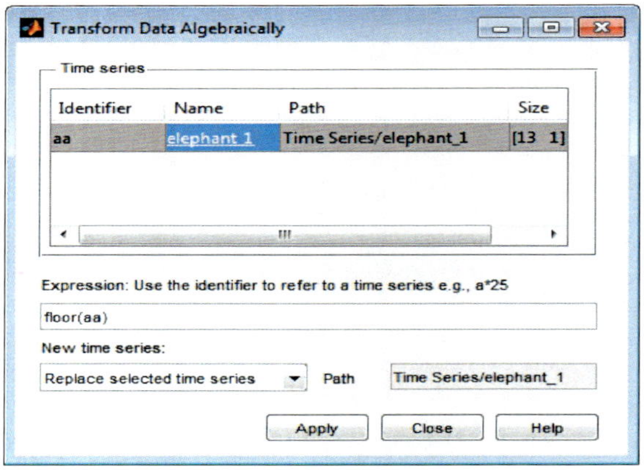

The interpolated values are 7311 and 8761 and they appear in place of the NaN values in the 'Data: 1' column of the 'Edit data for elephant_1' area.

Select the 'Detrend...' option in the 'Data' menu item and check the 'linear box' in the 'Remove trend type' item to remove trend data. A plot with the resulting values can be presented by using the 'Display' button in the 'Plot time series' area. Introduce the x-axis label 'Time' with the 'Property Editor', which can be selected from the box that appears when the plot window first opens or by clicking the 'Show Plot tool and Dock Figure' button in the toolbar of the 'Time Series Plots' window. The plot achieved is shown in the figure below.

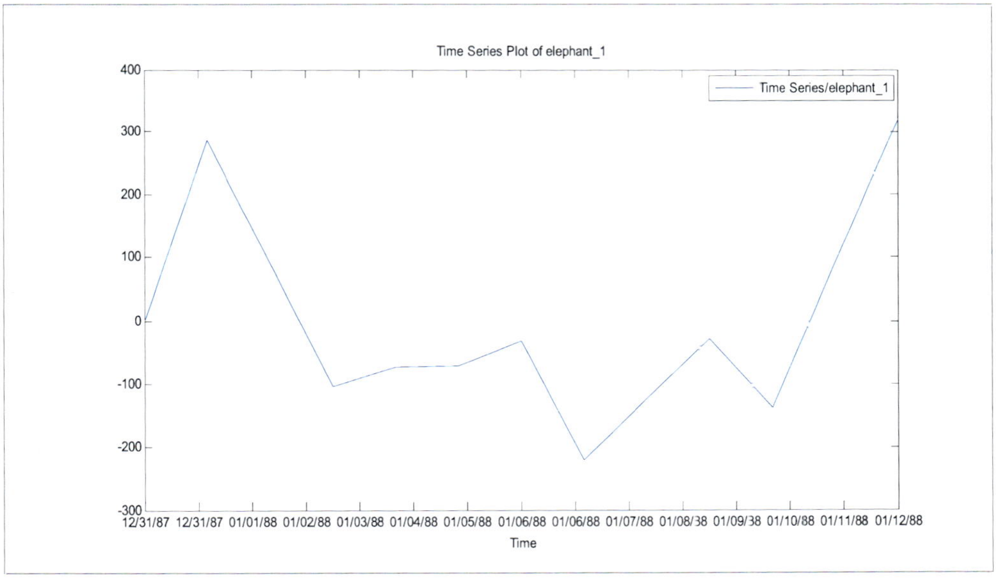

Export the detrended values to the workspace by selecting the appropriate option in the 'File' menu; after selecting this option, a box will appear with the following text: 'Object 'elephant_1 was exported to the base workspace'.

6.5. APPLICATION EXAMPLES

6.5.1. Fit for Thermal Conductivity of An Aqueous Solution

In a laboratory experiment, the thermal conductivities λ of 0.7 mol aqueous solution of the sodium chloride were measured. The values are 0.589, 0.577, 0.579, 0.560, 0.500, and 0.460 $Wm^{-1}C^{-1}$ for 25, 50, 75, 100, 125, 150 °C respectively.

Problem: Fit this data by the quadratic polynomial with:

a) The polyfit command. Write a program in the form of a function without parameters that prints the fit equation with defined coefficients and plot data together with the fit curve by the greater number of temperature points than in the original data;

b) The Basic Fitting tool, which shows the fit equation, fit coefficients, residuals and values of thermal conductivities at fitted temperature points.

To realize (a) the following program named `FA_6_5_1a.m` was written:

```
function FA_6_5_1a
%To run: >> FA_6_5_1a
Lambda=[0.589 0.577 0.579 0.560 0.5 0.46];
T=25:25:150;
Lambda_coeff=polyfit(T,Lambda,2); % quadratic fit
fprintf('Fit Equation: \nLambda=%11.6f*T^2+%7.5f*T%5.2f\n',Lambda_coeff)
T_fit=linspace(T(1),T(end),20); % T for the fit curve
Lambda_fit=polyval(Lambda_coeff,T_fit);% fitted lambda values
plot(T,Lambda,'o',T_fit,Lambda_fit,'-')
grid
xlabel('Temperature, ^oC'),
ylabel('\lambda, NaCl solution, W/(m^oC)')
legend('-Original Data','Second degree polynomial fit','location','best')
```

After running the program, a fit equation is displayed with a defined coefficients and outputs plot with the original thermal conductivity points and quadratic fit line as follows below:

```
>> FA_6_5_1a
Fit Equation:
Lambda=-0.000011*T^2+0.00092*T+0.57
```

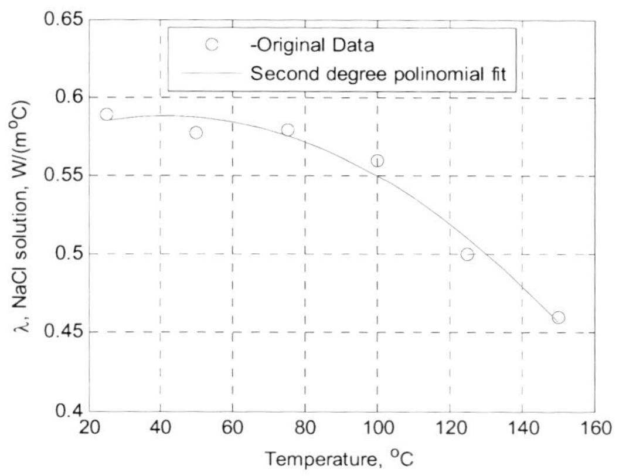

The solution for (b), fit with the Basic Fitting tool, follows these steps:

- Input the thermal conductivities and temperatures as two rows, vectors L and T respectively, into the Command Window and present these data on the plot of the Figure window with the following commands:

```
>> L= [0.589 0.577 0.579 0.560 0.5 0.46];T=25:25:150;
>> plot(L,T,'o')
```

- Select the Basic Fitting line in the Tool option of the Figure window menu, after which the Basic Fitting tool window appears. Click on the → button to open two additional panels.

- Mark the 'quadratic' options in the 'Check to display fits on figure' box of the 'Plot fits' panel; click the 'Show equation', 'Plot residuals', and 'Show norm of residuals' boxes in this panel. The fit equation, fit coefficients and norm of residuals will appear in the 'Numeric Results' panel.

  Note: x in the case described is temperature, and y is thermal conductivity of the NaCl solution.

- Print x values (temperature) for evaluation and y values (thermal conductivity); required x-points are: 25:25:150; then press the Evaluate button in the 'Find *y*=f(x)' panel. Inputted and computed values will appear in the adjacent table.

The Basic Fitting window and resulting plots with the problem solution are presented below:

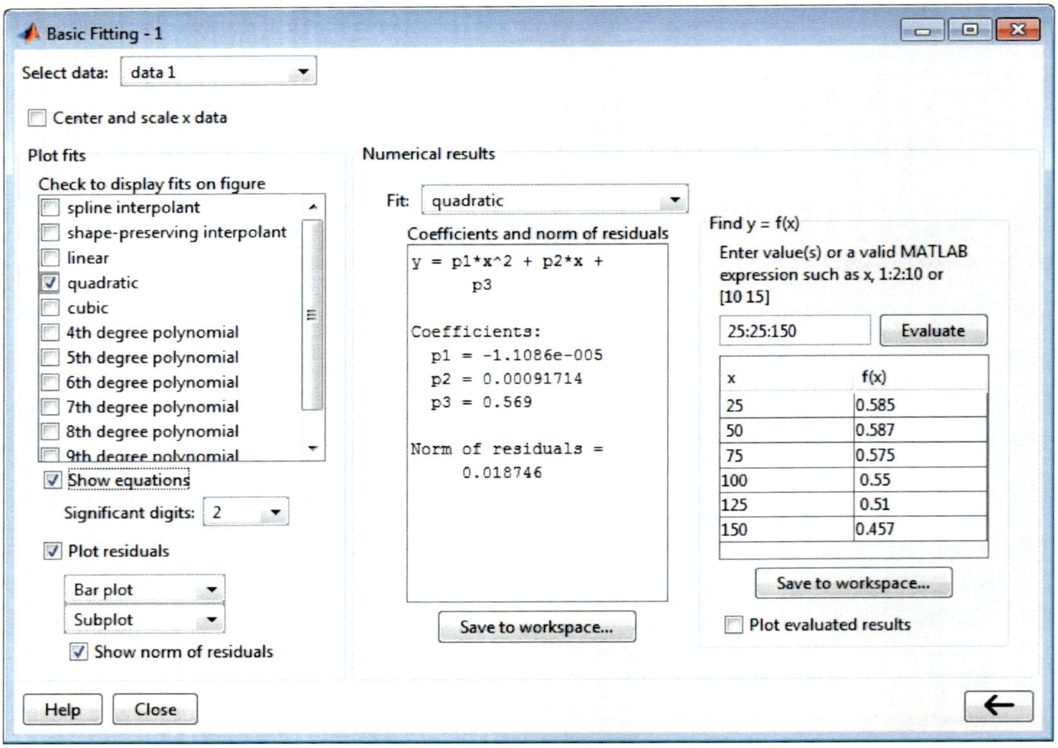

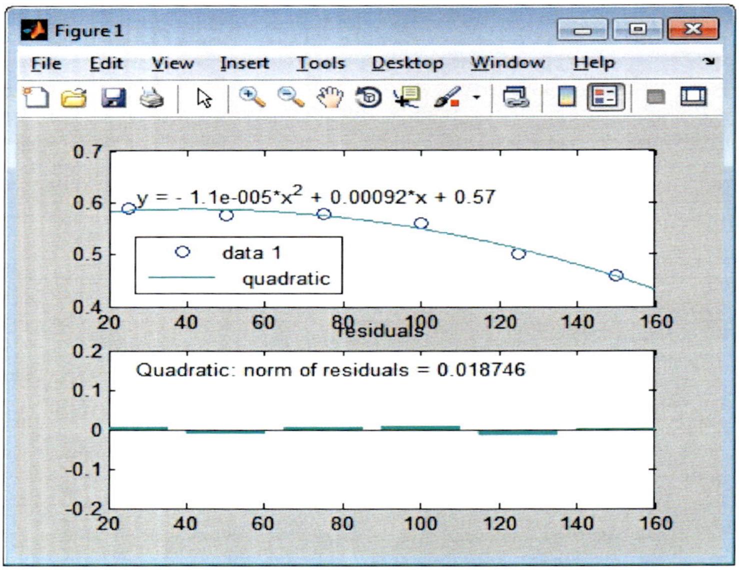

As shown above, the fit equation is identical in both the presented solutions.

6.5.2. Prediction of Air Temperature Monthly Average

The average monthly temperatures at a park in a North American city, during the period from January 31, 2009 to December 31, 2011 were:

-1, -1, 2, 7, 13, 21, 24, 24, 22, 12, 9, 4;

2, -1, 2, 7, 12, 20, 24, 24, 24, 16, 10, 2;

2, -1, 3, 7, 13, 21, 24, 26, 22, 17, 10, 3

degrees Celsius.

Problem: a) Predict the average temperature in December 2012 using time series prediction (see subsection 6.3.1), write a program in the form of function with the input parameter of the month number for forecasting and without the output parameter; display the predicted temperature value for December 2012 in an explanation string.

b) Import temperature data from the MATLAB workspace to the Time Series Tools; edit the time vector in respect to the given dates, plot the data, detrend the temperature data with linear options, and smooth obtained data by the first order filter; and export the obtained data to the workspace and display them in rows.

To solve (a) the following program-function named TSA_6_5_2a was written.

```
Function TSA_6_5_2a(month2predict)
% to run: >>TSA_6_5_2a(12)
Temp=[-1,-1,2,7,13,21,24,24,22,12,9,4,...
2,-1,2,7,12,20,24,24,24,16,10,2,...
2,-1,3,7,13,21,24,26,22,17,10,3];
year=2009:2011;
month=1:length(Temp); % month number
T_coeff=polyfit(month,Temp,1); % linear fit
T=polyval(T_coeff,month); % trend
Season_Rand=Temp-T; % seasonability+random
```

```
S=mean(reshape(Season_Rand,length(year),12));% monthly mean
months=length(month)+month2predict;
T_forecast=polyval(T_coeff,months)+S(month2predict);% prediction
fprintf('December, 2012: Forecasted Temp is%5.0f C\n',T_forecast);
```

After running the program, the forecast for December 2012 is displayed as follows:

```
>> TSA_6_5_2a(12)

December, 2012: Forecasted Temp is 12 C
```

To solve (b), use the Time Series Tools interface for detrending and then for smoothing, using the following steps:

- Input the vector of temperatures Temp into the workspace and enter the tstool command into the Command Window as follows:

```
>> Temp=[-1,-1,2,7,13,21,24,24,22,12,9,4,2,-1,2,7,12,20,24,24,24,16,10,2,...
2,-1,3,7,13,21,24,26,22,17,10,3];
>>tstool
```

- This will open the Time Series Tools window. Select the 'Array Data ...' line into the 'Import from Workspace' option of the 'File' menu. This opens the Import Wizard window;

- For the first step of the Wizard, select the 'MATLAB workspace' option in the 'Import from' field of the 'Data Source' panel and click the 'Next' button;

- For the second step, select the Temp variable from the list under the 'Specify data' panel;

- Check the 'define it now' options in the 'Specify time vector' panel in the 'Time-vector source' field; leave out the 'Units' field changes for editing the time vector at a further stage; click the 'Next' button.

- For the third step, check 'Create a new time series with the name'; input the name 'Temp_1' into this item field; click the 'Finish' button.

- The imported data appears in the table with two columns, the 'Time' and the 'Data:1' columns, in the 'Edit data for Temp_1' panel; they are arranged by time, not by the correct dates. Edit them by clicking the 'Uniform Time Vector ...' button; in the opened 'Define Uniform Time Vector' dialog box select: mm/dd/yy in the 'Display Format', print 12/31/09 in the 'Start Time:' field and 12/31/2011 in the 'End Time' field. After clicking the 'Apply' button, the time interval value is calculated automatically in days as the total number of days between the inputted dates divided by the number of data and appears in the 'Time interval' field; after clicking the 'Apply' button, a view of the dialog box will appear, as shown below:

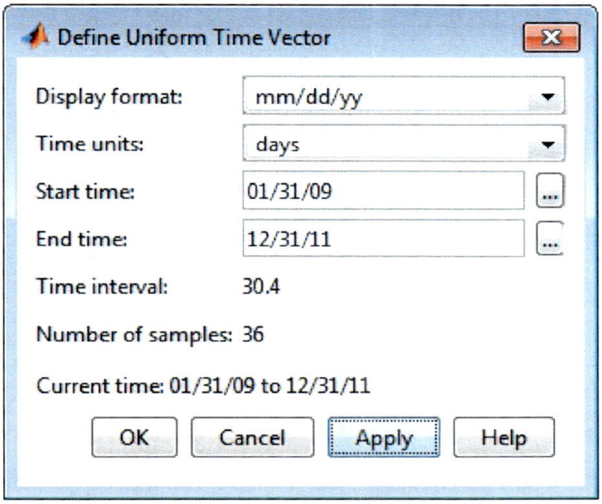

- Click the 'OK' button; the 'Time Series Tools' window looks now as follows:

- To plot, click the 'Display button into the 'Plot time series' panel, as presented in the figure below:

- To remove trend, select the 'Detrend ...' line under the 'Data' option of the tool menu; in the 'Process data' window that appears, check the 'Linear' option in the 'Remove trend type' item; click 'Apply' and 'Close'. The previous plot is corrected automatically and shows:

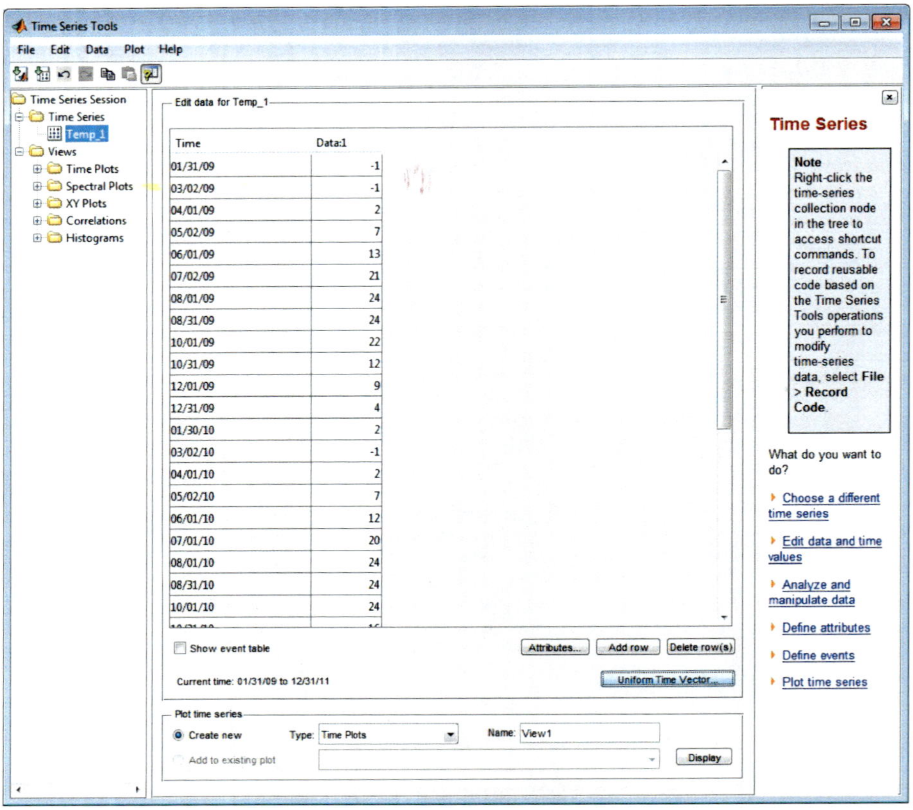
Time Series Tools
File Edit Data Plot Help
Time Series Session
Time Series
Temp_1
Views
Time Plots
Spectral Plots
XY Plots
Correlations
Histograms
Edit data for Temp_1
Time Data:1
01/31/09 -1
03/02/09 -1
04/01/09 2
05/02/09 7
06/01/09 13
07/02/09 21
08/01/09 24
08/31/09 24
10/01/09 22
10/31/09 12
12/01/09 9
12/31/09 4
01/30/10 2
03/02/10 -1
04/01/10 2
05/02/10 7
06/01/10 12
07/01/10 20
08/01/10 24
08/31/10 24
10/01/10 24
Show event table
Attributes... Add row Delete row(s)
Current time: 01/31/09 to 12/31/11
Uniform Time Vector...
Plot time series
Create new Type: Time Plots Name: View1
Add to existing plot
Display
Time Series
Note
Right-click the time-series collection node in the tree to access shortcut commands. To record reusable code based on the Time Series Tools operations you perform to modify time-series data, select File > Record Code.
What do you want to do?
Choose a different time series
Edit data and time values
Analyze and manipulate data
Define attributes
Define events
Plot time series

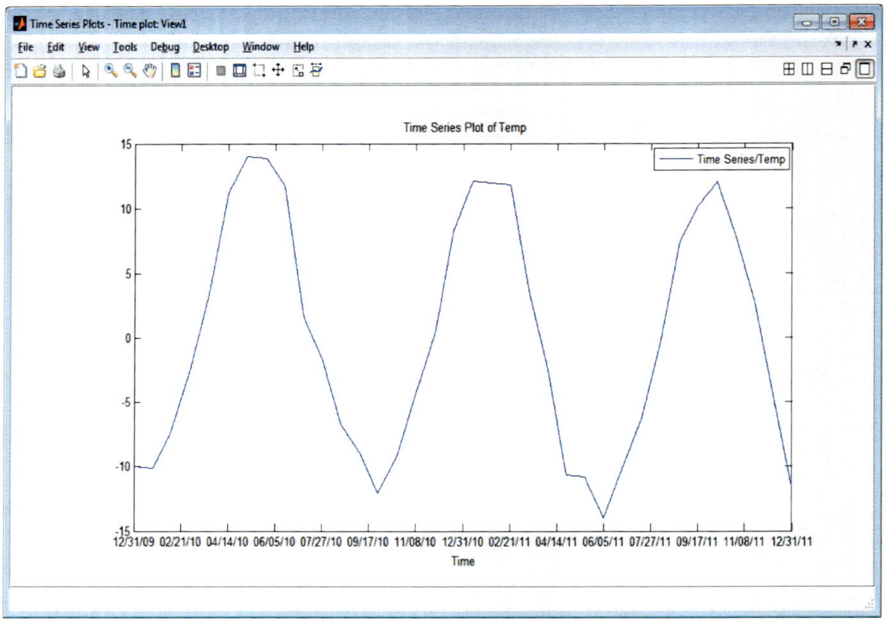
Time Series Plots - Time plot: View1
File Edit View Tools Debug Desktop Window Help
Time Series Plot of Temp
Time Series/Temp
15
10
5
0
-5
-10
-15
12/31/09 02/21/10 04/14/10 06/05/10 07/27/10 09/17/10 11/08/10 12/31/10 02/21/11 04/14/11 06/05/11 07/27/11 09/17/11 11/08/11 12/31/11
Time

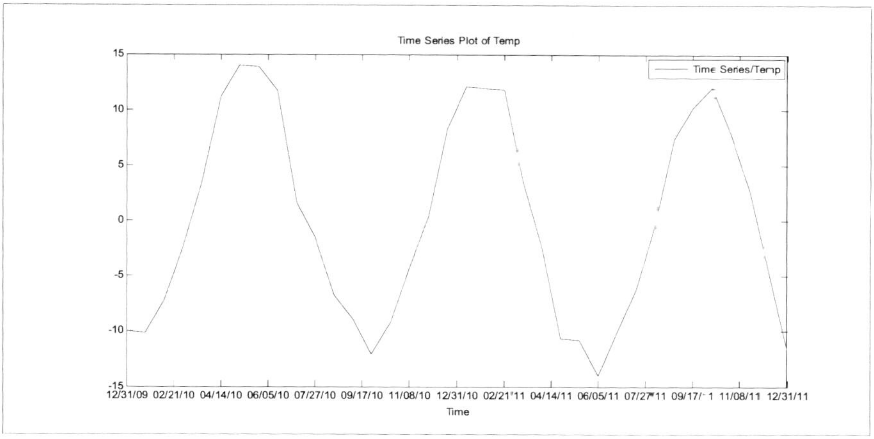

- For smoothing detrended data, select the 'Filter …' line under the 'Data' option of the tool menu; in the appeared 'Process data' window, click the 'Filter tab and 'check the 'First order (1/(1+time constant*s))' option in the 'Filter type' item; click then 'Apply' and 'Close'; previous plot are corrected automatically and smoothed data has form as follows.

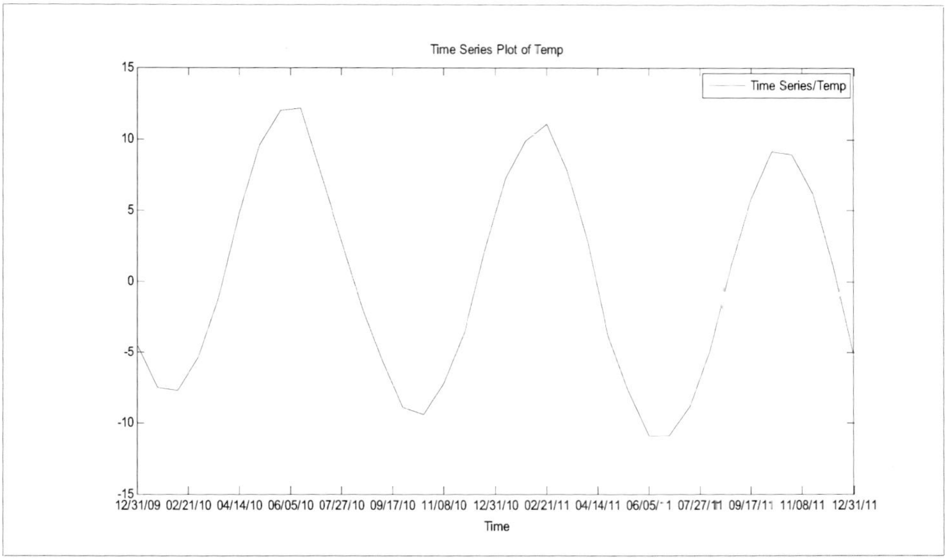

- To export data into the workspace, select the 'To workspace …' option with the 'Export…' line in the 'File' option of the 'Time Series Tools' menu. The data is immediately transmitted as column vector to the workspace and the Temp_1 icon appears in the Workspace window. These data have object type. This programming concept lies outside scope of this book; nevertheless, the data can be displayed in the Command Window by entering the following command:

```
>> Temp_1.data'
Temp_1.data'
Columns 1 through 10
-7.4865 -9.4981 -7.8840 -3.8590 1.5228 8.7419 12.6896 13.5686 12.1775 4.2350
Columns 11 through 20
-0.1335 -5.0928 -7.9599 -11.0452 -9.7026 -5.7462 -1.1290 5.8969 10.5429
11.5985
Columns 21 through 30
11.7464 5.6873 -0.4466 -8.0938 -10.1460 -13.0254 -10.8835 -7.4722 -2.2456
4.9343
Columns 31 through 36
8.8721 11.2430 8.7347 4.2457 -2.2385 -9.2270
```

The transpose (') operator is used in the command above for displaying results in rows.

6.6. QUESTIONS AND EXERCISES

1. To define fit coefficients with polynomial fit, which of the following commands should be used: (a) polyvalue, (b) polyfit, (c) interp1, (d) tstool.

2. To activate the Basic Fitting tool: (a) plot previously (y,x)- data points and select the Basic Fitting line into the Tools option of the Figure window menu, (b) select Basic Fitting option by clicking the 'Start' button of the MATLAB desktop, (c) both (a) and (b) answers are correct; (d) none of the answers are correct.

3. For detrend uniformly spaced time series data with the commands (*viz.* without the Time Series Tools) you need: (a) to interpolate the data, (b) to define average values at every period in time, (c) to

smooth the data, (d) to define a trend with the pclyfit command and remove the trend from the data values.

4. To open the Time Series Tools window you need: (a) to plot previously time series data and to select the Time Series Tools line in the Tools option of the Figure window menu, (b) to select Time Series Tools line from the MATLAB option of the 'Start' button in the bottom of the MATLAB Desktop, (c) enter the tstool command in the Command window, (d) both answers (b) and (c) are correct.

5. To smooth the time series values with the Time Series Tools which of the following operations should be executed: (a) select the 'Interpolate…' line in the 'Data' option of the tool menu; (b) select the 'Filter…' line in the 'Data' option of the tool menu and then select the necessary filter type and time constant; (c) right-click inside the plot with the time series data and select the 'Filter …' option and then select the necessary filter type and time constant; (d) both latter options are correct.

6. The annual biomass energy consumptions in 1973, 1975, 1980, 1985, 1990, and from 1995 to 2008 were: 4.410, 4.687, 5.428, 6.084, 6.040, 6.560, 6.600, 6.610, 6.490, 6.520, 6.100, 6.260, 6.430, 6.380, 6.270, 6.229, 6.608, 6.540, 7.221, quadrillion BTU (British Thermal Units), respectively. Fit these data by cubic polynomial, for which you must write the function with polynomial degree as input parameter and norm of residuals $\sqrt{\sum_{i=1}^{n} R_i^2}$ as output parameter; use the year values centered and scaled by the expression

$$X_i = \frac{x_i - \bar{x}}{\sigma_x}$$

where x – year value, $\bar{x}$ and σ_x is the year mean and standard deviation respectively, X is the value of x after centering and scaling, i is the point number.

Present the data and fit curve in the plot.

7. Fit the data from Exercise 6 using the Basic Fitting tool; select cubic polynomial, display polynomial coefficients, fit expression and norm of residuals in the Result panel of the tool window, give Figure window with two subplots of fit curve with fit equation and of residuals with residual norm.

8. In a process of an enzyme producing by fermentation, the following pH values are measured 8.88, 8.78, 8.60, 8.50, 8.70, 8.30, 8.30, 8.20 at times 8, 8.3, 9, 9.3, 10, 10.3, 11, 11.3 hours respectively. Fit the data by using the Basic Fitting tool, display polynomial coefficients, fit expression, and norm of residuals in the Result panel of the tool; give Figure window with two subplots of fit curve with fit equation and of residuals with residual norm.

9. Bimonthly mean concentrations of atmospheric carbon dioxide between the years 2008 and 2011 were: 771, 773, 776, 771, 766, 770, 774, 778, 780, 774, 769, 773, 778, 784, 785, 778, 774, 778, 783, 786, 788, 782, 778, and 782 parts per million. Write the script that uses the data for the years 2008, 2009, and 2010 for obtaining the linear trend and seasonality components and predict carbon dioxide concentrations in the 2011 year, calculate error as differences between predicted and observed values; display results as a two-column table with predicted values in the first column and error values in the second; generate the plot with the original data points for 2011 and line with predicted values signed by asterisk.

10. Use the Time Series Tools with the data from Exercise 9 for 2008 (January 31) ...2011 (December 31) years, detrend by the liner option and smooth obtained data by the first-order filter type option; present the tool window and time series plot with the smoothed data.

11. The monthly mean air pressure differences between two adjoining African animal parks during the years 2009 and 2010 were: 16.5, 16.8,

NaN, 15.4, 9.5, 6.1, 10.1, 9.3, 5.3, 11.2, 16.6, 15.6, 12.0, 11.5, 8.6, 13.8, 8.7, NaN, 8.6, NaN, 12.8, 13.2, 14.0, 13.4, and 14.8 mbar. Data are missing for March 2009, June 2011 and August 2011 (marked as NaN, not a number, in air pressure series). Use the Time Series Tools to define missing data by the 'Interpolate…' option. Present the resulting Time Series Tools table and Time series plot pressures series that include values defined for months when the data were missed; mark date with the asterisk by the 'Set Line Properties …' options of the 'Plot' item of the Time Series Tools menu.

6.7. ANSWER TO SELECTED QUESTIONS AND EXERCISES

2. a) to plot previously (y,x)- data points and select the Basic Fitting line into the Tools option of the Figure window menu.

4. d) both answers (b) and (c) are correct.

6.

```
>> norm_of_residuals=Ch6_6(3)
norm_of_residuals =
0.9123
```

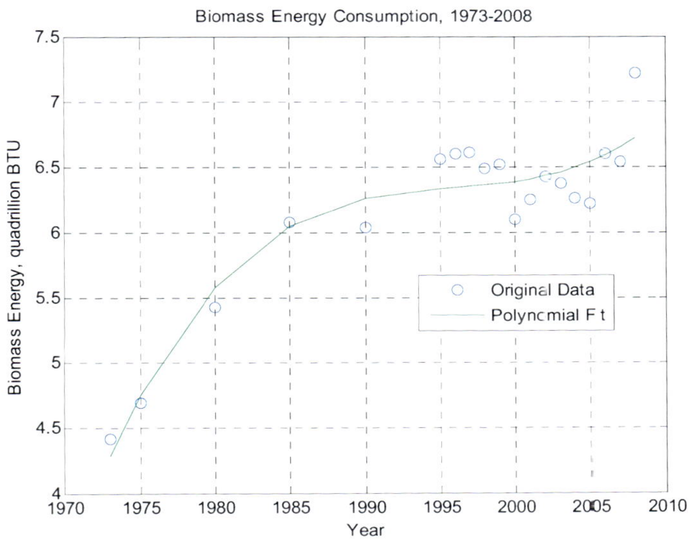

8. In the Command Window

```
>>pH =[8.88 8.78 8.6 8.5 8.7 8.3 8.3 8.2];
>>t=[8 8.3 9 9.3 10 10.3 11 11.3];
>>plot(t,pH,'o')
```

Select the Basic Fitting line in the Tools option of the Figure Window menu.

After providing solution the Basic Fitting and Figure windows appear as follows:

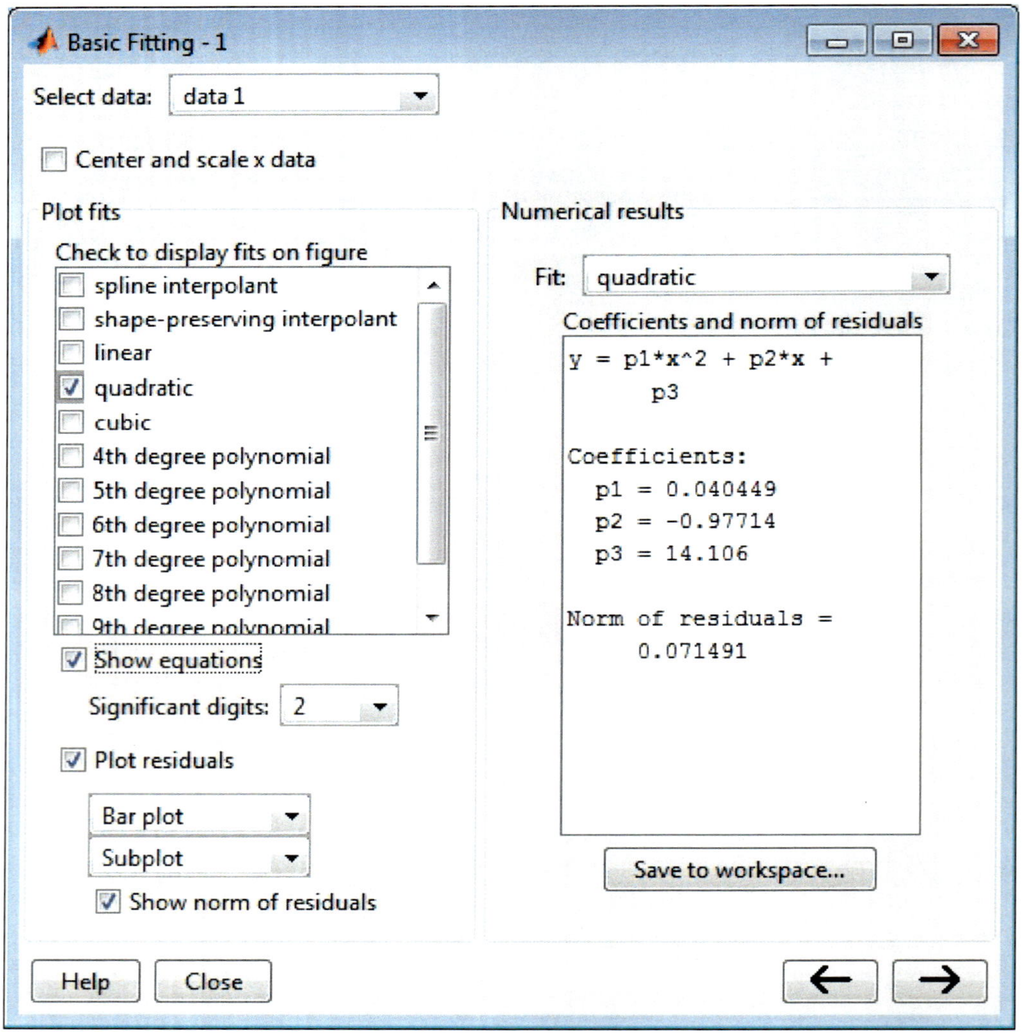

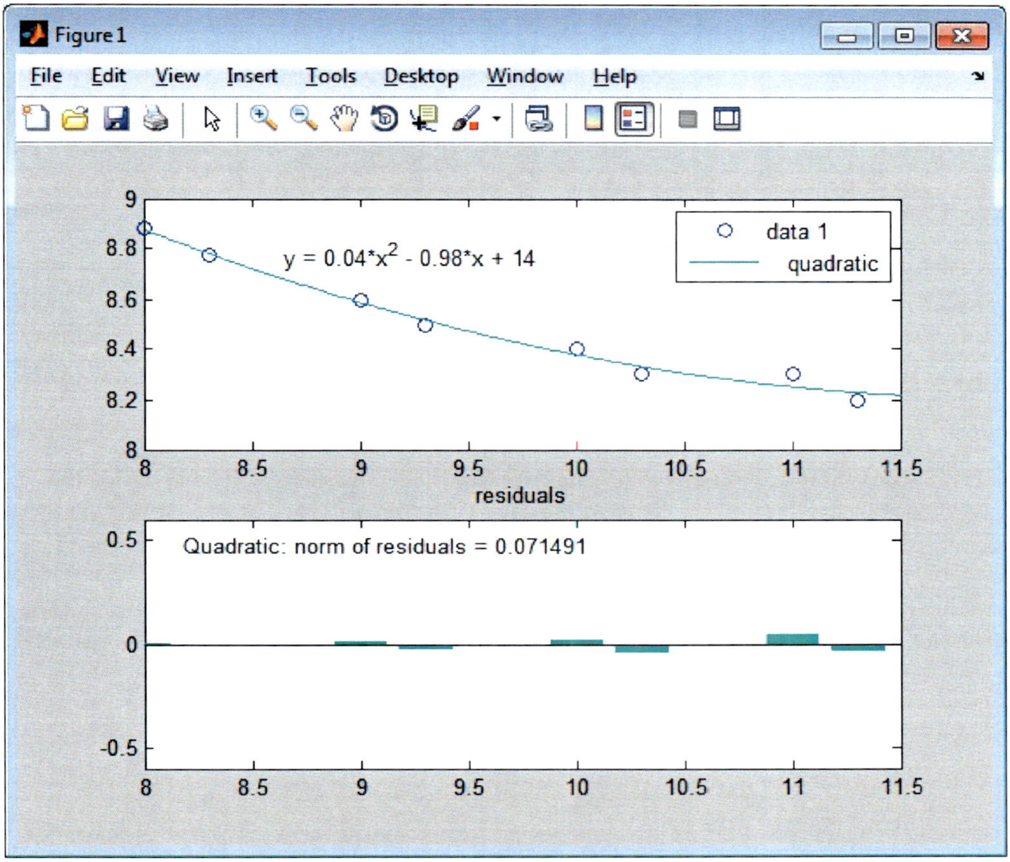

10. In the Command Window

>> CO2=[771, 773, 776, 771, 766, 770, 774, 778, 780, 774, 769, 773, 778, 784, 785, 778, 774, 778, 783, 786, 788, 782, 778, 782];

>> tstool

After execution the operations necessary to solve the problem, the Time Series Tools and Time Series Plot windows will look like the one below:

11. In the Command Window

>>dp=[16.5, 16.8, NaN, 15.4, 9.5, 6.1, 10.1, 9.3, 5.3, 11.2, 16.6, 15.6, 12.0, 11.5, 8.6, 13.8, 8.7, NaN, 8.6, NaN, 12.8, 13.2, 14.0, 13.4, 14.8];

```
>> tstool
```

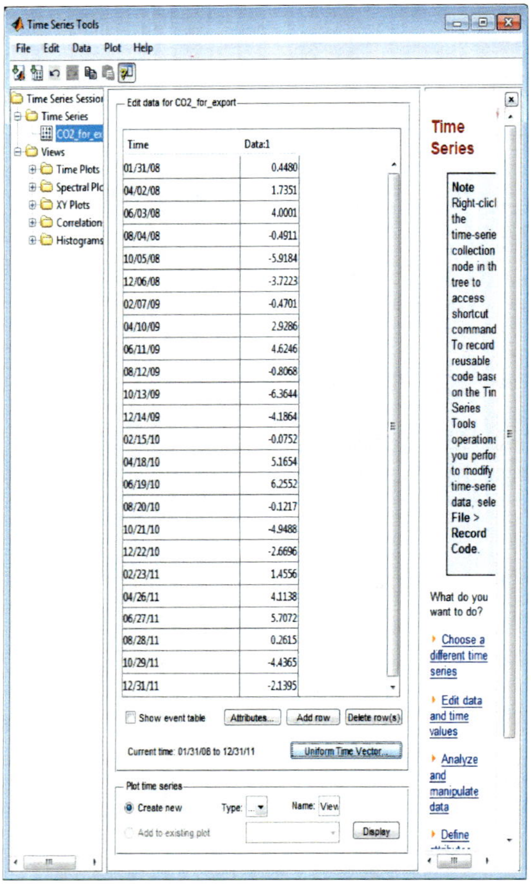

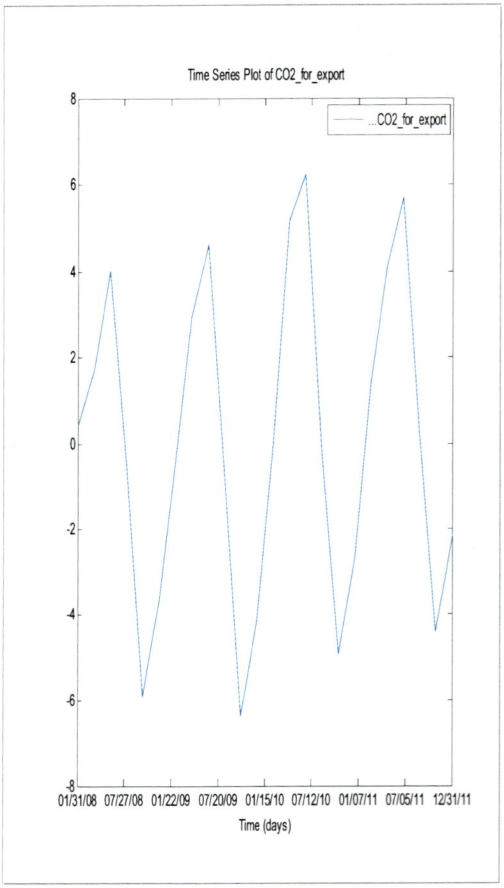

After executing the operations necessary to solve the problem, the Time Series Tools window and Time Series Plot windows will look like the one below:

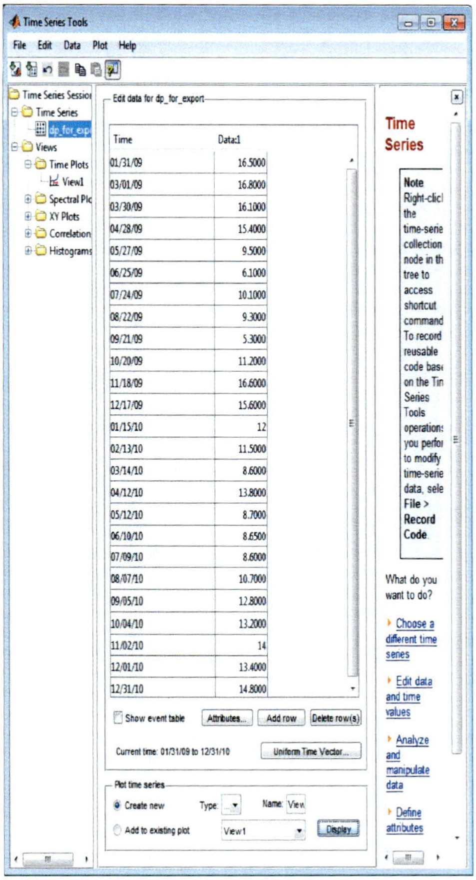
Time Series Tools
File Edit Data Plot Help
Time Series Session
Time Series
dp_for_exp
Views
Time Plots
View1
Spectral Plots
XY Plots
Correlation
Histograms
Edit data for dp_for_export
Time Data:1
01/31/09 16.5000
03/01/09 16.8000
03/30/09 16.1000
04/28/09 15.4000
05/27/09 9.5000
06/25/09 6.1000
07/24/09 10.1000
08/22/09 9.3000
09/21/09 5.3000
10/20/09 11.2000
11/18/09 16.6000
12/17/09 15.6000
01/15/10 12
02/13/10 11.5000
03/14/10 8.6000
04/12/10 13.8000
05/12/10 8.7000
06/10/10 8.6500
07/09/10 8.6000
08/07/10 10.7000
09/05/10 12.8000
10/04/10 13.2000
11/02/10 14
12/01/10 13.4000
12/31/10 14.8000
Show event table
Attributes...
Add row
Delete row(s)
Current time: 01/31/09 to 12/31/10
Uniform Time Vector...
Plot time series
Create new
Type:
Name:
Add to existing plot
View1
Display
Time Series
Note
Right-click the time-series collection node in the tree to access shortcut commands. To record reusable code based on the Time Series Tools operations you perform to modify time-series data, select File > Record Code.
What do you want to do?
Choose a different time series
Edit data and time values
Analyze and manipulate data
Define attributes

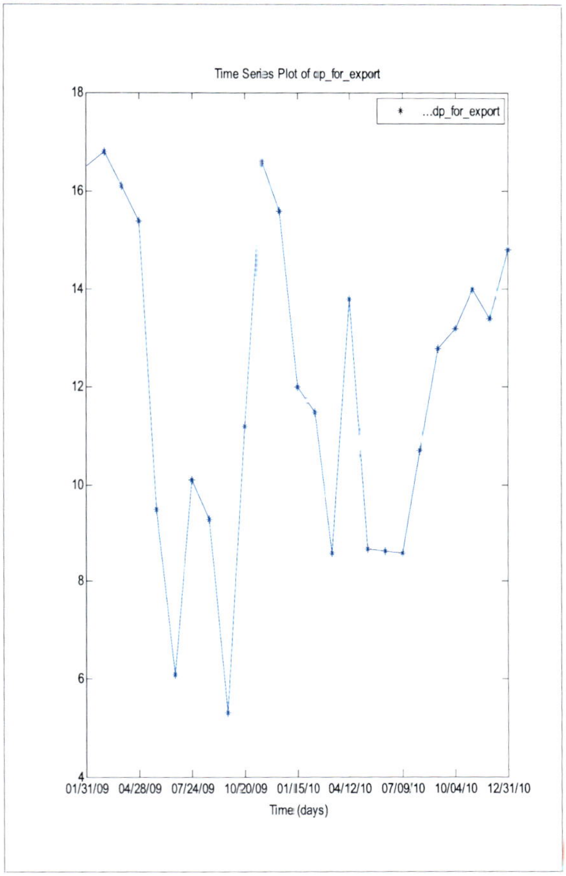
Time Series Plot of dp_for_export
...dp_for_export
18
16
14
12
10
8
6
4
01/31/09
04/28/09
07/24/09
10/20/09
01/15/10
04/12/10
07/09/10
10/04/10
12/31/10
Time (days)

REFERENCES

[1] The MathWorks, Inc., *MATLAB Documentation*. Retrieved April, 2013, From http://www.mathworks.com/products/index.html?s_cid=pl_prodandservices

[2] L. Burstein, *MATLAB® in Bioscience and Biotechnology*. Biohealthcare Publishing (Oxford) Limited, Oxford-New York, 2011.

[3] A. Gilat, *Matlab® An Intoduction With Applications*. Wiley, NJ, 2004.

[4] J. Tranquillo, *MATLAB for Engineering and the Life Sciences*, Morgan & Claypool Publishers, 2011.

[5] M. R. King, N. A. Mody, *Numerical and Statistical Methods for Bioengineering: Applications in MATLAB*, Cambridge University Press, NY, 2010.

[6] R. W. Shonkwiler, J. V. Herod, *Mathematical Biology: An Introduction with Maple and Matlab*, Springer, Heidelberg-London-New York, 2009.

[7] G.Strang, *Linear Algebra and Its Applications,* Thomson, Brooks/Cole, 2006.

[8] L. A. Seidman, C. J. Moore. *Basic Laboratory Methods for Biotechnology: Textbook and Laboratory Reference*. Prentice-Hall, NJ, 2000.

[9] N. S. Mosier, M. R. Ladish. *Modern Biotechnology. Connecting Innovations in Microbiology and Biochemistry to Engineering Fundamentals*. Wiley, New York, 2009.

[10] P. Henrici, *Elements of Numerical Analysis*, John Wiley & Sons Inc., 1964.

[11] N. J. Higham, *Accuracy and Stability of Numerical Algorithms,* SIAM, Philadelphia, PA, 2002.

[12] E. Hairer, S. P. Nørsett, G. Wanner, *Solving Ordinary Differential Equations I: Nonstiff Problems*, Springer, Berlin *etc.*, 1993.

Leonid Burstein

APPENDIX 1

MATLAB® Characters, Operators and Commands

Abstract: The list of MATLAB® special characters, scalar and matrix operators, commands and functions are presented in the alphabetical order.

Keywords: MATLAB® commands; special characters, scalar and matrix operators.

OPERATORS OF SCALAR, ARRAY AND MATRIX ARITHMETIC

	Operator and description	Location, page
+	Addition	12, 32
-	Subtraction	12, 32
*	Scalar and matrix multiplication	12, 33
.*	Element-wise multiplication	36
/	Right division	12, 35
./	Element-wise right division	36
\	Left division	12, 35
.\	Element-wise left division	36
^	Exponentiation	12
.^	Element-wise exponentiation	36

SPECIAL CHARACTERS

	Character and description	Location, page
=	Assignment	14
%	Percent; is used for comments and for output format specification	12, 22
( )	Parentheses; is used for input arguments and in matrix addressing	12, 30
[ ]	Brackets; use for vector, matrix, array elements input	27
(space)	Space; separates elements into arrays, and adds into output specifications	21, 27
:	Colon; creates vectors, used also for loops iterations and for selecting all array elements	27, 30, 57
,	Comma; separates elements into arrays and commands on the same line	12, 27, 29
;	Semicolon; suppresses printing if wrote after the command. Separates matrix rows and commands on the same line	11
...	Ellipsis; signs that a long statement to be continued on the next line	12, 29
'	apostrophe; array or matrix transpose quotation mark; is used for a text string generation	21, 31, 42

RELATIONAL AND LOGICAL OPERATORS

Operator and description		Location, page
==	Equal; element-wise	51
>	Greater than; element-wise	51
>=	Greater than or equal to; element-wise	51
<	Less than; element-wise	50
&	Logical AND	52
~=	Not equal; element-wise	51
|	Logical OR	52
<=	Lower than or equal to; element-wise	51
~	Logical NOT	52

ALPHABETICAL LIST OF COMMANDS AND PREDEFINED VARIABLES

Command and description		Location, page
abs	Absolute value	12
acos	Inverse cosine for angle in radians	14
acosd	Inverse cosine for angle in degrees	14
acot	Inverse cotangent for angle in radians	14
acotd	Inverse cotangent for angle in degrees	14
and	Logical AND	52
ans	Last calculated or defined value	14
asin	Inverse sine for angle in radians	13
asind	Inverse sine for angle in degrees	14
atan	Inverse tangent for angle in radians	14
atand	Inverse tangent for angle in degrees	14
axis	Controls axis scaling and appearance	83
bar	Generates a vertical bars on the plot	108
bar3	Generates 3D vertical bars on the plot	109
clabel	Labels iso-level lines	107
clc	Clear the command window	12
clear	Remove variables from the Workspace	19
close	Closes one or more Figure Windows	77
colormap	Sets colors	95
contour	Creates a 2D-contour plot	107
contour3	Creates a 3D-contour plot	108
cos	Cosine for angle in radians	13
cosd	Cosine for angle in degrees	13
cot	Cotangent for angle in radians	13
cotd	Cotangent for angle in degrees	13

cylinder	Generates a cylinder	107
det	Calculates a determinant	41
diag	Creates a diagonal matrix from a vector	40
diff	Calculates a difference, approximates a derivative	151
disp	Display output	21
doc	Displays HTML documentation in the Help window	16
else, elseif	Is used with if; conditionally executes if statement condition	56
end	Terminates scope of for, while, if statements, or serves as last index	29,56
errorbar	Creates a plot with error bounded points	101
exp	Exponential	12
eye	Creates a unit matrix	40
factorial	Factorial function	14
figure	Creates the Figure window.	106
find	Finds indices of certain elements of array	53
floor	Round off toward minus infinity	13
for	Is used to repeat execution of command/s	57
format	Sets current output format	19
fplot	Creates a 2D plot of a function	106
fprintf	Display formatted output	22
function	Function Creates a new function	137
fzero	Solves a one-variable equation	145
global	Declares a global variable	140
grid	Adds grid lines	83
gtext	Adds a text with the help of the mouse	84
help	Displays explanations in the Command Window	15
help graph2d	Displays list of 2D graph commands	105
help graph3d	Displays list of 3D graph commands	105
help specgraph	Displays list of specialized graph commands	105
hist	Plots a histogram	102
hold on/off	Keeps current graph open/ends hold on	78
i	$\sqrt{-1}$	19
if	Conditionally execute	56
inf	Infinity, is produced by dividing by 0	19
input	Prompt to user input	135
interp1	One-dimensional interpolation	144
inv	Calculates the inverse matrix	35
j	The same as i	19
legend	Adds a legend to the plot	86
length	Number of elements in vector	39
linspace	Generates a linearly spaced vector	28
log	Natural logarithm	12
log10	Decimal logarithm	13
loglog	Generates a 2D plot with log axes	106
lookfor	Search for the word in all help entries	16

sqrt	Square root	13
stairs	Creates star-like plot	110
std	Calculates standard deviation	41
stem	Creates a 2D stem plot	109
stem3	Creates a 3D stem plot	109
strvcat	Concatenates strings vertically	40
subplot	Places multiple plots on the same page	79
sum	Calculates sum of elements	41
surf	Creates a 3D surface plot	93
surfc	Generates surface and counter plots together	108
tan	Tangent for angle in radians	13
tand	Tangent for angle in degrees	13
text	text Adds a text to the plot	84
title	Adds a caption to the plot	84
transpose (')	Transposes elements of an array	31
trapz	Numerical integration with the trapezoidal rule	149
ver	Displays versions of the MATLAB products	18
view	Specifies a viewpoint for 3D graph	96
while	Repeat execution of command/s	57
who	Displays variables stored in the Workspace	19
whos	Displays Workspace variables and additional information about the variables	19
xlabel	Adds a label to x-axis	84
ylabel	Adds a label to y-axis	84
zeros	Creates an array with zeros	40
zlabel	Adds a label to z-axis	89

APPENDIX 2

The Desktop, Help and Editor Windows in MATLAB R2012b

Abstract: The MATLAB® windows modifications, introduced by the R2012b version, are briefly described. The Desktop and Editor toolstrips, and redesigned Help Window is presented.

Keywords: MATLAB® R2012b; toolstrips; Desktop; Editor Window; Help Window.

INTRODUCTION

When this book manuscript was prepared, a new version MATLAB®, R2012b, was appeared; in this version the Desktop, Help and Editor Windows have been modified. The changes compared to the version presented in the book are described briefly below.

DESKTOP

The changes in the Desktop view are connected with the strip in the top of the window. The located here, so-called, toolstrip collects the main MATLAB® purpose operations and functions in three tabs: the Home, Plots and Apps. Tabs are divided into sections that contain a series of related controls: buttons, drop-down menus and other user interface elements (Fig. **A1.2**). The tabs contain a number of buttons that are grouped in sections by its functionality (file, variable, code, *etc.*), the sections include buttons to execution of operations (*e.g.*, Open, New Variable, Preferences and so on). In more details:

- The Home tab includes general purpose operations like creating new files, importing data, managing your workspace, and setting your Desktop layout;

- The Plots tab displays a gallery of plots available in MATLAB and any toolboxes that you have installed;

- The Apps tab contains a gallery of applications from the toolboxes;

Leonid Burstein

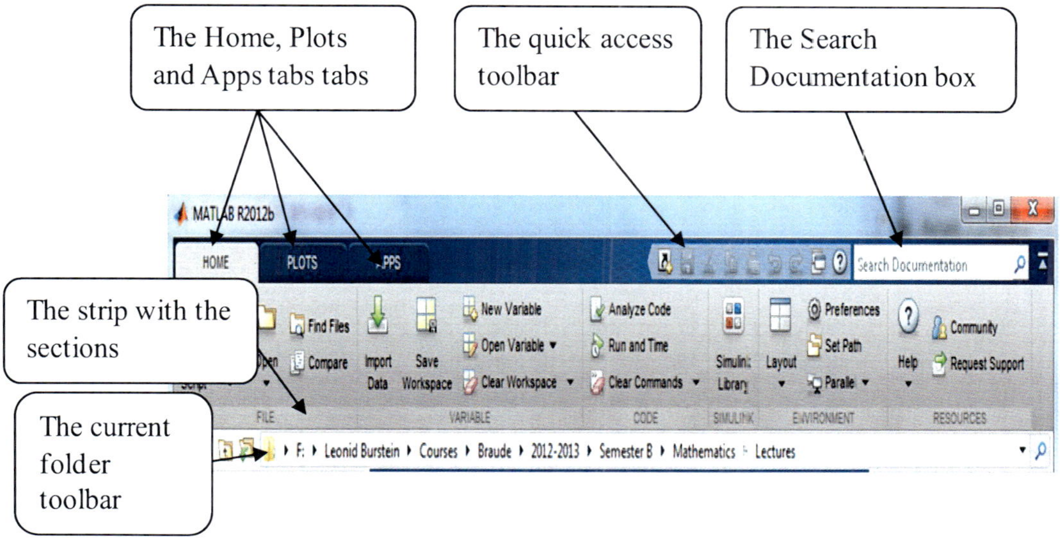

Figure A2.1: The Desktop toolstrip. MATLAB® R2012b version.

To the right of the top of the strip, the quick access toolbar is located; this toolbar contains frequently used options such as cut, copy, paste, *etc.*

In the bottom part of the strip, the current folder toolbar line is placed; analogously to previous versions, it is intent to control the current working directory;

Located next to the quick access toolbar, the Search Documentation box enables to search the documentation for functions and other topics of interest.

The Aps tab and quick access toolbar are customizable.

Help Window

The R2012b release includes a redesigned Help window, represented below (Fig. **A2.2**). The window appears with list of the toolboxes.

Each product's documentation is now presented by categories of functionality, such as Graphics or Simulation, rather than by information type, such as Function Reference or User's Guide. Categories include links to related reference pages, examples, and topics.

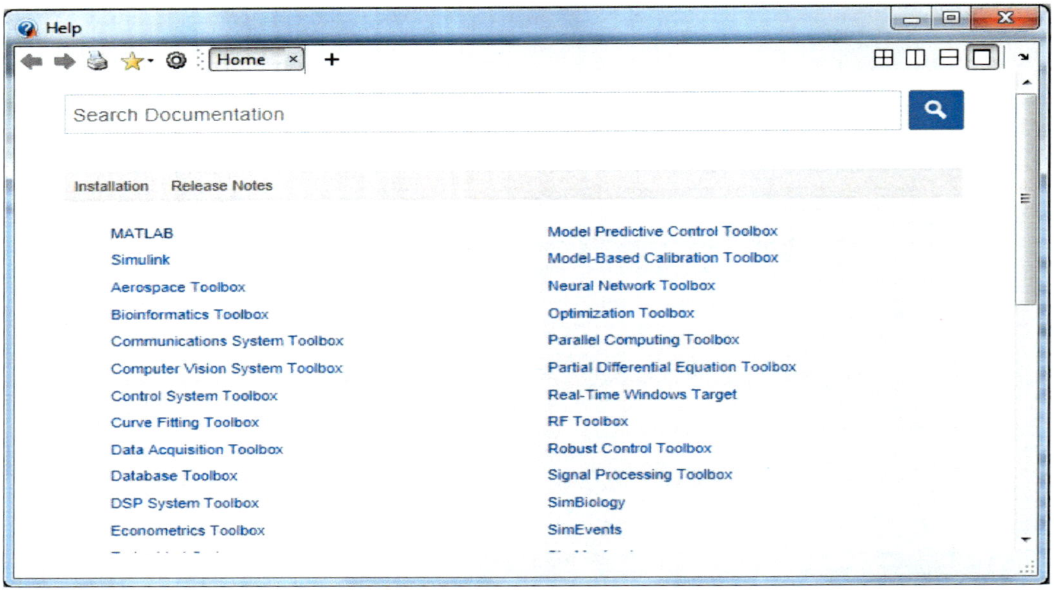

Figure A2.2: The Help window. MATLAB® R2012b version.

Most features of the previous Help browser are available in the new browser, although some features has a different appearance or location. For example:

- The table of contents does not appear in this Help Window version; to open it you need to click the Table of Contents button, ≡, that appears when the toolbox or the actual topics were chosen.

- Tasks performed in previous versions by the Help browser menu items (such as setting preferences or viewing page locations), can be accessed now *via* right-click menus, keyboard shortcuts, or toolbar buttons.

- 'Demos' are now marked as 'Examples', and are accessible from the top of each product page.

EDITOR

The Editor Window also has a toolstrip with three tabs: the Editor, Publish, and View. When the Editor is docked in the Desktop, these tabs appear to the right of the Desktop tabs. The toolstrip of the separate Editor Window is normally looks as:

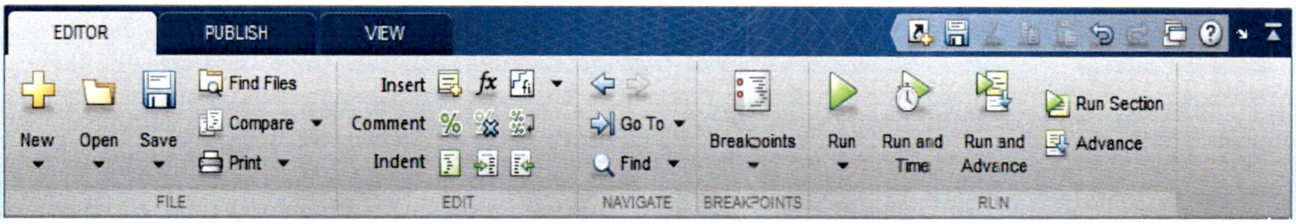

Figure A2.3: Toolstrip of the Editor Window. MATLAB® R2012b version.

The Editor tab contains the functions to the file edition; these functions are grouped, similarly to those in the Desktop toolstrip, into the sections (File, Edit, Navigate, *etc.*).

The Publish tab takes the controls that are needed to create, format, and present in a view suitable for publishing the programs and other documents.

The View tab is intent to control the layout and appearance of files in the Editor.

The Debug section of the Editor tab replaces the Run section, when a breakpoint is put in the file and after the program is running. The Debug section contains the controls that are necessary to debug the program. The Editor toolstrip in this case have the view:

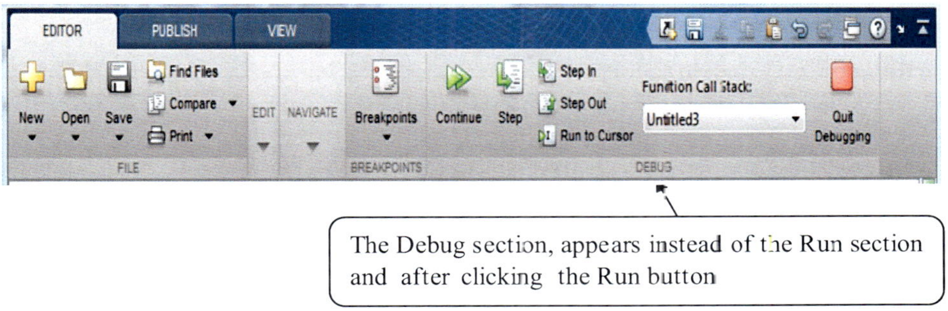

Figure A2.4: Toolstrip of the Editor Window after clicking the Run button. MATLAB® R2012b version.

With the exception of the changes above, all other MATLAB® windows, functions, and commands presented in the book, can be used exactly so as they are described.

Index

Leonid Burstein

C

E

O

P

S

T

V

Made in United States
North Haven, CT
04 November 2026

21719581R00155